RACE, RAGE, AND RESISTANCE

This timely collection asks the reader to consider how society's modern notion of humans as rational, isolated individuals has contributed to psychological and social problems and oppressive power structures.

Experts from a range of disciplines offer a complex understanding of how humans are shaped by history, tradition, and institutions. Drawing upon the work of Lacan, Fanon, and Foucault, this text examines cultural memory, modern ideas of race and gender, the roles of symbolism and mythology, and neoliberalism's impact on psychology. Through clinical vignettes and suggested applications, it demonstrates significant alternatives to the isolated individualism of Western philosophy and psychology.

This interdisciplinary volume is essential reading for clinicians and anyone looking to augment their understanding of how human beings are shaped by the societies they inhabit.

David M. Goodman is interim dean at the Woods College of Advancing Studies at Boston College, associate professor of the practice in the Philosophy department, director of *Psychology and the Other*, and a teaching associate at Harvard Medical School/Cambridge Hospital.

Eric R. Severson is author of the books *Levinas's Philosophy of Time* and *Scandalous Obligation*, and the editor of seven other volumes. He lives in Kenmore, Washington, with his wife Misha and their three children, and teaches philosophy at Seattle University.

Heather Macdonald's scholarly research focuses on the interface between relational ethics and clinical practice. Her first monograph, titled *Cultural and Critical Explorations in Community Psychology*, further considers the implications of psychological assessment and historical trauma.

PSYCHOLOGY AND THE OTHER

Series Editor: DAVID M. GOODMAN
Associate Editors: BRIAN W. BECKER, DONNA M. ORANGE and
ERIC R. SEVERSON

The *Psychology and the Other* Book Series highlights creative work at the intersections between psychology and the vast array of disciplines relevant to the
human psyche. The interdisciplinary focus of this series brings psychology into
conversation with continental philosophy, psychoanalysis, religious studies,
anthropology, sociology, and social/critical theory. The cross-fertilization of
theory and practice, encompassing such a range of perspectives, encourages the
exploration of alternative paradigms and newly articulated vocabularies that speak
to human identity, freedom, and suffering. Thus, we are encouraged to reimagine
our encounters with difference, our notions of the "other," and what constitutes
therapeutic modalities.

The study and practices of mental health practitioners, psychoanalysts, and scholars in the humanities will be sharpened, enhanced, and illuminated by these
vibrant conversations, representing pluralistic methods of inquiry, including those
typically identified as psychoanalytic, humanistic, qualitative, phenomenological,
or existential.

For a full list of titles in the series, please visit the Routledge website at:
www.routledge.com/Psychology-and-the-Other/book-series/PSYOTH

RACE, RAGE, AND RESISTANCE

Philosophy, Psychology, and the Perils of Individualism

Edited by David M. Goodman, Eric R. Severson, and Heather Macdonald

LONDON AND NEW YORK

First published 2020
by Routledge
2 Park Square, Milton Park, Abingdon, Oxon OX14 4RN

and by Routledge
52 Vanderbilt Avenue, New York, NY 10017

Routledge is an imprint of the Taylor & Francis Group, an informa business

© 2020 Taylor & Francis

British Library Cataloguing-in-Publication Data
A catalogue record for this book is available from the British Library

Library of Congress Cataloging-in-Publication Data
Names: Goodman, David, 1980- editor. | Severson, Eric R., editor. |
Macdonald, Heather (Psychologist), editor.
Title: Race, rage, and resistance : philosophy, psychology, and the perils of
individualism / edited by David M. Goodman, Eric Severson, and Heather
Macdonald.
Description: New York, NY : Routledge, 2020. | Includes bibliographical
references and index.
Identifiers: LCCN 2019015408 (print) | LCCN 2019016890 (ebook) |
Subjects: | MESH: Race Factors | Ethnopsychology | Psychology, Clinical |
Psychology, Social | Individuality | United States
Classification: LCC RC455.4.E8 (ebook) | LCC RC455.4.E8 (print) |
NLM WA 305 AA1 | DDC 362.196/89--dc23
LC record available at https://lccn.loc.gov/2019015408

ISBN: 978-0-367-21779-2 (hbk)
ISBN: 978-0-367-21782-2 (pbk)
ISBN: 978-0-429-26605-8 (ebk)

Typeset in Bembo
by Taylor & Francis Books

David Goodman: For my Gramps, whose inexhaustible attention, glowing smile, and generous love kept my eyes open.

Eric Severson: For Grandma Louise, whose gentle strength, realism, and constancy stabilize the world.

Heather Macdonald: To my Nona, whose love of adventure inspired me to maintain a stance of open hearted curiosity about people and to pay attention to the variegated forms of ethos across cultures.

CONTENTS

FIGURES

PREFACE

The preface to any book serves a peculiar role. The authors, or in this case editors, stand between the reader and the text, before its face. The preface also serves as a welcoming, the opening words of a conversation, as an invitation to participate. In this case, readers are invited into movement underway in psychology, philosophy, and theology. A growing community of clinicians and scholars are disregarding the traditional boundaries between disciplines, and working fruitfully and energetically on interdisciplinary conversations. A number of the chapters before you began as presentations or dialogues at the 2017 *Psychology and the Other Conference*, a biannual gathering that attends, explicitly, to this groundswell of interest in the power of interdisciplinary research and practice. Academia has long trended toward the fortification of scholarly silos. Conferences and publications tend to reinforce these fortifications, and sharing between disciplines is often discouraged or even belittled. This approach impoverishes the academy, denying scholars the palpable benefit of cross-disciplinary wisdom. Even worse, this isolation of disciplines represents a fundamental failure of higher education. Universities do not exist for their own sake; the ideas they research, nurture, develop, and teach should forever be in conversation with the world in which they are nestled. Interdisciplinary movements like this one are essential for the academy to do its work. The *Psychology and the Other* movement earnestly cultivates these conversations, and insists that the labors of psychologists, philosophers, and theologians be ever mindful of their obligation to therapists, ministers, clinicians, politicians, social workers, and so many more.

Psychology and the Other, which first met in 2011, has become a farmer's market for ideas. Rather than pushing ideas toward the security of disciplinary silos, contributors descend on Boston with earnest, and often hard-won, findings that they hope to submit to a burgeoning conversation. Many of these ideas are experimental, creative, irreverent, and daring. The ideas in this volume coalesced around themes related to generationality, with particular interest in the ways human beings transmit trauma, racism and sexism across generations. The book is also about hope, particularly the way attentiveness to this transmission can lead us to better ways of living together, healing from trauma, and breaking patterns of racism, sexism, and exploitation.

The editors of this volume have had the great pleasure of being its very first readers. A collection of dedicated, sincere, and talented scholars and clinicians have offered here their hard-won insights. To edit a book is more than just to read it first; we have had the honor of sitting with these words and ideas long enough to be reshaped by their power. This makes it easy for us to not only highly recommend the chapters ahead, but also to feel tremendous gratitude toward their authors.

The *Psychology and the Other Conference* takes place with the tremendous support of specific individuals that deserve to be recognized in these pages. As always, we cannot name each person involved, but we wish to underscore our gratitude for the many members of the Psychology and the Other community that pour their energies into seeing these conversations take place. These individuals range from undergraduate student volunteers to prominent scholars from across the planet who invest in participating and bringing their wisdom and presence to these events. More specifically, a small team of colleagues and students who put in incalculable time and creative energy to form this event included Ben Arcangeli, Sam Arcangeli, Carrie Buddington, Sara Carabbio, Abigail Collins, Adeline Dettor, Teresa Goodman, David House, Katie Lyle, and Cacky Mellor. Their spirit is deeply evident at every level during the conference.

Furthermore, each chapter in this book has been very carefully read and analyzed by Taylor Kelliher, whose insightful reading and poetic voice sharpened each chapter. We are grateful for the careful eye of the Routledge editorial staff and copy editor Rebecca Wise. Administrative and institutional support is also important here as generations transmit through these vehicles as well. Several institutions have remained committed to seeing this conversation grow, including Lesley University, Boston College, and the Danielsen Institute at Boston University. In addition to contributing his own exceptional scholarly input, Brian Becker fought the logistical battles that allowed for space on Lesley University's campus in Cambridge, MA. Colleagues from Boston College, including Richard Kearney, Vanessa Rumble, and David Blustein, have been deeply hospitable as they invite students and fellow scholars into this conversation. George Stavros and Lauren Kehoe, at the Danielsen Institute at Boston University, consistently go above and beyond to support the conference and ensure that it is accessible to clinicians by providing CEUs.

It is our ongoing hope that this conversational community grows in its ability to call us to greater vigilance and speak more fully to one another about our world.

NOTES ON CONTRIBUTORS

Mark Freeman is Distinguished Professor of Ethics and Society and Professor of Psychology at the College of the Holy Cross in Worcester, Massachusetts. His writings include *Rewriting the Self: History, Memory, Narrative* (Routledge, 1993); *Finding the Muse: A Sociopsychological Inquiry into the Conditions of Artistic Creativity* (Cambridge University Press, 1994); *Hindsight: The Promise and Peril of Looking Backward* (Oxford University Press, 2010); *The Priority of the Other: Thinking and Living Beyond the Self* (Oxford University Press, 2014); and numerous articles and chapters on issues ranging from memory and identity to the psychology of art and religion. Winner of the 2010 Theodore R. Sarbin Award in the Society for Theoretical and Philosophical Psychology, he also serves as editor for the Oxford University Press series "Explorations in Narrative Psychology."

Robert Bernasconi is Edwin Erle Sparks Professor of Philosophy and African American Studies at the Pennsylvania State University. He formerly taught at the University of Essex and the University of Memphis. He works extensively in critical philosophy of race as well as in nineteenth- and twentieth-century continental philosophy, especially Hegel, Heidegger, Sartre, Levinas, Derrida, and Fanon. In addition to numerous articles in these areas he has published three books: *The Question of Language in Heidegger's History of Being, Heidegger in Question*, and *How to Read Sartre*. He edits three journals: *Critical Philosophy of Race, Levinas Studies*, and *Eco-Ethica*.

Nahanni Freeman earned her PhD in clinical psychology from Rosemead School of Psychology at Biola University. She completed a post-doctoral fellowship in Medical Psychology at the Oregon Health Sciences University, where she studied neuropsychological assessment. Dr Freeman is a licensed clinical psychologist, and formerly worked as a unit psychologist at the Oregon State

Hospital. In Colorado, she previously engaged in clinical work with a geriatric population. Currently, Dr. Freeman works as an associate professor at Colorado Christian University, in the College of Undergraduate Studies. Her research explores the psychology of religion, social cognition and psychological aesthetics.

Jeff Sugarman is Professor of Education and Psychology at Simon Fraser University. His major interests are the psychology of personhood, the socio-political influence of psychology, the psychology of neoliberalism, and the application of historical ontology to psychological inquiry. He is a past President of the Society for Theoretical and Philosophical Psychology, former Associate Editor of the *Journal of Theoretical and Philosophical Psychology* and *New Ideas in Psychology*, and fellow of the American Psychological Association and American Educational Research Association. He is co-editor of *The Wiley Handbook of Theoretical and Philosophical Psychology* (Wiley-Blackwell, 2015), and co-author of *Persons: Understanding Psychological Selfhood and Agency* (Springer, 2010), *Psychology and the Question of Agency* (SUNY Press, 2003), and *The Psychology of Human Possibility and Constraint* (SUNY Press, 1999).

Sam Binkley is Professor of Sociology at Emerson College, Boston. His research examines the social production of subjectivity, identity, and personhood through lifestyle literatures and popular texts. Drawing on Michel Foucault's notions of bio-power and governmentality, but also from a range of critical theorists, he has undertaken studies of self help literature and popular psychology, lifestyle movements of the 1970s, anti-racist and multi-cultural discourses, and the affective, corporeal, and emotional cultures of neoliberalism, all with an eye toward the fashioning of subjectivity in these contexts. He has authored two research monographs; *Happiness as Enterprise: An Essay on Neoliberal Life* (SUNY, 2015) and *Getting Loose: Lifestyle Consumption in the 1970s* (Duke, 2007), and is co-editor of *A Foucault for the 21st Century* (Cambridge Scholars, 2010). He has published articles in such journals as *Body & Society, History of Human Sciences, Time and Society, Foucault Studies, Cultural Studies, Rethinking Marxism, Subjectivity* and the *Journal for Cultural Research*.

Sheldon George is a Professor of English and a scholar of American and African-American literature. His work focuses upon cultural and literary theory with a particular emphasis on Lacanian psychoanalytic theory. He is an associate editor of *Psychoanalysis, Culture & Society* and a guest editor of two special issues of the journal: "African Americans and Inequality" (2014) and "Lacanian Psychoanalysis: Interventions into Culture and Politics" (2018). His book *Trauma and Race: A Lacanian Study of African American Racial Identity* was published in 2016 by Baylor University Press. He is currently coediting a collection of essays on narrative form and racial ethics in the literature of African American and black British women authors and a collection on Lacan and Race.

Tracy Sidesinger, PsyD is a psychoanalytic psychologist in private practice in New York City, working with adult individuals and couples. She has postgraduate training in both Jungian and Relational psychologies. She teaches at the interfaces of psychology and religion, and psychology and the body. Her writing focuses on feminism and spirituality, as well as collaboration between all psychologies of the unconscious in order to make the creative potential of the unconscious more accessible in contemporary culture.

Educated in philosophy, clinical psychology, and psychoanalysis, **Donna M. Orange, PhD, PsyD** teaches at NYU Postdoc (New York University Postdoctoral Program in Psychoanalysis and Psychotherapy) and at IPSS (Institute for the Psychoanalytic Study of Subjectivity, New York); and in private study groups. Recent books are *Thinking for Clinicians: Philosophical Resources for Contemporary Psychoanalysis and the Humanistic Psychotherapies* (Routledge, 2010), and *The Suffering Stranger: Hermeneutics for Everyday Clinical Practice* (Routledge, 2011), *Nourishing the Inner Life of Clinicians and Humanitarians: The Ethical Turn in Psychoanalysis* (Routledge, 2016), and *Climate Justice, Psychoanalysis, and Radical Ethics* (Routledge, 2017). Her next project concerns hearing the voices of those silenced by history, by culture, by ourselves.

Robin R. Chalfin is a practicing psychotherapist and clinical supervisor in Boston, MA. She teaches in the Graduate Counseling and Psychology Program at Lesley University and serves as board member and frequent lecturer for the New England Center for Existential Therapy (NECET). At the intersections of philosophy and psychotherapy, her work attends to formations of identity and difference, interpersonal violence, and the vulnerabilities of existence. Her recent chapter *Being Broken and Unbroken: Trauma, Heidegger, and Befindlichkeit* is included in the anthology *In the Wake of Trauma: Psychology and Philosophy for the Suffering Other.*

Nancy McWilliams teaches at Rutgers University's Graduate School of Applied & Professional Psychology and has a private practice in Lambertville, NJ. She is author of *Psychoanalytic Diagnosis* (The Guilford Press, 1994; rev. ed. 2011), *Psychoanalytic Case Formulation* (The Guilford Press, 1999), and *Psychoanalytic Psychotherapy* (The Guilford Press, 2004). She has edited, co-authored, or contributed to several other books, and is Associate Editor of the *Psychodynamic Diagnostic Manual* (The Guilford Press, 2006; 2nd ed. 2017). A former president of the Division of Psychoanalysis (39) of the American Psychological Association, she is on the editorial board of *Psychoanalytic Psychology*. Dr McWilliams is a graduate of the National Psychological Association for Psychoanalysis and is also affiliated with the Center for Psychotherapy and Psychoanalysis of New Jersey.

The American Psychological Association chose her to represent psychoanalytic therapy in a 2011 remake of the classic film, "Three Approaches to Psychotherapy," and asked her to be a plenary speaker for the 2015 APA convention in Toronto. Dr McWilliams is an honorary member of the American Psychoanalytic Association, the Moscow Psychoanalytic Society, the Institute for Psychoanalytic Psychotherapy of Turin, Italy, and the Warsaw Scientific Association for Psychodynamic Psychotherapy. Her writings have been translated into twenty languages.

Doris Brothers is a co-founder and faculty member of the Training and Research in Intersubjective Self Psychology Foundation (TRISP). She served as co-editor with Roger Frie of *Psychoanalysis, Self and Context* from 2015 to 2019 and is chief editor of *eForum*, the online newsletter of the International Association of Psychoanalytic Self Psychology (IAPSP). She serves on the executive board, advisory board, and council of IAPSP. Her books include: *Toward a Psychology of Uncertainty: Trauma-Centered Psychoanalysis* (Routledge, 2008), *Falling Backwards: An Exploration of Trust and Self-Experience* (W. W. Norton & Company, 1995), with Richard Ulman, *The Shattered Self: A Psychoanalytic Study of Trauma* (The Analytic Press, 1988). A book with Koichi Togashi, *Psychoanalytic Narratives for a Traumatized World* is forthcoming, She is in private practice in Manhattan, New York, USA.

Koichi Tagashi is a certified clinical psychologist and licensed psychologist in Japan and a licensed psychoanalyst in the State of New York, is a faculty and training and supervising analyst at the Training and Research in Intersubjective Self Psychology Foundation, a professor and clinical supervisor at Konan University, Kobe, Japan. He is a member of the Council of the International Association of Psychoanalytic Self Psychology. He has published numerous books and articles in Relational Psychoanalysis and Cotemporary Self Psychology in the US, Japan, and Taiwan. His co-authored book, *Kohut's Twinship across Cultures: The Psychology of Being Human* was published by Routledge in 2015.

The authors of this volume share a deep concern for shaping language that leads toward healing and reconciliation. They sometimes utilize different strategies in this vein, with varying approaches to language as it points to gender, race, and ethnicity. For instance, the authors have been given the leeway to choose when to capitalize categories of ethnic identity.

INTRODUCTION

Intergenerational Strains

Eric R. Severson and David M. Goodman

A number of the deities in ancient Rome correlated with characters in Greek mythology. Jupiter is reminiscent of Zeus, Neptune of Poseidon, Ares of Mars, Mercury of Hermes, and so forth. One deity, however, factored routinely into everyday Roman life and had no Greek corollary[1]—Janus, the namesake for the month of January, the god of passage from old to new. This unique deity was the two-faced god, with one face pointed toward the past and the other toward the future. Modern New Year celebrations continue the ancient tradition of turning attention toward both past and future. Janus is the god of *auld lang syne*. For the Romans, he was the god of beginnings, endings, and transitions. His temple doors were opened at the outset of war, and closed as peace again settled over the realm.[2] Janus never loses track of the past, or fails to be turned toward the future; his role is to stabilize the present between the fading past and the indeterminate future.

If the Western philosophical tradition has a patron god of generations, it's Janus. This deity had a particular brand of knowledge and understanding: the omniscience of time. Janus is the reminder that someone, something, somewhere, glues together the chaos of time into a coherent unity and narrative. Traditional practices rest on an understanding of time held by the gods, by Janus in particular, and that means individuals need not fully understand *why* they are called to particular practices. Generations may come and go; Janus will keep track. Children will be summoned to believe and obey the traditions and practices of the past, whether or not they understand. There is, in these ancient myths, a reverence for the movement of tradition across generations, an obedience to religious or cultural practices that stabilize human life against the ravages of time.

When philosophy began to chip away at the authority of mythology, Janus was not spared. Even before Plato and Aristotle, Western philosophy began to prioritize and elevate the philosophical importance of the eternal and unchanging truth. This move simultaneously emphasizes the individual over community, minds over bodies, knowledge over tradition and biology over society. These trends find expression in modern philosophy, perhaps reaching their most obvious manifestation when Descartes endeavors to rebuild philosophy and the foundations of knowledge on the isolated, thinking self. It is impossible to track the vast consequences of this emphasis, which twists and contorts nearly every avenue of inquiry and discipline. This move serves to define the boundaries of psychology in particular, where the individualized mind is paramount. By beginning with the isolated self, philosophy often discovers that it has relegated social and relational aspects of the human person to secondary importance. Descartes doubts all things; only the *cogito* is indubitable. And, as Descartes rebuilds philosophy on that firm foundation, he only slowly and reluctantly returns to the other person. Society, culture, and history play no role whatsoever in Descartes' reconfiguration of epistemology. The so-called Age of Reason turned in disdain away from antiquated traditions and idiosyncratic cultural practices. Beset and preset by Enlightenment reductionist assumptions, the modern discipline of psychology suffers the same generational myopia and emphasis on individual and social rationality, divorced from history, gender, ethnicity, and bodies.

Among the most devastating problems we inherit from this modern turn is a seemingly pervasive inclination to minimize the significance of society, history, and generationality. As these are pushed to the periphery, a new framework for human life and society emerges. To be human is first of all to be rational individuals, with bodies programed by genetics. The traditions and practices of society, and intergenerational relationships, are replaced by the putative transmission of pseudo-scientific knowledge and truth. Only problems that register at this material level can be addressed. Racism and sexism can be easily dismissed as irrational and immoral positions, yet these scourges continue to flourish. The problem is, in part, a catastrophic failure to think about human beings as fundamentally social, relational, ethical, historical creatures. These facets of human personhood are not, and cannot, be handed down as facts of knowledge. The transmission of what it means to be human happens generationally through a vast network of relationships. And, as current literature on the intergenerational transmission of trauma shows us, it happens through unformulated experience, subtly prohibited emotions, invisible cultural habits and preferences, family structures, and through language: the very means we have of communicating distress to ourselves and others.[3] The embodied nature of intergenerational transmission demands a far more dimensional conceptualization of our social pain points and open wounds.

In many voices, and from many angles, this book argues that to be human is first to be embedded in society, to exist in porous and complex social and ethical relationships. This volume seeks to expose the way individualistic philosophy and psychology contributes to oppression, racism, and sexism. The scholars collected here offer a rich understanding of *Homo sapiens* as fundamentally temporal, ethical, and social creatures. In no small way, the authors seek to restore Janus's gaze, holding a present that remains attuned to the past and its relationship to our future. This is critically important for the purpose of establishing a means to vigilantly watch for our repetitions, hauntings, recapitulations, and the deeper historical streams that act through our premises and practices. We are destined to repeat, if no one is watching. And even a watchfulness does not ensure the past won't merely slip through in new form. We must have eyes communally trained to see and witness together if there is to be hope for a new mode of relating.

The lost urgency of generationality

Humans today, particularly those who live in more developed countries, enjoy an almost unimaginably long lifespan compared to our ancestors. During the Bronze Age, life expectancy at birth was just under 29 years of age.[4] Even the lucky few individuals who made it into their twenties were unlikely to see 40 years of age, and anyone who broke 50 years would have seemed ancient. Grey hair was a rare sign of wisdom and maturity, since most people did not live long enough to experience greying hair or balding scalps. Technological advancement, which has produced steady benefits for longevity since the Stone Age, has brought with it a host of dangers and perils that have kept human lifespan at bay. As recently as the year 1900, the average global lifespan was only 31 years of age.[5] Today, the average global lifespan exceeds 70.[6] Humans today live almost three times as long as our recent and ancient ancestors. This dramatic spike has many contributing factors, though the decreased mortality rate of both mothers and new-borns are almost certainly the most significant. Life was most precarious at its most important point: when an infant entered the world. We should remain mindful that this remains the case, today, in many parts of planet earth.

There may be no way to adequately appreciate the way this disparity in lifespan between modern humans and our ancestors impacts our understanding of morality, responsibility, and temporality. The brevity of life packed generations in together tightly, both in terms of households and chronology. In the world today, the median age of a mother giving birth to a first child is about 26 years, with averages in Japan, Austria and Switzerland exceeding 30 years of age.[7] In ancient times, across the planet, the median age for first childbirth would have been the early teenage years. Typically, a generation is quantified as that gap between the birth of a girl and the birth of her first child. In the old world—from which all the major cultures, philosophies and religions of the world originate—generational turnover occurred at more than twice their current rate. People in their early twenties would have been the elders and leaders in many communities. The urgency to procreate would have been intense and ubiquitous, as necessary as it was dangerous. The birth of a human life was the most crucial moment in the life of the community, but also among the most risky, with exceedingly high maternal mortality rates. Furthermore, the importance of establishing the mode of transmission of wisdom between generations would have been paramount, because the time of transmission was limited to the short lifespan of the individuals. Until recently, these dynamics shaped the notion of what it meant to belong to a generation. This aspect of human existence is attuned to the precariousness of life, to the delicate and painstaking work necessary to sustain meaning across time, and through the harrowing process of reproduction. This must have been, in part, what sustained the mythology of deities like Janus.

Mythology served as a kind of connective tissue that bound communities and social networks together across time and formed the bedrock for cultural memory. Cultures and communities across the planet developed a variety of traditions and practices relative to the rapid cycle of generations, and the urgency to succeed in passing forward vital components of society. All cultures, everywhere and across all of time, have borne some form of concern for what we call *generationality*. The very idea of culture implies the transmission of ideas, values or narratives across time, and this means passing such treasures from parents to children. The importance of generations, historically, was not primarily about the transmission of a body of knowledge. Rather, parents and elders sought to transmit what it means to be human, what it means to live, love, and die well. By thinking of every human person as a fresh *tabula rasa*, Western philosophy has minimized the rich and nuanced way that we pass along what is best and worst about ourselves. This problem is psychological, religious, and sociological, as much as philosophical. The forces of generational movements shape the psychological constitution of human persons. We are configured by the flow of a particular history and uniquely constelled into local forms with rather specific, generational, experiential parameters.[8] Western psychology, by adopting these same philosophical notions, has too often cut off the individual from the flow of history that constitutes the human person. This is especially true in the experience of historical human catastrophes (e.g. slavery, genocide) that have reverberating impact over multiple generations and operate with a kind of exponential osmolality that is not well understood.

Whatever we discover about the dynamics of generations in our current research, we must first account for the fact that human societies have been historically configured in the face of the acute precariousness of life, the tenuousness of the future, and an intensely urgent mandate to transmit vital values. The pressure to accurately transmit morality is evident in the way children memorized religious texts, illiterate scribes carefully copied documents, rituals were repeated with precision, and punishments for deviation were severe. In many cultures, this pressure also created an incredible tension between generations, or a powerful resistance to the insistence that new generations sustain the practices of their elders.

Global mythologies offer a staggering repetition of patricide and filicide, which are obvious rejections of generationality. One example is Cronus, who overthrew his father Uranus to take his place as master of the universe, and—terrified that the next generation of gods would do the same to him—he devoured each of his offspring before they had the chance to threaten his reign. Eventually, however, Cronos himself was murdered by his own son, Zeus. Human ancestors, around the globe, were captivated by anxious worry about the proper movement between generations. This idea also extends forward to modern psychological theorists such as Freud, who draws deeply from the wells of this anxiety, whether one considers his employment of Oedipus Rex or his pitting of civilization and its traditions and practices against the biological instincts of individual beings. Generational transmission is a complicated and fraught process, from the perspective of ancient mythologies and modern thinkers alike.

Another obvious example of concern about generationality comes from the great creation epic of Babylon, the *Enûma Elish*. The first table narrates the dawn of creation, with two eternal deities dwelling peacefully: Apsû, god of fresh water, and Tiamat, goddess of oceanic water. Their "waters mingle" and they begin to produce a host of gods. But the Babylonian pantheon of gods is profoundly noisy, and has "their way" of doing things, which creates great annoyance for both Apsû and Tiamat.[9] The new generation refuses to conform to the ways of their parents, persistently and flagrantly ignoring instruction. Apsû decides to kill all the young gods, but their mother Tiamat intervenes and undermines his murderous plan. Ultimately, Apsû is murdered by his son, and Tiamat's reward for sparing the younger generation is her own slaughter at the hands of her grandson Marduk. The *Enûma Elish* is written to describe the ascension of Marduk to the position of universal dominion, but the plot is moved by anxiety about change, death, and especially the necessary risks of introducing to the universe a new "generation." The first parents desperately desire to produce a generation that sustains tradition, but chaos ensues when the offspring fail to capitulate.

In a wide swath of ancient global mythology, the gods echo the anxieties of the people who search for meaning and who tell their stories. They procreate, but then fret endlessly about the chaos introduced by their children. The result is a wide range of approaches around the globe to the tension of generationality. In the ancient world, this often led to an insistence that *tradition precedes understanding*. Some traditions can be easily conveyed between generations; it's easy to explain to a five-year-old that certain berries are poisonous and should not be eaten. Other traditions are counterintuitive, hazardous, baffling, and oppressive. Children may not understand why they are asked to speak in a hushed voice, to remove their shoes, to wear a covering on their heads, to eat bitter foods, to stay away from matches and light switches on Shabbat, to fast during daylight hours, to wear a red dot on their foreheads, to walk long pilgrimages, and nearly countless other rituals. They are taught to obey first and understand second. This remains important in both religious and cultural communities today, but the intense pressure to communicate these ways of being human to young children has been slackened by the lengthening of average lifespans, and the resulting lengthening of the time for training and educating the young. There is more time, at least seemingly, for children to understand the reasoning behind traditional practices. Yet sometimes these traditions do not exist to conform to the demands for rational accounts of their usefulness. In *Fiddler on the Roof*, Tevye ponders the origins of traditions that prescribe certain items of clothing: "You may ask, how did this tradition get started? I'll tell you...I don't know. But it's a tradition and because of our traditions every one of us knows who he is and what God expects him to do."[10]

Surely these myths, traditions, and practices belie a deep nervousness in the face of the tenuous transition between generations. Nothing could be more important than the production and training of a new generation, but there is no formula for succeeding in this endeavor. This process is riddled with perils, and dependent upon unsteady and uncertain factors. Given the history of mythology and its social importance, it is not hard to see why Plato, and then Descartes, diverted attention away from history, culture, and reproduction, which generated some of the major tectonic fault lines for philosophy. The same is most certainly true for the modern enterprise of psychology. Its temptation has been to build upon universal characteristics, substrates of experience, shared biological principles, procedural protocols, and empirically generalizable findings to establish a picture of persons largely denuded of generational complexity. Though there are caveats in the literature that nod to differences in cultures, psychology, too, has sought a means of decontextualizing our notions of human identity such that history does not need to be accounted for.[11] Bypassing a deeper picture of history and establishing ideas on a "surer" footing was and is an attractive proposition for the young psychological sciences who attempted to model themselves on the natural sciences. In its own anxieties for existence it, too, sought foundations that might circumvent the perils of generational transmission. Such is the seduction of a reason-based paradigm. Rationality and its various methods, it seemed, might allow for smooth transmission as it is not reliant on bodies, communities, and tradition.

Myth, tradition, and gender

In the Western world, the ancient tendency to pass on traditions without sufficient understanding was challenged by Plato, who was more successful than Chronos at grinding to a halt the momentum of tradition, society, and culture. Plato points to eternal ideas, to unchanging truth, and to probing rational inquiry into all responsibilities and duties. In *Euthyphro*, Plato narrates a telling encounter between Socrates and Euthyphro. Their conversation involves piety, or holiness, especially whether and how a person might know that their behavior was indeed pious. Euthyphro has a vague, fragmented collection for his understanding of piety, and Socrates makes easy work of showing that his position on piety is problematic. On the question of reverence to tradition, Euthyphro makes unsuccessful several attempts to mount an adequate defense. Tradition, piety, holiness, and reverence are no match for the power of reason. Socrates, at the time of the dialogue, is seeking to create his own defense against the charge of impiety. What Socrates may not realize is that his debate with Euthyphro demonstrates the very impiety for which he seeks a rebuttal. Socrates elevates reason over tradition, interrogating practices and insisting that they conform to the synchronizing force of reason. This emphasis is a great gift to humanity, but it accelerates the forgetfulness of time, tradition, bodies, and generationality.

This forgetfulness is particularly intriguing as it relates to gender. The notion of a generation is inherently social, and deeply dependent on bodies, particularly female bodies. To be part of a generation is to receive and embody a complex history. Generation requires reproduction, and elevates the importance of child-birth, storytelling, rituals, and traditions. All of these themes are marginalized, to varying degrees, in modern philosophy and psychology. Furthermore, it is quite extraordinary to witness how mothers are represented as a mitigating influence in this intense generational tension. Or, to express it more clearly, females often appear in these myths with an alternative approach to the traditional dynamics of generational transmission. Yet, as has been repeatedly the case in the history of philosophy and culture worldwide, the voices of women have been muted, ignored, or worse. Rhea, wife of Chronus, gave birth to Zeus in secret, then swapped the swaddled thunder god with a stone so the angry Chronus ate a rock instead of his son.[12] In the epic Hindu text the *Mahabharata*, Babruvahana killed his father Arjuna in battle, but the deed was undone by the goddess Ulupi, Arjuna's wife.[13] Ulupi both condemned the violence and found creative means to unravel its sting; she traveled far to find the gem that would resuscitate her husband, who awoke grateful to be reunited with the son who killed him. In the *Enûma Elish*, Tiamat attempts to mediate the impending genocide of her children by Apsû, even as it leads to her own eventual slaughter. Whatever these universal concerns about generationality might be, we are wise to take note of the way mothers and daughters have often pushed for alternative approaches to these tensions. Against the seesaw of patricide and filicide, Tiamat, Ulupi, Rhea, and others make moves full of trust and care. This alternative approach to generations is intriguing and warrants more extensive treatment and investigation. Tracy Sidesinger's chapter in this volume, "The Nasty Woman: Destruction and the Path to Mutual Recognition," is a good example of such work. Sidesinger follows Simone de Beauvoir's suspicion that what passes for "human" has been heavily inflected by masculine frameworks and structures. She explores the way reflection on the "nasty woman" trope can help topple the abiding cultural perspective on social relationship, which is based primarily on dominance.

The Age of Reason, the era of European philosophical development between the seventeenth and eighteenth centuries, involved an even more overt turn against any and all practices that could not be connected by reason for validation. This involved, most obviously, a rejection of authority derived from myths, miracles, superstition, stories, and other sources that could not be verified by plain and clear rationalization. Immanuel Kant claims that the Enlightenment is a release from the *immaturity* of humankind, a sort of graduation from the ignorant sort of knowledge that characterizes childhood. Children must be told not to touch a stove before they can understand why; but to continue to avoid stoves into adulthood without understanding them would be immature. So, for Kant, the Enlightenment is liberation from the priority of obedience over understanding. As Kant puts it, and this really captures the gist of the problem before us, "immaturity is the inability to use one's own understanding without the guidance of another."[14] Understanding liberates the modern person from the need for guidance, the need for others.

Rethinking the generationality of humankind after modernity requires the reconsideration of these historical themes, and the way their neglect has led to contemporary psychological and social problems, racism, sexism, and a host of other issues. Collective and individual healing will require frameworks that narrow the gaps between public discourse, embodied experience, historical trauma, structural violence, and pragmatic political and ethical action. This idea also requires that restitution and resilience be seen as phenomena that are *embedded* in social, relational, ethical, and historical processes. In other words, the primary source of healing will come from an ability to understand the power and complexity of intergenerational relatedness.

The task before us

This book focuses attention on what happens when we fail to take measure of culture, history, tradition, and the body as we seek to understand human experience. In contemporary theories across many academic and clinical traditions, there is a significant countertrend underway that upsets some of the valorization of reason and modern seductions that unlinked the individual from the social and historical. Whether through Merleau-Ponty's work on the body, Gadamer's re-discovery of tradition and historically affected consciousness, Judith Butler's notions of precarity and embodiment, or the burgeoning literature on intergenerational transmission of trauma within psychoanalysis and psychology, there are growing resources for linking some of our contemporary social ailments and blindspots with the reproduction of modernity's bleaching of generationality. A particular set of foci in this book are the ways that race and gender are impacted by this failure.

The time is right, we think, to push back against the forgetfulness of bodies and history, and the way neglecting these leads to the entrenchment of racism and sexism. In the United States, for instance, seemingly intractable problems of racism continue to be manifest in educational inequality, mass incarceration, and police brutality. Myopic, and nationalistic, perspectives on history have exacerbated phobias about immigration, leading to an escalated obsession with borders, including physical and legal barriers. The #MeToo and Black Lives Matter movements serve, in part, as reminders of what modernity has made us forget. Racism, sexism, and xenophobia are produced and reinforced by the way we think about bodies, time, history, tradition. The work before us, in this book and beyond, is to investigate the deep history that steadily and surreptitiously perpetuates these scourges.

In Mark Freeman's chapter, he points out how the pervasive fixation on the individual in traditional psychoanalysis overlooks and obscures what he calls the "deep history" of the cultural past. Beneath the veneer of history, as a roster of commonly known past events, there is an unseen and often unacknowledged cultural past that relates to the "narrative unconscious." Race and racism take center stage in this chapter, as Mark Freeman investigates the complex cultural memory that inhabits contemporary racial tension. Michael Eric Dyson wrote of a Black intuition, a kind of deep history that "is passed down from generation to generation in the cellular memory of our vulnerable black bodies."[15] To think seriously about this aspect of human existence, and the implications it has for the crucial problems like racism, Freeman proposes a careful process of discerning, owning, and narrating deep history.

As Franz Fanon identifies in *Black Skin, White Masks*, the failure to attend to the function of society and history in the psychological formation of persons is complicit in the entrenchment of racism. Robert Bernasconi's chapter in this volume, "Frantz Fanon and Psychopathology," unpacks Fanon's critique. Fanon's frustration was partly with the modern tendency to frame human psychology according to individual psyches, biology, and heredity, and therefore minimize or ignore the social dimension of human existence and entanglement of human identities. Bernasconi draws attention to Fanon's claim, as important now as ever, that traditional psychology has thus framed the human experience as the White experience. To be human is first of all to be formed in a social environment, in a cultural milieu. To frame the human psyche as predominantly hereditary and biological is therefore to misunderstand mental illness, to fail to see the impact of institutions and the effects of society on individuals. This is no trivial oversight; Fanon argues that this failure entrenches and ensures the continuance of racism.

If Plato and company launched a long war on mythology, and if this war has led to a loss of the full understanding of human personhood, it will be helpful to investigate the way mythology remains nevertheless active in our social conscience. In her chapter, "American Cultural Symbolism of Rage and Resistance in Collective Trauma," Nahanni Freeman takes a look at the roles of transcendence, symbolism, and mythology in loosening the contemporary atmosphere of dehumanizing politics, racism, and sexism. Her chapter suggests that ignoring or oppressing reverence for the transcendent leads to intolerance and rage. Freeman sees promise in a renewal of rich engagement in spiritual and cultural practices, particularly those that foster reverent intercultural encounters.

Michel Foucault offers his own analysis of the vast consequence of the modern turn. For Foucault, the turn toward scientific knowledge is far from an innocent evolution of Western ideas. Knowledge is not neutral, but becomes useful socially in the establishment and fortification of political power. Foucault notes that terms like "madness" were used to ostracize and disempower anyone who failed to conform politically. Modernity, and its liberalism, has cast a unifying blanket over all human experience. Individuality and particularity are threats to the dominating power structures. Despite his dire assessment of our modern situation, Foucault offers hope. We can learn from the way these power structures dominate and oppress our lives, chiefly by attending to the particularities and details of human life, culture, and identities. Foucault is leery of the way these particularities are forced, again by the overarching power structures of modernity, into normalized behaviors. These routines, practices, and patterns reinforce oppression, even as they emerge from seemingly banal, everyday practices.

Two chapters in this volume, written by Jeff Sugarman and Sam Binkley, explore Foucault's angle on the problem before us. Sugarman's chapter, "Neoliberalism and the Ethics of Psychology," provides an insightful overview of the way the discipline of psychology, along with all modern disciplines, has been forcibly framed by Neoliberalism. Utilizing Foucault's critique, Sugarman incisively points out the indoctrination involved in the neoliberal agenda, which ignores the diversity of race, class, and gender in lieu of an individualistic meritocracy. What matters for the neoliberal self, Sugarman points out, is successful competition in the pursuit of values that reinforce structures of power. Autonomy is valued, but the options open to individuals are often prescribed and limited; all alternatives lead to the reinforcement of systemic power structures. Sugarman underscores the way neoliberalism therefore opposes any effort toward the collective good, as well as energies that might address the collective revulsion to *difference* that neoliberalism engenders.

Binkley's chapter, "Black Rage and White Listening: On the Dispositif of Racial Emotionality," utilizes Foucault's theory of normalization. Binkley is able to demonstrate the connection between the institutional pressure to normalize and the framing of race as abnormality. Racial tensions frequently result in expressions of rage from people of color, which operate alongside a phenomenon Binkley calls "White listening." The resulting emotional ensemble appears to challenge systemic racism but often leads to a delicate but manageable equilibrium. Black rage and White listening depressurize racial tension, which stabilizes and entrenches racialized positions. Binkley, like Sugarman, invites readers to a realistic assessment of the vast invasion of neoliberalism into the framing of what a person can become. We are offered hope, though, that through awareness of this function of the neoliberal political order we might recover racial emotion that does not simply reproduce and fortify racism.

Sheldon George's chapter, "Jouissance and Discontent: A Meeting of Psychoanalysis, Race and American Slavery," provides a captivating account of Freud's contribution to these problems. Freud contended that civilization served to usurp the individual, and interrupt the impulse gratification that is more natural and instinctive for human beings. George points out that this places the blame for human misery on civilization and culture, which renounce the pursuit of pleasure. For Freud, then, ethnicity and racial identity are regressive. Civilization moves toward unity, but ethnicity and racial identification pull us back toward the aggressive and antisocial instincts. George provides a fascinating account of the consequences of Freud's thesis, both for psychoanalysis and the broader cultural problem of racism. Utilizing Lacan, he offers a fresh analysis of the phenomenon of American slavery and demonstrates the way race mediates the way people access *jouissance*. The problem at hand runs deep, and George's chapter provides a unique perspective on the development of the modern idea of "race" and its many consequences.

Donna Orange looks to the underappreciated Danish ethicist Knud Løgstrup for help rethinking the devaluation of human life that results from Western fixation on ethics as rational and deeply individualistic. These approaches to ethics are largely based on risk and reward, and focus on individual choices rather than the complex systems that generate and sustain prejudice, ecological destruction, and oppressive economic forces. The alternative, according to Orange, must involve some radical approach to ethics, for all reasonable approaches only reinforce individualism. Løgstrup points to the Christian responsibility to love the neighbor, acknowledging that this is a radical command, as difficult as it is radical. In the relation with the neighbor, Løgstrup suggests that this command is one-sided and genuinely impossible. The impossibility of this injunction is only reason to abandon if one needs a rationally achievable ethic. Orange, following Løgstrup, suggests a return to the radically obligated sense of human *trust*. It rarely makes sense to radically trust other persons, particularly in troubled times, which Orange asserts that we inhabit. She claims that while radical ethics can orient everyday life, it becomes essential in times of emergency. Life arrives as a gift, and Orange suggests that we have a fundamental and radical duty to take care of one another.

Like Orange, Nancy McWilliams takes stock of the troubled times in which we live. In her chapter, "Finding the Other in the Self," McWilliams explores the psychological process whereby contemporary humans so frequently demean and objectify the other person. Keeping a close eye on the importance of these insights for clinicians, McWilliams evaluates the remarkable diversity of human communities and the way "othering" appears in everyday events. In the face of difference and diversity, McWilliams suspects that people are inclined toward a subconsciously defensive posture that gives rise to fear, rage, envy, and shame. Diversity training and cultural competencies are ineffective at addressing the deep origin of these responses. McWilliams suggests respect and vulnerability as key components to addressing the deeper problem, particularly in clinical practice. She advocates a "willingness to let ourselves be taken over by an intersubjective process that will psychologically enrich both our patients and ourselves."

Pressing for a more existential and embodied sense of personhood, Robin Chalfin's chapter appeals to Heideggerian insights on the language of identity and difference. Identity, she argues, is not something a people possess but something that persons *live*. We do not *have* gender identity and sexual orientation, as some artifacts attached to fixed identities. These are lived and embodied, and identity is the event of their embodiment. With an eye for clinical application, Chalfin explores and critiques the life and work of Martin Heidegger. She finds, in the arduous embodiment of differing identities, the emergence of what she calls a "psychic unease." This unease relates to undefined and undetermined facets of identity, but it need not lead to despair. Instead, Chalfin hopes that this perspective leads to a deeper understanding of the interconnectedness of human existence, as well as the intense vulnerability of human persons.

The authors of this book each identify resources to help unravel thorny and dense problems that arise from modern, Enlightenment articulations of human personhood. Doris Brothers and Koichi Togashi turn in two different directions to think otherwise: Japanese ethics and the unique philosophy of Emmanuel Levinas. Brothers and Togashi compare the way these approaches help us understand diverse responses to wide-scale catastrophic events. They look at various responses to the September 11, 2001 terrorist attacks and the Great Hanshin-Awaji Earthquake in Japan, and outline some striking cultural differences. Both Japanese and Levinasian approaches to ethics reject the fundamental egocentrism that emerges in Western philosophy. Through introductions to these ways of thinking, clinical vignettes, and suggested applications, Brothers and Togashi demonstrate significant alternatives to the isolated individualism of Western philosophy and psychology.

This book is an act of resistance, or rather a series of actions, against the modern Enlightenment; it is a turn towards the rich complexities of human community. As the individual is elevated above the deep and complex generational history of humanity, serious problems emerge that entrench, reinforce, and reproduce racism and sexism. This is a realistic text; none of these scholars and clinicians pretends that the task before us is simple, and some of them concede that it is downright impossible. Nevertheless, each chapter of this book urges its readers to think deeply, patiently, humbly, and openly about ways to rethink human experience. These suggestions will enliven and enrich clinical work, and inspire scholars to press resolutely down pathways that are opened here.

Notes

1 L. Schmitz, "Janus," in *Dictionary of Greek and Roman Biography and Mythology* (London: Taylor and Walton, 1890), 550–552.
2 Edith Hamilton, *Mythology: Timeless Tales of Gods and Heroes* (Boston: Little, Brown and Company, 2011), 51.
3 See the following list of recent edited volumes that bring together theorists and clinicians who are pioneering the intergenerational transmission of trauma literature within psychoanalysis: Sue Grand and Jill Salberg, eds., *Transgenerational Trauma and the Other* (New York: Routledge, 2013); Jill Salberg and Sue Grand, eds., *Wounds of History* (New York: Routledge, 2016); Adrienne Harris, Margery Kalb, and Susan Klebanoff, eds., *Ghosts in the Consulting Room* (New York: Routledge, 2016).
4 Oded Galor and Omer Moav, "Natural selection and the evolution of life expectancy," *CEPR Discussion Paper No. 5373* (London: Centre for Economic Policy Research, 2005), 32.

5 Thomas Prentice, "Health, history, and hard choices: Funding dilemmas in a fast-changing world," *Nonprofit and Voluntary Sector Quarterly* (2008), accessed July 2018, http://www.who.int/global_health_histories/seminars/presentation07.pdf.

6 World Health Organization, "Global Health Observatory Data: Life Expectancy," accessed July 2018, http://www.who.int/gho/mortality_burden_disease/life_tables/situation_trends/en/.

7 Center for Disease Control, "Trends in Characteristics of Birth by State, United States, 1990, 1995, and 2000–2002," accessed July 2018, https://www.cdc.gov/nchs/data/nvsr/nvsr52/nvsr52_19acc.pdf.

8 Philip Cushman, *Constructing the Self, Constructing America: A Cultural History of Psychotherapy* (Garden City, NY: DaCapo Press, 1995).

9 Leonard William King, *Enuma Elish (2 volumes in one): The Seven Tablets of Creation* (New York, NY: Cosimo, 2010), 7–9.

10 Joseph Stein (Author), Sheldon Harnick (Lyrics) and Jerry Bock (Music), *Fiddler on the Roof,* (Original Broadway production 1964), based on *Tevye and his Daughters* by Sholem Aleichem (1914).

11 Philip Cushman, *Travels with the Self: Interpreting Psychology as Cultural History* (New York: Routledge, 2018). See also Kurt Danziger, *Constructing the Subject: Historical Origins of Psychological Research* (Cambridge: Cambridge University Press, 1990).

12 Hamilton, 81.

13 Krishna Dharma (narrator), *Mahabharata: The Greatest Spiritual Epic of All Time* (New Delhi: Torchlight Publishing, 1999), 882–884. She also convinced Babruvahana not to commit suicide when he repented for his patricide.

14 William Bristow, "Enlightenment," in *The Stanford Encyclopedia of Philosophy* (Summer 2011 Edition), ed. Edward N. Zalta, accessed July 2018, https://plato.stanford.edu/archives/sum2011/entries/enlightenment/.

15 Michael Eric Dyson, *Tears We Cannot Stop: A Sermon to White America* (New York: St. Martin's Press, 2017), 174.

1

OPEN WOUNDS

Discerning, Owning, and Narrating Deep History

Mark Freeman

It seems only fitting to begin this chapter with some words penned by James Baldwin.

> History, as nearly no one seems to know, is not merely something to be read. And it does not refer merely, or even principally, to the past. On the contrary, the great force of history comes from the fact that we carry it within us, are unconsciously controlled by it in many ways, and history is literally present in all that we do. It could scarcely be otherwise, since it is to history that we owe our frames of reference, our identities, and our aspirations.[1]

A premise of this chapter is that beneath the veneer of commonly shared knowledge about one's cultural background is some measure of either unseen or unacknowledged cultural history. Following on this basic premise, this chapter goes on to underscore the importance of moving beyond the exterior of common knowledge about the cultural past, toward the deep history that lies beneath. More specifically, drawing on the idea of the "narrative unconscious,"[2] this chapter addresses the importance of discerning, owning, and narrating deep history. *Discerning* means opening oneself up to the untold stories of the cultural past. *Owning* means integrating and metabolizing these stories into cultural identity. *Narrating* means making these stories visible and public and thereby casting off the shroud of secrecy heretofore in place. This triune process need not eventuate in enhanced health and well-being. On the contrary, it may well eventuate in a deep and thoroughgoing sense of shame or the supposition that there is no making right the wrongs of the past. Whatever the outcome, there will have been some measure of substantial social transformation, and with it, the seeds of both personal and cultural growth.

In what follows, I focus my attention on the situation of African Americans in the United States. On the surface, it would appear—or it *would* have appeared—to many both within and outside the United States that the racial hostilities and violence that had existed before the civil rights era had largely passed. This is not to say that there weren't remnants or that all the troubles of the past had simply vanished. Far from it. All it meant, or appeared to mean, is that we in the States, especially upon electing the country's first Black president, had moved to a different stage. Judging by what has gone on over the course of the past few years, some of which will be considered shortly, some of this "progress" has been cast into question, and wounds that many had thought to be closed have turned out to be quite open. With this, some of our own blindness—to our history and to its sundry manifestations in the present—has become frightfully more apparent. In what follows, I shall try to make sense of this turnabout, drawing especially on the aforementioned concept of the "narrative unconscious." Before doing so, it may be useful to provide a sketch of the empirical landscape within which some of these ideas have taken shape. I shall do so in the form a brief enumeration of the "cases" in question.

Erasure

In some ways, it seems fitting to begin with a case that happened long ago, back in 1955. I am referring to the well-known case of Emmett Till, a fourteen-year-old boy from Chicago, visiting relatives in Mississippi, who was mercilessly lynched for having allegedly "molested" a young white woman at a local grocery store. As Timothy B. Tyson writes in his (2017) book *The Blood of Emmett Till*, "The ruthless attack inflicted injuries almost certain to be fatal" and "reveal a breathtaking level of savagery, a brutality that cannot be explained without considering rabid homicidal intent or a rage utterly beyond control." Indeed, by all indications, "Affronted white supremacy drove every blow."[3] This would seem confirmed by the fact that the "victim" herself, nearing 80, finally confessed that some of what she had said in the trial that took place to prosecute Till's killers—including the alleged molestation—was simply untrue.

For present purposes, the main thing to be emphasized is that, appearances notwithstanding, the United States remains in the clutches of much the same sort of hostility, if not outright savagery, that brought Emmett Till to his untimely death. As Tyson writes,

If we refuse to look beneath the surface, we can simply blame some Southern white peckerwoods and a bottle of corn whiskey. We can lay the responsibility for Emmett Till's terrible fate on the redneck monsters of the South and congratulate ourselves for not being one of them. We can also place … some percentage of the blame on Emmett, who should have known better, should have watched himself, policed his thoughts and deeds, gone

> more quietly through the Delta that summer.... . That we blame the murderous pack is not the problem; even the idea that we can blame the black boy is not so much the problem, though it carries with it several absurdities. The problem is *why* we blame them. We blame them to avoid seeing that the lynching of Emmett Till was caused by the nature and history of America itself and by a social system that has changed over the decades, but not as much as we pretend.[4]

I don't know whether "pretend" is the right word here. One way or the other, there is no question but that the Emmett Tills of the world are very much with us still.

First, there was Trayvon Martin: a 17-year-old African American gunned down in Florida by one George Zimmerman, a kind of vigilante volunteer policeman, who had apparently taken upon himself the responsibility of ensuring that his streets would remain emptied of the sort of riffraff that always seemed to be lurking about. Martin was wearing a hoodie; that seemed to signal danger. A tussle ensued, culminating in his being shot dead. Was he culpable in some way? Might he actually have posed a threat—a sufficient enough threat that Zimmerman had to spring into action in self-defense? I don't know. No one does. But Zimmerman's profile points in the direction of the killing being "overdetermined," shall we say, fueled by motives other than his and his community's safety.

Then there was Michael Brown, of the now-infamous Ferguson, Missouri: an 18-year-old man who had allegedly tried to steal from a convenience store and who, in view of the threat he supposedly posed, was eventually shot multiple times, the final bullet to his head sealing the deal. Brown had been unarmed and, as a recently released video showed, he hadn't actually been stealing; he had returned to the convenience store to retrieve some "cigarillos" that were rightfully his. Rather than Brown being the "demon" that had been described by the (white) police officer who shot him, who said he had "felt like a 5-year-old holding on to Hulk Hogan" (Brown was 6-foot-4, 292 lbs.), he seems to have been another victim, scary and threatening enough to be erased. Was *he* culpable? Had he done some things that posed a real threat to the policeman who gunned him down? Perhaps; it is difficult to say. But not unlike the other cases, there is also compelling reason to assume that there was a disconnect between the "crime" and the horrible magnitude of the punishment.

The list continues. That same year, there was 43-year-old Eric Garner, father of six, who had been suspected of selling loose cigarettes on a street corner in Staten Island, New York City, only to be put in a chokehold on the ground. Garner, asthmatic and obese, had apparently cried out "I can't breathe!" some eleven times; and in relatively short order he was gone, the victim of what was eventually ruled as a homicide. And Freddie Gray, 25, arrested in Baltimore, Maryland, for allegedly carrying an illegal switchblade, who died of injuries to his spinal cord, sustained while in the back of a police van. And Philando Castile, 32, in Falcon Heights, Minnesota, who had informed the shooter-policeman that he was licensed to carry a weapon and who, upon reaching into his pocket for his ID, was shot seven times. And 37-year-old Alton Sterling, shot several times at close range in Baton Rouge, Louisiana, while held down on the ground by two (white) policemen.

We have heard mainly about the plight of Black men, but there have been women too—for instance, Renisha McBride, 19, who, having crashed her car, knocked on someone's door and was blown away with a shotgun in Dearborn Heights, Michigan; and Marlene Pinnock, a 51-year-old homeless woman who had been severely beaten by a California Highway Patrol officer for walking barefoot on a highway. Unlike the others, Pinnock lived, but she was irreparably damaged.

I could go on. As I have already suggested, there were complications in several of these cases and different sides to the story. One could also argue that this spate of killings over a period of two years or so is just a random cluster, an unfortunate series of tragic coincidences that may not be as revealing as many have assumed. Finally, it may be the case that, during this same period of time, comparable numbers of white men met their untimely demise in much the same way, their own deaths buried in obscure columns of local newspapers. These sorts of "qualifications" notwithstanding, there was something extremely alarming about this sequence of killings, something that called attention to wounds mistakenly thought to have been a thing of the past.

This brings us back to Tyson's contention that things haven't changed quite as much as we "pretend"—or at least would like to believe. Consider the Black Lives Matter movement that emerged in the States and the demonstrations that eventually took place following this recent spate of killings. "Much like the Emmett Till protests of the 1950s," Tyson writes,

> these demonstrations raged from coast to coast and fueled scores of local campaigns. Police brutality against men and women of color provided the most urgent grievance but represented a range of festering racial problems: the criminalization of black bodies; the militarization of law enforcement; mass incarceration; racial injustice in the judicial system; the chasms of inequality between black and white and rich and poor; racial disparities in virtually every measure of well-being, from employment and education to health care.[5]

All of this had been going on since the Till era, but surreptitiously somehow, under the collective radar. "Yes," Tyson acknowledges, "many things have changed; the kind of violence that snatched Till's life strikes only rarely." But "America is still killing Emmett Till, and often for the same reasons that drove the violent segregationists of the 1950s and 1960s,"[6] not the least of which is the fact that "we have not yet killed white supremacy."[7] As for what is to be done, "all of us," he asserts, "must develop the moral vision and political will to crush white supremacy—both the political program and the concealed assumptions." And to do so, "We have to come to grips with our own history."[8] Until then, there will be open wounds, gaping at times, and what Michelle Alexander has referred to as the *new* Jim Crow era will continue apace.[9]

"Not everything that is faced can be changed," James Baldwin has written, "but nothing can be changed until it is faced."[10] This is surely so. But what does it mean? And how might I myself be implicated? "That great Western house I come from is one house," Baldwin has also written, "and I am one of the children of that house. Simply, I am the most despised child of that house. And it is because the American people are unable to face the fact that I am flesh of their flesh, bone of their bone, created by them. My blood, my father's blood, is in that soil."[11] The implication: "History is not the past. It is the present. We carry our history with us. We *are* our history. If we pretend otherwise, we literally are criminals." There is that word again: "pretend." *Is* that what I and others have been doing? Are *we* criminals? Baldwin continues: "I attest to this: the world is not white; it never was white. White is a metaphor for power, and that is simply a way of describing Chase Manhattan Bank."[12] Chase Manhattan is one of the banks I do business with. What shall I make of it?

I have already noted, with Tyson, that the Emmett Tills of the world are with us still; they are part of our history—indeed, on some level, part of *my* history. I cannot say that I "remember" the killing of Emmett Till; the year of his death was the year of my birth. Nor do I remember much of what has gone on since that time—although in point of fact, there was much more going on throughout the years than I fully saw. Back in grade school, a big, tough Black boy got into a fistfight with a crude white boy, and at one point the white boy called his formidable opponent a "black bitch," which immediately brought that big, tough boy to terrible tears. What *was* that? I sort of knew, but didn't. Plus, it seemed exceptional—like those "rednecks" Tyson wrote about. There were other events too, strewn throughout the years. I even felt some of them. But most faded into the nether reaches of the past, where they would remain essentially locked away.

Excursus: the narrative unconscious and the psycho-politics of erasure

We shall hear more about the fate of Black bodies shortly, especially through the work of Ta-Nehisi Coates[13] and Michael Eric Dyson.[14] For now, I want to suggest that all of the stories considered thus far have served to disclose some salient characteristics of what I earlier referred to as the "narrative unconscious." The idea of the narrative unconscious arose in a quite different context, and may be traced back to an extremely unsettling experience I had during my first time in Berlin. The story, in short, is that after several days of exploring the city and gaining some concrete sense of its brutal past during the Holocaust era, I had something of an emotional breakdown. It was utterly unanticipated. Troubled though I had been by the many spectacles I had been encountering, I had little idea of the profound way in which they were registering in my mind and soul. In the aftermath, and on further inspection, I could only conclude that there was much that I had brought with me to the city—enough, apparently, in the way of information, ideas, and images, to "activate the undercurrents" of the spectacles observed. Memory thus becomes "a curious amalgam of fact and fiction, experiences and texts, documentary footage, dramatizations, movies, plays, television shows, fantasies, and more."[15] It was this very experience that led me to this notion of the "narrative unconscious," which "refers not so much to that which has been dynamically repressed as to that which has been lived but which remains unthought and untold, i.e., to those culturally-rooted aspects of one's history that have not yet become part of one's story."[16]

This initial site of the narrative unconscious was largely personal in nature, and led me to explore some under-acknowledged aspects of my own identity, especially as a Jew. I simply didn't know this was as much a part of my identity as it seemed to be. The experience at hand thus proved revelatory and allowed me to think further about those dimensions of identity that had theretofore been largely unseen and unknown. In speaking of the narrative unconscious in the present context, the focus is less on my particular identity as Mark Freeman, ambivalent American Jew, filled with all manner of bric-a-brac from numerous sources outside the perimeter of my first-hand experience, and more on my identity as a "white" American, living in a culture and climate and with a history that had remained on the periphery of my consciousness at best. I am not suggesting that I have had some sort of earth-shattering epiphany, some shocking moment of sudden illumination, in which the history just referred to was made clear. On the contrary, this history remains quite obscure. Fortunately, it is a bit less obscure than it was, thanks to both the cases I have recounted and the ways these have been processed and analyzed by some important thinkers, whose aim is nothing less than to reveal the narrative unconscious of America.

I have found the process of trying to come to terms with these stories and analyses painful at times. They have allowed me to see what, on some level, I had refused to see, or see clearly. I was (and remain) a liberal. I had some sense of the plight of Black Americans. I had lived on the South Side of Chicago—sheltered within the confines of the well-guarded University of Chicago, but in close proximity to real violence and degradation and suffering. I knew all that, and I had even felt some of it. But only in a cursory way. It's still somewhat cursory, partial, incomplete. Maybe it is destined to remain so. All I can do, it seems, is to try to move ahead, slightly less blind, slightly less oblivious, slightly less unconscious. But what else? Is there anything that I might actually *do* to redress the situation we have been considering?

Discerning

In referencing "open wounds," I am referring not only to those wounds suffered in Black America but also to those we in white America have suffered, and are continuing to suffer, on account of the pain we have inflicted. One can of course ask here: Who is the "we"? What pain have I, personally, inflicted? All things considered, I have been pretty good, haven't I? Perhaps. But it's quite immaterial, for the history in question is one to which I belong. It is time now not only to acknowledge these wounds but also to *feel* them. This requires, first, seeing more clearly aspects of my own unseeing.

Ta-Nehisi Coates's *Between the World and Me* [17] has been of great value in the process. But this isn't about me—certainly not in any personal sense. It's about being in a Black body in America, and takes the form of an extended letter Coates has written to his son. On another level, however, it *is* about me—me as a social subject and a participant in history. This is more explicitly stated in Dyson's book,[18] framed as "a sermon to White America," but it is part of Coates's story too. Can I truly read it? *Have* I?

It's too soon to tell. Coates has some harsh words to share with his son—especially harsh, perhaps, for those who believe they are white. Indeed,

> it must be said that washing the disparate tribes white, the elevation of the belief in being white, was not achieved through wine tastings and ice cream socials, but rather through the pillaging of life, liberty, labor, and land; through the flaying of backs; the chaining of limbs; the strangling of dissidents; the destruction of families; the rape of mothers; the sale of children; and various other acts meant, first and foremost, to deny you and me the right to secure and govern our own bodies.[19]

Part of the problem, Coates continues, is that "America believes itself exceptional, the greatest and noblest nation ever to exist, a lone champion standing between the white city of democracy and the terrorists, despots, barbarians, and other enemies of civilization." This is a strong claim, and it ought to be taken seriously—"which is to say, I propose subjecting our country to an exceptional moral standard. This is difficult," however, "because there exists, all around us, an apparatus urging us to accept American innocence at face value and not to inquire too much. And it is so easy to look away, to live with the fruits of our history and to ignore the great evil done in all of our names. But you and I have never truly had that luxury. I think you know."[20]

Why is Coates writing to his son now? It had to do with his son having witnessed Eric Garner being choked to death and Renisha McBride being shot and other such deadly assaults. On some level, he had to have known already. But it was time to put some flesh on this knowledge and to remind that young boy that "racism is a visceral experience, that it dislodges brains, blocks airways, rips muscle, extracts organs, cracks bones, breaks teeth."[21] Upon learning that Michael Brown's killers would go free, Coates's son retreated to his room and cried. There was no room for comfort, solace. "What I told you is what your grandparents told me: that this is your country, that this is your world, that this is your body, and that you must find some way to live within the all of it."[22]

Here I am, using Coates's words, in order to stock this chapter appropriately with something other than theories. Should I be sharing his words? Can I justify using them in this way? I suppose it's better than just reading the book and setting it aside; good to remember some of what he said, put it out there for another crowd. But am I really *discerning* what is being said? Can I? More to the point: Can I discern with enough care and attention to detail that I can begin to make the narrative unconscious conscious and to feel what emerges? I am part of the history about which Coates is speaking, and his story is a vehicle for making some of it visible. "You really ought to know," he is essentially telling us. "I *do* know," I might protest. But I really don't. Can I?

There was, there is, so much fear—for instance, of Coates's own potential demise when, in the sixth grade, the "boy with the small eyes reached into his ski jacket and pulled out a gun" and who, in those eyes, disclosed "a surging rage that could, in an instant, erase my body."[23] It was just another day. "Fear ruled everything around me, and I knew, as all black people do, that this fear was connected to the Dream out there, to the unworried boys, to pie and pot roast, to the white fences and green lawns nightly beamed into our television sets."[24] Are they really related? I always liked pie and pot roast! Was it really at the expense of all these terrified people, locked in their Black bodies? Through it all, through all this fear and terror and threat of violence, was the constant praise of nonviolence. But "Why," Coates asks, "were our only heroes nonviolent? I speak not of the morality of nonviolence, but of the sense that blacks are in especial need of this morality." It was difficult to make sense of it all. "The world, the real world, was civilization secured and ruled by savage means. How could the schools valorize men and women whose values society actively scorned? How could they send us out into the streets of Baltimore, knowing all that they were, and then speak of nonviolence?"[25] Not surprisingly, "I came to see the streets and the schools as arms of the same beast."[26]

There would be education, and more education, counter-narratives proclaiming Black beauty and nobility, and more counter-narratives, demythologizing the myths Coates had unwittingly embraced—so needed were they as antidotes, even if temporary, to the stories that had surrounded him and threatened to devour him. There were, however, some unassailable truths. "Never forget," he would tell his son, "that we were enslaved in this country longer than we have been free. Never forget that for 250 years black people were born into chains—whole generations followed by more generations who knew nothing but chains."[27]

Perhaps Coates is speaking to me too, I who believe (believed?) I am white? It would seem so:

> You must struggle to truly remember this past in all its nuance, error, and humanity. You must resist the common urge toward the comforting narrative

of divine law, toward fairy tales that imply some irrepressible justice. The enslaved were not bricks in your road, and their lives were not chapters in your redemptive history. They were people turned to fuel for the American machine.[28]

And that machine is still cranking along in the form of narrative, triumphal and redemptive, noble and proud.[29] "America first!" Donald Trump whoops. We had taken a wrong turn with Barack Obama, Trump argued. He was the "worst president," "a disaster," "unfit to serve." Things are going to be different under my watch, Trump promised. We're going to turn shame into pride, loss into gain, defeat into victory. We're going to wipe out the urban blight in Chicago and elsewhere, and when we do, you will be free once more to walk your streets in security, comfort, and pride. Maybe then there will be no more reminders of our awful history. Maybe then those 250 dreadful years of slavery will be forgotten. Maybe then we will have arrived at a state of purity, cleanliness, the dirt of the past having been swept away. *Erasure*, apocalypse-style.

Trump's "vision" is little more than a crude fantasy. And make no mistake: there is no separating the purity he seeks from the power tactics he has explicitly called for in addressing the social problems he has identified. Law and order, he has told us; that's what we need. And, of course, we need to secure our borders, make sure all of those threats to law and order are kept at bay, outside the confines of our peace-loving nation. And we need to get rid of those already here who mistakenly assumed that they might find a safe haven from the ravages of their own native worlds. Meanwhile, there are the ravages of this one—including, for Coates, the killing of his friend Prince Jones, who had apparently been hunted across three states and gunned down in terrible error, the hunt in question having been for someone else. Jones "was not killed by a single officer" in any case "so much as he was murdered by his country and all the fears that have marked it from birth."[30] As Coates writes, "This entire episode took me from fear to a rage that burned in me then, animates me now, and will likely leave me on fire for the rest of my days."[31]

Coates goes on to recount another incident that had left him filled with hot rage:

> Perhaps you remember that time we went to see Howl's Moving Castle on the Upper West Side. You were almost five years old. The theater was crowded, and when we came out we rode a set of escalators down to the ground floor. As we came off, you were moving at the dawdling speed of a young child. A white woman pushed you and said "Come on!" Many things now happened at once. There was the reaction of any parent when a stranger lays a hand on the body of his or her child. And there was my own insecurity in my ability to protect your black body. And more: There was my sense that this woman was pulling rank. I knew, for instance, that she would not have pushed a black child out on my part of Flatbush, because she

would be afraid there and would sense, if not know, that there would be a penalty for such an action... . I turned and spoke to this woman, and my words were hot with all of the moment and all of my history. She shrunk back, shocked. A white man standing nearby spoke up in her defense. I experienced this as his attempt to rescue the damsel from the beast. He had made no such attempt on behalf of my son. And he was now supported by other white people in the assembling crowd. The man came closer. He grew louder. I pushed him away. He said, "I could have you arrested!" I did not care. I told him this, and the desire to do much more was hot in my throat. This desire was only controllable because I remembered someone standing off to the side there, bearing witness to more fury than he had ever seen from me—you.[32]

The incident was devastating and shocking, and served to reveal much about the narrative unconscious. "I came home shook," Coates writes, partly due to the intensity of his rage and partly due to the depth of the history disclosed.

That history had, of course, been there all along. But it was only now, in the wake of this awful incident, that it had come to the surface in full force. There had no doubt been an awakening for his son too, who, in witnessing both the woman's arrogance and his father's unbridled rage, would also see the workings of the narrative unconscious. For present purposes, however, what is most important is that we, Coates's readers, especially those of us who believe we are white, are able to discern the many and profound ways in which the history in question, so often concealed by ourselves, has been operative in our lives. This seems to be the main purpose of his book. We need to see things more clearly. We need to see some of our own blind spots and refusals. We need to see how the narrative unconscious has been at work, creating a vast panoply of social and personal pathologies, symptoms of a still-diseased culture. Only upon such seeing is owning made possible.

Owning

Was the woman Coates wrote about a racist? In her own view, he ventures, probably not. "Had I informed this woman that when she pushed my son, she was acting according to a tradition that held black bodies as lesser, her response would likely have been, 'I am not a racist.'" For many, "the word racist ... conjures, if not a tobacco-spitting oaf, then something just as fantastic—an orc, troll, or gorgon... . There are no racists in America," it might be said, "or at least none that people who need to be white know personally."[33] The fact is,

The mettle that it takes to look away from the horror of our prison system, from police forces transformed into armies, from the long war against the black body, is not forged overnight. This is the practiced habit of jabbing out one's eyes and forgetting the work of one's hands. To acknowledge these horrors means turning away from the brightly rendered version of your country as it has always declared itself and turning toward something murkier and unknown. It is still too difficult for most Americans to do this. But that is your work. It must be, if only to preserve the sanctity of your mind.[34]

Son, Coates continues, "The entire narrative of your country argues against the truth of who you are."[35] Indeed, one might add, it argues against the truth, period. That remains hidden, veiled, unconscious. "We are captured, brother, surrounded by the majoritarian bandits of America. And this has happened here, in our only home, and the terrible truth is that we cannot will ourselves to an escape on our own." Help is needed, help that might break the spell of the long sleep of unconsciousness. "Perhaps that was, is, the hope of the movement: to awaken the Dreamers, to rouse them to the facts of what their need to be white, to talk like they are white, to think that they are white, which is to think that they are beyond the design flaws of humanity, has done to the world."[36]

What sort of awakening should it be? A gentle rousing? As in: "It's time to get up now, brothers and sisters"? That can't possibly be enough. No; there needs to be some shaking involved, and the rage that's there needs to be part of it. And yet, this cannot be his son's responsibility. "I do not believe we can stop them, Samori, because they must ultimately stop themselves." So, "do not struggle for the Dreamers. Hope for them. Pray for them, if you are so moved. But do not pin your struggle on their conversion. The Dreamers will have to learn to struggle for themselves."[37]

Through it all, Michael Eric Dyson states, "I believe that our moral and spiritual passions can lead to a better day for our nation" and that "when we get out of our own way and let the spirit of love and hope shine through we are a better people." On the face of it, Dyson's view would appear to be somewhat more upbeat than Coates's. "But," he quickly adds,

> such love and hope can only come about if we first confront the poisonous history that has almost unmade our nation and undone our social compact. We must face up to what we as a country have made of the black people who have been the linchpin of democracy, the folk who saved America from itself, who redeemed it from the hypocrisy of proclaiming liberty and justice for all while denying all that liberty and justice should be to us.[38]

Dyson, taking up his role of ordained Baptist minister (in addition to being a scholar, cultural critic, and activist), has his book take the form of "a sermon to White America." It is in a section of the book titled "Repenting of Whiteness" that we come face to face with what I am here calling the issue of "ownership." Having just provided some context for this notion of repentance, Dyson acknowledges: "*I know this is a lot* for you to take in. It must make you woozy and weak at the knees. So much has been invested in whiteness that it's hard to let it go. It is often defensive, resentful, full of denial and amnesia." But there is a solution, of sorts. "The only way to save our nation, and yes, to save yourselves, is to let go of whiteness and the vision of American history it supports."[39]

Here, then, we have a new twist to the set of ideas we are now exploring: there will be no owning until there is some measure of *dis*owning. Discerning is surely a requisite condition. Before one can engage in *distanciation*—in this case, the leaving-behind of a particular mode of knowing and being—there has to be the *recognition* that the mode in question is inadequate or faulty.[40] The challenge of spelling out how and why it is inadequate or faulty can be massive indeed, particularly in situations as loaded as this one. "*I must say to you*, my friends," Dyson continues,

> that teaching in your schools has shown me that being white means never having to say you're white. Whiteness long ago, at least in America, shed its ethnic skin and struck a universal pose. Whiteness never had to announce its whiteness, never had to celebrate or promote its unique features.
>
> If whites are history, and history is white, then so are culture, and society, and law, and government, and politics; so are logic and thinking and reflection and truth and circumstances and the world and reality and morality and all that means anything at all.
>
> Yes, my friends, your hunger for history is still pretty segregated. Your knowledge of American often ends at the color line. You end up erasing the black story as the American story, black history as American history.[41]

Again, doing otherwise is bound to be difficult. Indeed, Dyson suggests, the process in question "bears some resemblance to the five stages of grief a person passes through when they know they are dying." We need not traverse all of these stages here. But let us acknowledge, candidly:

> It is being wrong that leaves you distressed. There is often sorrow and anguish in white America when blackness comes in the room. It gives you a bad case of what can only be called, colloquially, the racial blues, but more formally, let's name it C.H.E.A.T. (Chronic Historical Evasion and Trickery) disorder. This malady is characterized by bouts of depression when you can no longer avoid the history that you think doesn't matter much, or when your attempts to deceive yourself and others—about the low quality of all that isn't white— fall flat. It's understandable that you experience mood swings.[42]

And it's understandable that you, *we*, might wish to keep things under wraps. In the present context, there is a markedly *dynamic* dimension to the narrative unconscious. When I initially introduced the idea I framed it mainly in terms of aspects of our histories that had yet to become part of our stories. In this respect, it was largely about coming to consciousness, making visible what may have been invisible, unseen and unknown. Here, following Dyson in broad outline, we are seeing something added to the picture—namely, an element of cultural *repression*, oftentimes manifested in the form of *resistance* to what, on some unconscious level, we know to be so.

The process of owning will thus entail breaking through the hardened crust of repression and breaking down resistance. As Freud reminds us in his essay, "Remembering, repeating, and working-through,"[43] it is bound to be fraught: rather than remembering, there will be repeating, which in turn signals that there has yet to be the necessary working-through. We see this process in full bloom with the rise of Donald Trump who, in his rally cry to "Make America great again!" is, in essence, issuing a refusal to work through the harsh realities of history, thereby condemning him and us to the illusory fictions many seem to need to rest comfortably with—and to retain—their dominant status. As Dyson puts the matter,

> It sounded the call to white America to return to simpler, better days. But the golden age of the past is a fiction, a projection of nostalgia that selects what is most comforting to remember. It summons a past that was not great for all; in fact, it is a past that was not great at all, not with racism and sexism clouding the culture. Going back to a time that was great relies on deliberate disremembering.[44]

Despite my bringing the idea of repression into the picture, I am not sure about the "deliberate" part of what Dyson has to say. In Trump's case, it probably is deliberate. In many other cases, it probably is too—even if not in a fully conscious way. Crude strategist that Trump is, he has no problem at all feeding people what he thinks they want to hear. Moreover, there are surely those who know enough about the "underside" of American history that they have done what they could to tamp it down. But for many of those who heard, and heeded, Trump's shrill call to return to better days, there may be no deliberate disremembering at all. The reason, which Dyson surely knows on some level, is that they were simply recycling the story they have been told time and time again about their beautiful country, beacon of democracy, able to provide "liberty and justice for all"—albeit, with a few kinks along the way. The idea of the narrative unconscious remains applicable here too: even if deep history hasn't been deliberately kept under wraps, it remains operative and alive, configuring the world in ways that may be unseen.

As Dyson goes on to point out, there is another dimension of the issue that needs to be addressed, one that is pertinent not only to this particular situation but to any and all situations in which responsibility for the crimes of the past is believed to rest with those who actually committed them. The Holocaust is one such situation. "*We* didn't do it," members of subsequent generations might say.

Apartheid is another. "That ended before we were even born." There are other such situations with similar reasoning: "We ought not to be held responsible for the crimes of our ancestors. They did it, not us. So, don't turn *us* into the victims of *their* moral depravity or short-sightedness. Plus, what's done is done." It's not at all clear that things are quite as "done" as this idea would suggest. Remnants of the Holocaust surely remain. And, as noted earlier, even though apartheid is officially over, there is no question that its remnants linger on quite visibly. As for the American situation, to imagine that things are even *close* to "done" is nothing short of a delusion. All those recent killings? Again, maybe they are just a statistical anomaly. "That's not who we are!" some might cry. The challenge is to take seriously the distinct possibility, indeed likelihood, that this is precisely who we are. As Dyson notes, "The 'them, not me' defense denies how the problem persists in the present day." Bearing this in mind, "It is best to think of systems and not individuals when it comes to racial benefit in white America."[45] Actually, it seems best to think of both, for alongside the large structures and systems Dyson is referring to here, there are still many individuals carrying the torch of "them." They sometimes do it quite proudly.

I just referred to "they"—the supposition being that "I" am somehow a member of another category. If we are talking about overt pride, it's true: it does not apply to me. But this is no time for splitting hairs. And as much as we in America might wish to blame Donald Trump for the awful spell he was able to cast over much of the country, we all need to look more closely at our history, and we need to own it. The reason isn't just that the history is ours. The reason is that it is still very much with us. How could it be otherwise?

Narrating

Okay, then; let's own it. But how? How can "white America" own not only the "old" fiction-filled history that has been told but the "new" history to come? It will be difficult. Following what I earlier called "distanciation," there must be a process of *articulation*, that is, of beginning to identify a way forward, a way that marks a significant difference from one's earlier way. That is not all. Alongside articulating this new way forward, there must be *appropriation*, which, in the present context, means beginning to *live* the stories we tell.[46]

But first things first—it is time for a new story to be told, the one that has been locked away in the secret corridors of America's history, locked away in the narrative unconscious. It will not only be about Black America. It will be about Native Americans too, and others who have been excluded, shut out from what Coates had called "the Dream." I won't begin to tell that story here. If truth be told, I don't know enough about it to speak with any real authority, and it feels presumptuous for me to even try. The good news, I suppose, is that I now *know* that I don't know enough about it. Let me therefore turn to Dyson once more to get us started. In a portion of the book titled *Being Black in America*, Dyson includes three sections, respectively titled "Nigger," "Our Own Worst Enemy?," and "Coptopia." Needless to say, these sections wouldn't be the sections I would—or could—write. Certain words cannot be spoken by the likes of me.

This is telling. Perhaps the first step of what I am here calling "narrating" is to truly (try to) *listen* to others' stories, especially those that are less about events and more about those sensibilities and intuitions that characterize lived worlds. So it is that Dyson writes about the process of having acquired "a sense about the world that outpaced my knowledge of it. It was black intuition that, in retrospect, was inevitable because all black people get it at one time or another. It is passed down from generation to generation in the cellular memory of our vulnerable black bodies."[47] Hearing what is sometimes referred to as "the N word" served to activate this memory for Dyson; and now, looking backward, one of the many challenges before him is to somehow explicate the lived world it brought to light. As for being deemed "our own worst enemy," killing each other off with abandon, that storyline needs a serious correction. What about "Coptopia"? Can we subscribe to the story Dyson's telling here? *Should* we? Part of me is reluctant. Of course there are racist cops—just like there are racist everything else. And yes, maybe there is a disproportionate concentration of them. Should we go any further? "Could you believe that most cops are good and well-intentioned when the history of harm forever hangs above your heads?" More questions: "Can you honestly say that if we just comply with the cops' wishes that we'll be safe? How many more black folk do you have to see get sent to their deaths by cops while doing exactly what they were told before you'll believe us?"[48] *Come on.* "If you're honest you'll see that the police force is a metaphysical collective with a gift for racial punishment that has never viewed black folk as human beings, because the law that they are charged to enforce has never seen us as human beings. And the Constitution that the law rests on did not write us in as fully human."[49]

This sort of storyline is bound to meet with some resistance. But there is a part of it that is unassailable—namely, the part that seeks to tell the story of how people have actually *experienced* the world they have come to inhabit. Dyson recounts a number of events in his own life entailing profound humiliation. "They've embarrassed me in front of my brother and my son. Most painfully, they've embarrassed me in front of myself. Every encounter with the police splits us into two selves, one a quiet, brooding figure cursing the cops from within, the other a dawdling doppelganger, a concrete-staring shuffling Negro we are ashamed to admit lives inside of us."[50] There is more.

> Terror and shame go hand in hand. There is fear in realizing we are help-
> less to persuade others that we are human. In that moment, there is also
> deep shame, shame that you do not take our humanity for granted. We are
> ashamed that there is nothing we can do to keep you from seeing us as
> worthless.[51]

There is nothing to resist in these words. Dyson is simply telling it like it is, at least for some. "You cannot know the terror that black folk feel when a cop car makes its approach and the history of racism and violence comes crashing down on us. The police car is a mobile plantation, and the siren is the sound of dogs hunting us down in the dark woods."[52] He's right; we cannot know the terror, certainly not in the way he does. But we can know, or begin to know, *something*. As we have just seen, narrating is key.

"Beloved," Dyson writes, "your voices are crucial because the doubt of black humanity, the skepticism of black intelligence, and the denial of the worth of black bodies linger in our cultural unconscious and shadow our national politics." As I have suggested throughout this chapter, this cultural unconscious is intimately tied to narrative: the narrative of what hasn't been told and the narrative of what needs to be. "If you challenge white ignorance, or indifference, to the plight of people of color, it will lend our cause needed legitimacy."[53]

Yes, this is surely so. But I ask once more: what does it mean? When I presented the story of my experience in Berlin, I wrote about my process of essentially "uncovering" certain aspects of history and identity about which I had been largely unaware; the experience had "activated the undercurrents," as I put it, with the result that I came to see and to know "that which has been lived but which remains unthought and untold." There are aspects of this process that apply to the present context as well. In reading books like Coates' and Dyson's, among others, I sometimes find myself looking backward and thinking anew about what I have seen through the years, only to let go by. There was plenty there, but I didn't do much to metabolize it. And I certainly didn't do much to *act* on what I saw and, on some level, knew.

But there is a difference too between the process pertaining to the Berlin experience and this one. I am referring here to the fact that there is much about the history at hand that I simply don't know and have never known. It is not lying in waiting, such that the undercurrents might be activated. Rather, it is one that all but escaped the gaze of many of those who, like me, have been comfortable enough with the reigning renditions of things: Yes; things were bad back then; remnants remain. But let's not dwell too much; let's take solace in the remarkable gains and just do our best to keep our eyes open.

These reigning renditions are not only illusory—which is to say, based on our wishes—but as I have come to learn, they can be flat out false, serving to justify and perpetuate the status quo. I take minimal solace in having acquired some of this learning. On the contrary, I find it profoundly humbling, at times shameful. I ought to have known more. I ought to know more.

After completing the first draft of this chapter, I had the opportunity to read a number of other texts, including Michelle Alexander's *The New Jim Crow: Mass Incarceration in the Age of Colorblindness.*[54] In it, Alexander compellingly argues that "mass incarceration is, metaphorically, the New Jim Crow and that all those who care about social justice should fully commit themselves to dismantling this new racial caste system." For Alexander, "The popular narrative that emphasizes the death of slavery and Jim Crow and celebrates the nation's 'triumph over race' with the election of Barack Obama, is dangerously misguided." Indeed, "The colorblind public consensus that prevails in America today—i.e., the widespread belief that race no longer matters—has blinded us to the realities of race in our society and facilitated the emergence of a new caste system."[55] Given what has gone on in the United States since Alexander penned the first edition of the book (in 2010), there may be somewhat less blindness than there had been beforehand. Perhaps, some have said, we haven't gotten quite as far as we had imagined. Perhaps it's time to look anew at our history and see what we have failed to see.

For some time, Alexander herself seems to have been at least partially blinded to the realities being considered. Now, however,

> the new caste system is ... as obvious as my own face in the mirror. Like an optical illusion—one in which the embedded image is impossible to see until its outline is identified—the new caste system lurks invisibly within the maze of rationalizations we have developed for persistent racial inequality. It is possible—quite easy, in fact—never to see the embedded reality. Only after years of working on criminal justice reform did my own focus finally shift, and then the rigid caste system slowly came into view. Eventually it became obvious. Now it seems odd that I could not see it before.[56]

This strikes me as a wonderfully clear example of the workings of the narrative unconscious.

I won't pretend to have acquired anything near the knowledge or the vision of Alexander or any of the others discussed in these pages. All I can say is that I have come to see certain aspects more clearly and that, in addition, I have come to see others for the very first time. And if there is a reason I have quoted Coates, Dyson, and others so extensively, it's that it is important to have *them* speak—to hear *their* words—rather than have me try to speak for them. For all that I have come to know, it has become radiantly clear that there is infinitely more that I do not—and perhaps cannot. Their words have helped me see that. It is humbling to begin to see the narrative unconscious in action, particularly in situations like this one, in which there is no small measure of culpability involved.

Whose wounds are the open wounds of the title of this chapter? First and foremost, they are those of the people who have suffered, owing to slavery, to Jim Crow, to the New Jim Crow, and more. But the wounds at hand are not theirs alone. They are also those of any and all of us who have been complicit in the history we have been considering. The nature and magnitude of these wounds cannot, and should not, be compared. But insofar as "the great Western house" that Baldwin spoke of is indeed "one house," the wounds, and the history that produced them, are shared. By discerning, owning, and narrating it, in some manner akin to what has been described herein, we may be better poised to live out the justice so desperately needed. The process is bound to be painful. But it might plausibly be said that the wounds of the suffering Other can only begin to close to the degree that our own, *mine*, open further and yield the measure of pain that severe wounds bring in tow. This means truly beholding the "face" of the Other,[57] and in so doing, recognizing and upholding its priority.[58] Only this will call forth, in experience, the responsibility that has been there all along. Narrative—hearing and heeding the untold stories of the Other, revising the larger stories within which they have emerged, and, not least, re-imagining our own—is key to the process. We might think of it as a kind of deep affirmative action, one that isn't about this or that policy but about the burden of deep history and the requirements of moral life.

Notes

1 James Baldwin, "The White Man's Guilt," *Ebony* 20, no. 10 (1965): 47.
2 Mark Freeman, "Charting the narrative unconscious: Cultural memory and the challenge of autobiography," *Narrative Inquiry* 12, no. 1 (2002): 193–211. See also Freeman's *Hindsight: The Promise and Peril of Looking Backward* (New York: Oxford University Press, 2010).
3 Timothy B. Tyson, *The Blood of Emmett Till* (New York: Simon & Schuster, 2017), 206.
4 Ibid., 208.
5 Ibid., 213.
6 Ibid., 214.
7 Ibid., 216.
8 Ibid., 217.
9 Michelle Alexander, *The New Jim Crow: Mass Incarceration in the Age of Colorblindness* (New York: The New Press, 2012).
10 James Baldwin, "As much truth as one can bear," in *James Baldwin: The Cross of Redemption: Uncollected Writings,* ed. Randall Kenan (New York: Pantheon, 2010); cited in Tyson, *Emmett Till*, 217.
11 James Baldwin, *I Am Not Your Negro* (New York: Vintage International, 2017; compiled and edited by Raoul Peck), 50.
12 Ibid., 107.
13 Ta-Nahisi Coates, *Between the World and Me* (New York: Spiegel & Grau, 2015).
14 Michael Eric Dyson, *Tears We Cannot Stop: A Sermon to White America* (New York: St. Martin's Press, 2017).
15 Mark Freeman, "Charting the narrative unconscious: Cultural memory and the challenge of autobiography," *Narrative Inquiry* 12, no. 1 (2002), 199.
16 Ibid., 193.
17 Coates, *Between.*
18 Dyson, *Tears.*
19 Coates, *Between*, 8.
20 Ibid., 8–9.
21 Ibid., 10.
22 Ibid., 11–12.
23 Ibid., 19.
24 Ibid., 29.
25 Ibid., 32.
26 Ibid., 33.
27 Ibid., 70.

28 Ibid.,
29 See Dan P. McAdams, *The Redemptive Self: Stories Americans Live By* (New York: Oxford University Press, 2005).
30 Coates, *Between*, 78.
31 Ibid., 79.
32 Ibid., 93–94.
33 Ibid., 97.
34 Ibid., 98–99.
35 Ibid., 99.
36 Ibid., 146.
37 Ibid., 151,
38 Dyson, *Tears*, 4–5.
39 Ibid., 49.
40 See Mark Freeman, *Hindsight: The Promise and Peril of Looking Backward* (New York: Oxford University Press, 2010). See also Mark Freeman and Rick Robinson, "The development within: An alternative approach to the study of lives," *New Ideas in Psychology* 8, no. 1 (1990): 53–72.
41 Dyson, *Tears*, 65.
42 Ibid., 72.
43 Sigmund Freud, "Remembering, repeating, and working-through," *Standard Edition* XII (London: Hogarth, 1958[1914]): 147–156.
44 Dyson, *Tears*, 77–78.
45 Ibid., 79.
46 See Freeman and Robinson, "The development within": 53–72. See also Freeman, *Rewriting the Self: History, Memory, Narrative* (London: Routledge, 1993).
47 Dyson, *Tears*, 131.
48 Ibid., 173.
49 Ibid., 174.
50 Ibid.
51 Ibid.
52 Ibid., 181.
53 Ibid., 208.
54 Alexander, *The New Jim Crow*.
55 Ibid., 11–12.
56 Ibid., 12.
57 See, for instance, Emmanuel Levinas, *Ethics and Infinity* (Pittsburgh, PA: Duquesne University Press, 1985); *Alterity and Transcendence* (New York: Columbia University Press, 1999).
58 Mark Freeman, *The Priority of the Other: Thinking and Living Beyond the Self* (New York: Oxford University Press, 2014).

References

Alexander, Michelle. *The New Jim Crow: Mass Incarceration in the Age of Colorblindness*. New York: The New Press, 2012.

Baldwin, James. "The White Man's Guilt." *Ebony*, 20, No. 10(1965): 47–51.

Baldwin, James. "As much truth as one can bear." In R. Kenan, ed., *James Baldwin: The Cross of Redemption: Uncollected Writings*. New York: Pantheon, 2010.

Baldwin, James. *I Am Not Your Negro*. New York: Vintage International, 2017 (compiled and edited by Raoul Peck).

Coates, Ta-Nehisi. *Between the World and Me*. New York: Spiegel & Grau, 2015.

Dyson, Michael Eric. *Tears We Cannot Stop: A Sermon to White America*. New York: St. Martin's Press, 2017.

Freeman, Mark. *Rewriting the Self: History, Memory, Narrative*. London: Routledge, 1993.

Freeman, Mark. "Charting the narrative unconscious: Cultural memory and the challenge of autobiography." *Narrative Inquiry*, 12, no. 1(2002): 193–211.

Freeman, Mark. *Hindsight: The Promise and Peril of Looking Backward*. New York: Oxford University Press, 2010.

Freeman, Mark. *The Priority of the Other: Thinking and Living Beyond the Self*. New York: Oxford University Press, 2014.

Freeman, Mark & Rick E.Robinson. "The development within: An alternative approach to the study of lives." *New Ideas in Psychology*, 8, no. 1(1990): 53–72.

Freud, Sigmund. "Remembering, repeating, and working-through." *Standard Edition XII:* 147–156. London: Hogarth, 1958 (originally 1914).

Levinas, Emmanuel. *Ethics and Infinity*. Pittsburgh, PA: Duquesne University Press, 1985.

Levinas, Emmanuel. *Alterity and Transcendence*. New York: Columbia University Press, 1999.

McAdams, Dan P. *The Redemptive Self: Stories Americans Live By*. New York: Oxford University Press, 2005.

Tyson, Timothy B. *The Blood of Emmett Till*. New York: Simon & Schuster, 2017.

2

FRANTZ FANON AND PSYCHOPATHOLOGY

The Progressive Infrastructure of *Black Skin, White Masks*

Robert Bernasconi

Frantz Fanon's writings, like his life, were a call to action, a call that still resonates today, but the arguments that he used to promote action—or *praxis* as he preferred to call it in key moments of *The Wretched of the Earth* [1]—are not always understood in all their complexity. I largely confine myself here to clarifying the overall argument of his first book, *Black Skin, White Masks*. I will focus on the book's sixth chapter, "The Negro and Psychopathology," as I believe it is the key chapter. The book's original title, before Francis Jeanson proposed a change, was *Essay on the Disalienation of the Black Man*. [2] In keeping with the original title, Fanon described *Black Skin, White Masks* as "a mirror with a progressive infrastructure where the black man can find the path to disalienation." [3] That is to say, the reader—and for reasons I will explain, particularly the Black man as reader— is invited to follow a progressive path. This gives the book its *dialectical* structure (to employ a term Fanon himself made use of on several occasions), but one must always be aware of the point within the overall argument in which any one of Fanon's dramatic and eminently quotable lines is to be found. As I proceed, I will give some examples of claims that Fanon makes that some of his commentators have treated as if they were his final view, when in fact they are modified or even reversed by him later in the book.

Fanon published *Black Skin, White Masks* when he was only 27 years old. In the previous year he had submitted his dissertation at the University of Lyon medical school under the title "Mental Alterations, Character Modifications, Psychic Disorders and Intellectual Deficit in Spinocerebellar Heredodegeneration." [4] The dissertation helps our reading of *Black Skin, White Masks* insofar as it shows his preoccupation with unpicking the links between hereditary neurological disturbance and the psychiatric symptoms to which it gives rise under specific social and cultural conditions. Much of *Black Skin, White Masks* is a continuation of this polemic. It takes the form of an attack on the way many psychological accounts emphasize biology and heredity at the expense of the social dimension of existence.[5]

I am not going to address the vexed question of the role of women, and especially Black women, in Fanon's account because it is a subject of its own and by no means an easy one to negotiate. The strategy of concealing the problem by assuming that whenever he says *le Noir* he means both men and women will not work in every case and I will avoid doing so here. When Fanon used the term *le Noir,* I will usually translate it as "the Black man" even though it is only in some cases that one can be sure that he meant specifically to exclude women from the descriptions that follow; and so in other cases the translation is over determined. But there is another translation issue that is at least equally offensive to our ears, if not more so. He frequently used the term *le Nègre,* which I will translate as "the Negro," because on certain occasions the distinction between *le Noir* and *le Nègre* is important. Fanon frequently, although not always, uses *le Nègre* with all its negative connotations, not as a synonym, but to highlight how Blacks are seen by Whites in a racist context. On this, as on many points, neither the Markmann translation, nor the Philcox translation, are remotely adequate.[6]

Fanon's starting point was that one must never lose sight of the role of society, not just culturally but also economically[7] Contrary to the exaggerated focus on the individual that he associated with Sigmund Freud, Fanon's own position was that "the alienation of the black man is not an individual question." He believed that genuine disalienation would occur only when *"in the most materialist sense"* things had resumed their rightful place.[8] In other words, one cannot address the psychological problems facing Blacks by relying only on psychology to the neglect of the other sciences.[9] He explained at the end of chapter 3: "We shall see that another solution is possible. It implies restructuring the world."[10]

This solution was predicated on the conviction that psychological problems were not hereditary, but were caused by the environment. For that reason, significant portions of the book were devoted to combating the way in which, in much of the psychological literature, problems that were caused by the environment and its culture were being misattributed both explicitly and implicitly to the patient's constitution. That was the theme of chapter 2 of *Black Skin, White Masks,* where he posed the question of "whether the *basic personality* is a constant or a variable."[11] At the same time Fanon sought to show the inapplicability of standard theories to Blacks. One would never guess from the secondary literature that the primary purpose of his discussion of Mayotte Capécia's novels, a discussion that has caused heated debate, was largely directed at showing that the withdrawal of the ego, which Anna Freud described as "a normal stage" in the development of the ego, is impossible for Blacks because they seek White approval.[12] Turning to Abdoulaye Sadji's novel *Nini,* which in its first incomplete version was published in installments in *Présence Africaine,* Fanon highlighted how its heroine, Dédée, gained white approval through marriage.[13] (Fanon called this particular form of abnormal behavior which supported Dédée "affective ereth-ism," with the implication again that this was "a cultural phenomenon" and not something constitutive.)[14]

Similarly, when in the third chapter Fanon gave a reading of *Un homme pareil aux autres* (*A Man Like the Others*), René Maran's semi-autobiographical novel, it was primarily the occasion for him to demonstrate that, even if a problem with a patient persists after a change of environment, it does not prove the environment was not the main cause.[15] Maran's hero, Jean Veneuse, wonders whether he has not been betrayed by everyone around him, both by the Whites who deny him recognition as one of their own and by the Blacks who repudiate him.[16] But by reading the novel through the lens supplied by Germaine Guex's *The Abandon-ment Neurosis*, Fanon showed that Veneuse's sense of betrayal is nothing other than a classic symptom of the negative-aggressive type.[17] On this basis Fanon sought to demonstrate that the changes Veneuse prescribed for himself were intended only to corroborate his externalizing neurosis.[18] Fanon described Veneuse as someone who is "accidentally black" but who is a neurotic who needs to be released from his infantile fantasies.[19] In other words, the novels of Capécia, Sadji, and Maran were not Fanon's real subjects; their books were merely the backdrop of an engagement with the psychological literature in ser-vice of the larger issue of improving understanding between Blacks, as well as between Blacks and Whites.

The most egregious error in the psychological literature that Fanon wanted to expose in the book's early chapters was represented by Octave Mannoni's Prospero and Caliban, explored in chapter 4. Mannoni, drawing on the theories of Alfred Adler, placed responsibility for the colonization of the Malagasy not so much on the colonizers as on the dependency complex that he attributed to the Malagasy themselves.[20] Fanon returned to this critique in chapter 7, where he suggested that an Adlerian would conclude from a reading of Mannoni that the Malagasy should accept their place in society and not strive for anything else.[21] Fanon believed that the error arose from an insistence on locating psychological problems in the indi-vidual, whereas "in some circumstances the *socius* is more important than the indi-vidual."[22] In support of this conclusion Fanon cited Pierre Naville's critique of Sigmud Freud, according to which the real conditions in which the individual's sexuality is expressed are explained by the economic and social conditions of the class struggle.[23] Hence Fanon's judgment in the context of his reading of Mannoni that "Freud's discoveries are of no use to us whatsoever."[24] This is one of the basic themes of the book. Fanon made a similar critique when, in the context of his reading of Lacan's account of the mirror stage, he announced that he had already demonstrated that for the Black man, as compared with the White man, one must take into account historical and economic realities.[25] Echoing what he had written at the end of chapter 3, the main conclusion of chapter 4 was that the source of the conflict lay not in the dependency complex but in the social structure—the solu-tion therefore was to change it.[26]

Chapter 5, "The Lived Experience of the Black," is the most accessible and best-known chapter in Fanon's book. It was originally published as a stand-alone essay,[27] but when read in isolation it is misleading for three reasons. First, it exaggerates Fanon's distance from Sartre as I have explained elsewhere.[28] Secondly, it ends with the words "I began to weep," thereby giving a false impression of where Fanon ended up;[29] this is especially clear if one compares it with the calls for action as well as the more hopeful tone adopted at the end of the book where he asked the reader to feel the open dimension of every consciousness.[30] Above all, thirdly, the fifth chapter highlights the lived experience of the individual at the expense of the individual's social and economic context and so, when read in isolation, runs counter to the main thrust of *Black Skin, White Masks*.

The fifth chapter is not my main topic here, but for the sake of my theme of the progressive structure of the book it is important to make one observation. In "Black Orpheus," a Preface written for Léopold Sédar Senghor's *Anthologie de la nouvelle poésie nègre et malgache de langue française*, Sartre, taking his cue from some of the Marxist poets anthologized there, applied the dialectic, conceived in a somewhat elementary and vulgar form to make the point that Blacks were called upon to sacrifice their negritude in favor of "the realization of the human in a raceless society."[31] Every reader of *Black Skin, White Masks* seems to remember that this led Fanon to say that "Jean-Paul Sartre has destroyed black enthusiasm";[32] but, in part because of the poor translations, few English-speaking readers realize that Fanon himself had already in the Preface warned against enthusiasm.[33] These same commentators also tend not even to comment on the fact that what Sartre had destroyed was described by Fanon himself as an illusion, an "unthinking position."[34] Certainly there is a criticism of Sartre here, but it largely derives from the fact that Sartre was White and so could forget that "the negro suffers in his body differently than the White."[35] In other words, in Fanon's view, Sartre was in no place to make the comment.[36] Most commentators assume that Fanon was saying Sartre should not have applied the dialectic so as to look beyond the present to a time when negritude had given way to a society without race. They ignore Fanon's statement in chapter 6, where he says very clearly in the context of a reading of Aimé Césaire "we can understand why Sartre sees in the black poets' Marxist stand the logical end to negritude."[37] The point is that Fanon's dramatic rejection of "Black Orpheus" is only one stage on the reader's journey, one that he explicitly re-evaluated later.

Another aspect of the book's progressive structure is revealed when one compares the provisional claim at the end of the second chapter that both Freud and Adler would "help us understand the notion of the world of the man of color,"[38] to the beginning of chapter 6 when he questioned the extent to which the psychoanalytic findings of Freud and Adler could be applied "in an attempt to explain the vision of the world of the man of color."[39] In chapter 6 he highlighted the incongruity between the psychoanalytic schema and the reality of the Black man,[40] just as in chapter 7 when he eventually turned to Adler and explained his opposition to any application of Adler's theory to the Black man again because of its concentration on the individual to the neglect of society: "If there is a flaw, it lies not in the 'soul' of the individual, but in his environment."[41] What Fanon did not appear to deny was that Freud and Adler could help us understand Whites, and this meant that they could contribute to what it was that Blacks had to deal with in negotiating the White world. Indeed, the majority of the chapter is devoted more to Whites than to Blacks.

The broader perspective that Fanon argued for in *Black Skin, White Masks* was not simply a theoretical concern but was at the heart of the approach he developed in his own psychiatric practice as an intern at Saint-Alban under the direction of Francois Tosquelles, the founder of "social psychotherapy" (later known as "institutional psychotherapy"). Subsequently, Fanon adopted it in his own right at the psychiatric hospital in Blida in Algeria. There is some uncertainty about when Fanon actually completed *Black Skin, White Masks* and thus some uncertainty about whether the manuscript was already complete by the time Fanon came under Tosquelles' direction. Certainly there was a synergy between the two men. Félix Guattari, who also collaborated with Tosquelles, wrote a description of "institutional psychotherapy" in terms of its determination, first, never to isolate the study of mental illness from its social and institutional context, and secondly, to analyze institutions always in terms of the real, symbolic and imaginary effects of society on individuals.[42] This is Fanon's approach in a nutshell, and nobody before him seems to have thought to apply it to the investigation of the effects of racism as rigorously as he did.

The sixth chapter of *Black Skin, White Masks* already shows Fanon moving in the direction of social psychotherapy. The chapter begins with the immediate contrast between the environment of the Antillean and the very different environment that psychoanalysis takes for granted. Against Jacques Lacan's claim that "the psychic object and circumstance" is the family,[43] Fanon responded that the model of the family among Europeans is very different from that in the Antilles. In other words, universal structures had been presupposed where what was called for is "a concrete understanding."[44] He extended this observation to include the fact that there is a proportionality between the White family and the social milieu that is lacking for the Black family as a result of the racist context.[45] The trauma that Black children suffer when confronted with images of themselves in magazines and nursery rhymes means that "a normal black child, having grown up with a normal family, will become abnormal at the slightest contact with the white world."[46] Fanon turned to the French translation of Sigmund Freud's 1909 *Five Lectures on Psycho-analysis* to show that he believed that the origins of psychic traumas are repressed in the unconscious.[47] In response, Fanon argued that this was simply not the case for the Black man for whom everything takes place at the level of existence: "he exists his drama."[48] This difference—Fanon calls it at this point a "dialectical substitution"—is even more apparent if the Black man leaves Antilles for Europe, as Fanon did, thereby indicating how the discussion in chapter 5 fits into chapter 6 as a kind of evidence, but now presented in the form of a testimony that initially did not fully understand itself, for the reasons given above.

The inapplicability of Freudianism to a discussion of the man of color, like the inapplicability of Adlerism later, should not be read as a total dismissal of psychoanalysis. It is necessary to remember Fanon's statement from the Introduction: "only a psychoanalytic interpretation of the black problem can reveal the affective disorders responsible for this network of complexes."[49] But what did he have in mind? This remark was made in the context of his announcement that the book was aiming at the lysis of the morbid universe, a reference to Angelo Hesnard's book *L'univers morbide de la faute* (*The Morbid Universe of Transgression*).[50] When he returned to that book in chapter 6 it was to make the point that both Jews and Blacks are scapegoats for a society that is suffering from collective guilt.[51] Psychoanalysis helps us understand how White guilt cannot be separated from White supremacy and so is very much part of the problem that creates the Black world. This shows how this book, so often read as if it were written almost exclusively about Blacks, hinges on the account of Whites given in this chapter, which is concerned with "the deep-rooted myth" concerning the Black man as he exists in the White unconscious.[52] This myth impacts both Blacks and Whites and contributes to the alienation of both of them.

In chapter 6, Fanon also explored two prevalent myths about the Black man that contributed to how he was seen and thus also to how he came to see himself under oppressive conditions. According to the first, the Black man is genital, and here Fanon again referred to Freudianism, even though the word *imago*, which he used to describe the mechanism at work here, is more properly associated with Jung and Lacan.[53] According to the second myth, the Black man is evil, and this led Fanon to initiate a critique of Jung's account of the collective unconscious in this context. Initially he called the collective unconscious indispensable to an account of a racist society,[54] but subsequently he introduced serious qualifications on the grounds that Jung confused instincts, which are invariable, with habits, which are acquired.[55] Once that distinction is made it becomes clear that what Fanon calls the figure of the bad negro is not an archetype in Jung's sense.[56] In an effort to dispel that confusion, Fanon replaced the role of collective unconscious in Jung with a mechanism to which he gave the name "cultural imposition."[57]

In addition to identifying these two myths, Fanon highlighted in chapter 6 two "errors of analysis."[58] What is important about these two errors is that they represent positions that are readily attributed to Fanon himself if one takes some of his remarks out of the context of the dialectical presentation of the argument in which they are embedded. The first error he identified was that of insisting that there is "only one type of negro."[59] The refutation of this error turns out to be more complex than it might seem at first. In chapter 5, in the context of a discussion of Sartre's "Black Orpheus," he had written: "The negro experience is ambiguous, for there is not *one* negro—there are *many* negroes."[60] In keeping with this criticism, in the following chapter, he quoted, seemingly approvingly, Gabriel d'Arbousier's critical remarks on Sartre's "Black Orpheus." The long quotation from d'Arbousier begins:

> This anthology that puts Antilleans, Guyanese, Senegalese, and Malagasies on the same footing creates a regrettable confusion. It thus poses the cultural problem of overseas territories by detaching the cultural issue from the historical and social reality of each country as well as the national characteristics and different conditions imposed on each of them by imperialist exploitation and oppression.[61]

Fanon commented: "The objection is valid. It concerns us too. At the start, we wanted to confine ourselves to the Antilles."[62] This is a reference to his comment in the Introduction that "our observations and conclusions are valid only for the French Antilles."[63] But Fanon had in his own account deliberately failed to abide by this restriction that he had placed on himself at the beginning of the book.

Although Fanon conceded that d'Arbousier's objection could be used against him just as it could be used against Sartre, that was not his last word. He began chapter 6 by focusing on the Antilles, but after conceding the validity of d'Arbousier's point, he tried to explain to d'Arbousier that "dialectics, whatever the cost, got the upper hand and we have been forced to *see* that the Antillean is above all a Black (*Noir*)."[64] Fanon acknowledged that "the universal situation of the Negro is ambiguous," which is not exactly the same as what he said earlier when he acknowledged the ambiguity of negro experience. In any event, the ambiguity was resolved in "concrete existence": "In order to counter the alleged obstacles above, we shall resort to the obvious fact that *wherever he goes, a negro remains a negro.*"[65] As the concluding chapter showed, Fanon was not insensitive to the different forms of alienation suffered by a physician from Guadeloupe and an African construction worker,[66] but he recognized that in concrete existence both of them were subject to the same inferiorizing gaze of Whites. Indeed, not only were both treated as Negroes by Whites, but they had a culture imposed on them that made them see themselves as Negroes, that is to say, see themselves as Whites see them, thereby compromising the diversity of Black experience. In spite of his admission that d'Arbousier's objection was valid, Fanon refused to concede the point because he recognized that in spite of local variations these two myths concerning the Negro are sufficiently widespread as a result of colonialism that they operated across all societies characterized by anti-Black racism. In short, the restriction of the analysis to the Antilles was overcome in the course of the book.

I quoted Fanon as saying that "the universal situation of the negro is ambiguous, but this is resolved in his concrete existence." He followed that comment with the sentence: "This in a way puts him alongside the Jew."[67] This takes us to what for him was the second error of analysis, which is said to be that of "equating anti-Semitism with negrophobia."[68] Throughout *Black Skin, White Masks,* Fanon drew parallels between these two forms of racism, mainly by way of Sartre's *Anti-Semite and Jew.* However, in chapter 5 he made the point that, as opposed to the Jew, as described by Sartre, the Black man is over determined from the outside.[69] In chapter 6 it was Joachim Marcus who exhibited the error, as illustrated by a long quotation in a footnote where it is said of anti-Semitism that the attitude finds the content.[70] But Fanon's point was that, whatever the formal similarities, one must take into account the concrete differences that can be traced back to the myths: "No anti-Semite, for example, would ever think of castrating a Jew. The Jew is killed or sterilized. The negro, however, is castrated."[71] To that extent, there is not racism as such: there are racisms.

Fanon's question about whether psychoanalysis can take account of the man of color gave way to two questions that are related to each other: "can the White man behave in a sane manner toward the Black man and can the Black man behave in a sane manner toward the White man?"[72] He was least hopeful about Whites. To make the point the chapter ends with an extended discussion of a White woman who had a fear of imaginary Negroes. Fanon had observed the woman in 1951 during his time at the Saint-Ylié hospital in Dôle.[73] Fanon's conclusion was that, even if one were to attribute part of her problem to her "constitution," her "alienation" was aggravated by predetermined circumstances and until those circumstances had been addressed any improvement in her illness was going to be limited.[74] The conclusion is clear: White people also need a change in the structures of the world if they are ever to become sane, or, as he also put it, if they are ever to achieve their ambition to become human.[75] Fanon did not exclude disalienation for either group: "Disalienation will be for those Negroes and Whites who have refused to let themselves be locked in the substantialized 'Tower of the Past.'"[76] He understood that the cause of the problems lay in the past, and so a knowledge of history was requisite for assessing the situation. But he highlighted an additional option for those Negroes who refused to treat their actuality as definitive.

More precisely, Fanon offered clear indications of what would constitute a solution for Blacks. Indeed, he used the word "solution" twice at the end of chapter 6 in conjunction with a discussion of Aimé Césaire.[77] The solution turns on the earlier diagnosis that the Black man suffers from a collapsed ego that renders him re-actional, in the sense that his actions are dependent on the "Other" as the source of valorization.[78] For Fanon the answer lay in action: "to induce man to be actional."[79] He had already said it in chapter 4: the Black man must choose action with regard to the true conflictual source, which is the social structure of society.[80] By the time the reader reaches chapter 6, Fanon was able to explain himself more clearly. The Black man must, once he has discovered the White man in himself, kill him.[81] This is the heart of *Black Skin, White Masks,* and it does not necessitate literal violence, although it does appear to entail risking one's life in the fight for freedom.[82] Chapter 5 may end in tears, but, as chapter 6 shows, the path to disalienation is ultimately by way of action directed toward a transformation of the very structures of society. This would be different depending on the situation, the context. The question of what kinds of action that necessitates, in the various contexts in which he found himself, exercised him in his subsequent works until his death in 1961 at the age of only 36.

Notes

1 Fanon, *Oeuvres*, 543; *Wretched*, 97–98.
2 Cherki, 24, 277 n41.
3 Fanon, *Oeuvres*, 211; *Black Skin*, trans. Philcox, 161.
4 Fanon, *Écrits sur l'aliénation*, 168–232; *Alienation and Freedom*, 203–275.
5 Khalfa, *Poetics*, 209–235.
6 Fanon, *Black Skin*, trans. Philcox; *Black Skin*, trans. Markmann. There is, in addition, a problem posed by the fact that Fanon sometimes capitalizes *le Noir* and *le Nègre* and sometimes not. In quoting Fanon I have followed his usage, but when speaking in my own voice I have followed current usage by always capitalizing *Black* and *Negro*.
7 Fanon, *Oeuvres*, 66; *Black Skin*, trans. Philcox, xv.
8 Fanon, *Oeuvres*, 66; *Black Skin*, trans. Philcox, xv. Emphasis mine.
9 Fanon, *Oeuvres*, 96; *Black Skin*, trans. Philcox, 31.
10 Fanon, *Oeuvres*, 125; *Black Skin*, trans. Philcox, 63.
11 Fanon, *Oeuvres*, 97; *Black Skin*, trans. Philcox, 31. Italicized phrase in English in the original.
12 Anna Freud, *Das Ich*, 120; *The Ego*, 102–103. Fanon, *Ouevres*, 99; *Black Skin*, trans. Philcox, 34.
13 Sadji, "Nini," 498.
14 Fanon, *Oeuvres, 105, 187; Black Skin, trans.* Philcox, 41, 130–131.
15 Fanon, *Oeuvres*, 124; *Black Skin*, trans. Philcox, 62.
16 Maran, *Un homme*, 36. Cited Fanon, *Ouevres*, 119; *Black Skin*, 55.
17 Guex, *La névrose*, 28; *Abandonment*, 18. Cited Fanon, *Ouevres*, 119; *Black Skin*, 55.
18 Fanon, *Oeuvres*, 124; *Black Skin*, trans. Philcox, 62.
19 Fanon, *Oeuvres*, 123; *Black Skin*, trans. Philcox, 61.
20 Mannoni, *Psychologie*, 71n; *Prospero*, 70n.
21 Fanon, *Oeuvres*, 237; *Black Skin*, trans. Philcox, 190–191.
22 Fanon, *Oeuvres*, 146; *Black Skin*, trans. Philcox, 86.
23 Naville, *Psychologie*, 151.
24 Fanon, *Oeuvres*, 145; *Black Skin*, trans. Philcox, 84.
25 Lacan, "Le complexe," 5. Cited Fanon, *Ouevres*, 194n; *Black Skin*, trans. Philcox, 139n.
26 Fanon, *Oeuvres*, 142; *Black Skin*, trans. Philcox, 80.
27 Fanon, "L'expérience."
28 Bernasconi, "On Needing."
29 Fanon, *Oeuvres*, 176; *Black Skin*, trans. Philcox, 119.
30 Fanon, *Oeuvres*, 251; *Black Skin*, trans. Philcox, 206.
31 Sartre, "Orphée Noir," xli; "Black Orpheus," 137. Quoted Fanon, *Oeuvres*, 171; *Black Skin*, trans. Philcox, 112.
32 Fanon, *Oeuvres*, 172; *Black Skin*, trans. Philcox, 113. Translation modified.
33 Fanon, *Oeuvres*, 64; *Black Skin*, trans. Philcox, xviii. Translation modified.
34 Fanon, *Oeuvres*, 175, 173; *Black Skin*, trans. Philcox, 116, 114. Translation modified.
35 Fanon, *Oeuvres*, 175; *Black Skin*, trans. Philcox, 117. Translation modified.
36 Bernasconi, "The European," 107.
37 Fanon, *Oeuvres*, 221; *Black Skin*, trans. Philcox, 174. Bernasconi, "The Assumption."
38 Fanon, *Oeuvres*, 107; *Black Skin*, trans. Philcox, 43. Translation corrected.
39 Fanon, *Oeuvres*, 179; *Black Skin*, trans. Philcox, 120. Translation corrected.

40 Fanon, *Oeuvres,* 186; *Black Skin,* trans. Philcox, 129.
41 Fanon, *Oeuvres,* 235; *Black Skin,* trans. Philcox, 188.
42 Guattari, "L'étudiant," 104.
43 Lacan, "Le complexe," 5. Cited Fanon, *Oeuvres,* 179; *Black Skin,* trans. Philcox, 120.
44 Fanon, *Oeuvres,* 75; *Black Skin,* trans. Philcox, 6. Translation corrected.
45 Fanon, *Oeuvres,* 180; *Black Skin,* trans. Philcox, 121.
46 Fanon, *Oeuvres,* 181; *Black Skin,* trans. Philcox, 122.
47 Sigmund Freud, *Psychologie collective,*140; *Two Short Accounts,* 52.
48 Fanon, *Oeuvres,* 186; *Black Skin,* trans. Philcox, 129. Translation modified.
49 Fanon, *Oeuvres,* 65; *Black Skin,* trans. Philcox, xiv.
50 Hesnard, *L'univers morbide.*
51 Fanon, *Oeuvres,* 218 (see also 210); *Black Skin,* trans. Philcox, 170 (see also 160).
52 Fanon, *Oeuvres,* 185, 222; *Black Skin,* trans. Philcox, 128, 175.
53 Fanon, *Oeuvres,* 199; *Black Skin,* trans. Philcox, 146.
54 Fanon, *Oeuvres,* 136, 181; *Black Skin,* trans. Philcox, 72, 123.
55 Fanon, *Oeuvres,* 214; *Black Skin,* trans. Philcox, 165.
56 Fanon, *Oeuvres,* 214; *Black Skin,* trans. Philcox, 164.
57 Fanon, *Oeuvres,* 216–19; *Black Skin,* trans. Philcox, 167–171.
58 Fanon, *Oeuvres,* 210; *Black Skin,* trans. Philcox, 160–161.
59 Fanon, *Oeuvres,* 210; *Black Skin,* trans. Philcox, 160. Translation modified.
60 Fanon, *Oeuvres,* 173; *Black Skin,* trans. Philcox, 115. Translation corrected.
61 D'Arbousier, "Une dangereuse," 38–39.
62 Fanon, *Oeuvres,* 202; *Black Skin,* trans. Philcox, 150.
63 Fanon, *Oeuvres,* 70; *Black Skin,* trans. Philcox, xviii.
64 Fanon, *Oeuvres,* 202; *Black Skin,* trans. Philcox, 150. Translation modified.
65 Fanon, *Oeuvres,* 202; *Black Skin,* trans. Philcox, 150. Translation corrected.
66 Fanon, *Oeuvres,* 245; *Black Skin,* trans. Philcox, 198.
67 Fanon, *Oeuvres,* 202; *Black Skin,* trans. Philcox, 150.
68 Fanon, *Oeuvres,* 210; *Black Skin,* trans. Philcox, 160.
69 Sartre, *Réflexions,* 102; *Anti-Semite,* 95. Fanon, *Oeuvres,* 158; *Black Skin,* trans. Philcox, 95.
70 Marcus, "Structures familiales," 282. Cited Fanon, *Oeuvres,* 191–192; *Black Skin,* trans. Philcox, 136.
71 Fanon, *Oeuvres,* 194; *Black Skin,* trans. Philcox, 140. Translation corrected.
72 Fanon, *Oeuvres,* 199; *Black Skin,* trans. Philcox, 146.
73 Macey, *Frantz Fanon,* 133–134.
74 Fanon, *Oeuvres,* 229; *Black Skin,* trans. Philcox, 184. Translation corrected.
75 Fanon, *Oeuvres,* 65; *Black Skin,* trans. Philcox, xviii.
76 Fanon, *Oeuvres,* 247; *Black Skin,* trans. Philcox, 201. Translation modified.
77 Fanon, *Oeuvres,* 219, 221; *Black Skin,* trans. Philcox, 171, 174.
78 Fanon, *Oeuvres,* 189, 235; *Black Skin,* trans. Philcox, 132, 187.
79 Fanon, *Oeuvres,* 243; *Black Skin,* trans. Philcox, 197.
80 Fanon, *Oeuvres,* 142; *Black Skin,* trans. Philcox, 80.
81 Fanon, *Oeuvres,* 222; *Black Skin,* trans. Philcox, 175.
82 Fanon, *Oeuvres,* 240; *Black Skin,* trans. Philcox, 194.

References

Bernasconi, Robert. 2002. "The Assumption of Negritude: Aimé Césaire, Frantz Fanon, and the Vicious Circle of Racial Politics." *Parallax* 8(2): 69–83.
Bernasconi, Robert. 2005. "'The European knows and does not know' Fanon's Response to Sartre." In *Frantz Fanon's 'Black Skin, White Masks,'* edited by Max Silverman. Manchester: Manchester University Press, 100–111.

Bernasconi, Robert. 2007. "On Needing Not to Know and Forgetting What One Never Knew: The Epistemology of Ignorance in Fanon's Critique of Sartre." In *Race and the Epistemologies of Ignorance*, edited by Nancy Tuana and Shannon Sullivan. Albany: SUNY Press, 231–239.

Capécia, Mayotte. 1948. *Je suis Martiniquaise*. Paris: Corrêa.

Capécia, Mayotte. 1950. *La négresse blanche*. Paris: Corrêa.

Cherki, Alice. 2006. *Frantz Fanon. A Portrait*. Translated by Nadia Benabid. Ithaca: Cornell University Press.

D'Arbousier, Gabriel. 1949. "Une dangereuse mystification: la théorie de la négritude." *La Nouvelle Critique* 1(7), June: 34–47.

Fanon, Frantz. 1951. "L'expérience vécue du Noir." *Esprit* 179, May: 657–679.

Fanon, Frantz. 1967. *Black Skin, White Masks*. Translated by Charles Lam Markmann. New York: Grove Weidenfeld Press.

Fanon, Frantz. 2005. *The Wretched of the Earth*. Translated by Richard Philcox. New York: Grove Press.

Fanon, Frantz. 2008. *Black Skin, White Masks*. Translated by Richard Philcox. New York: Grove Press.

Fanon, Frantz. 2011. *Oeuvres*. Paris: La Découverte.

Fanon, Frantz. 2015. *Écrits sur l'aliénation et la liberté*. Paris: La Découverte.

Fanon, Frantz. 2018. *Alienation and Freedom*. Translated by Steven Corcoran. London: Bloomsbury.

Freud, Anna. 1936. *Das Ich und die Abwehrmechanismus*. Vienna: Internationaler Psycho-analytischer Verlag.

Freud, Anna. 1973. *The Ego and the Mechanisms of Defense*. New York: International Universities Press.

Freud, Sigmund. 1950. *Psychologie collective et analyse du moi: Suivi de "Cinq Leçons sur la psychanalyse."* Paris: Payot.

Freud, Sigmund. 1962. "Five Lectures on Psycho-analysis." In *Two Short Accounts of Psychoanalysis*. Translated by James Strachey. Harmondsworth: Penguin, 31–87.

Guattari, Félix. 1969. "L'étudiant, les fous, et les Katangais." *Partisans* 46, February–March: 104–111.

Guex, Germaine. 1950. *La névrose d'abandon*. Paris: Presses Universitaires de France.

Guex, Germaine. 2015. *The Abandonment Neurosis*. Translated by Peter D. Douglas. London: Karnac.

Hesnard, Angelo. 1949. *L'univers morbide de la faute*. Paris: Presses Universitaires de France.

Khalfa, Jean. 2017. *Poetics of the Antilles*. Bern: Peter Lang.

Lacan, Jacques. 1938. "Le complexe, facteur concret de la psychologie familiale." *Encyclopédie française*, vol. 8, no. 40, 5–16.

Macey, David. 2001. *Frantz Fanon. A Biography*, New York: Picador.

Mannoni, Octave. 1950. *Psychologie de la colonization*. Paris: Seuil.

Mannoni, Octave. 1956. *Prospero and Caliban*. Translated by Pamela Powesland. New York: Frederick A. Praeger.

Marcus, Joachim. 1949. "Structures familiales et comportements politiques." *Revue française de psychanalyse* 2, April–June: 277–313.

Maran, René, 1947. *Un homme pareil aux autres*. Paris: Albin Michel.

Naville, Pierre. 1948. *Psychologie, Marxisme, Materialisme*. Deuxième editition revue et augmentée. Paris: Marcel Rivière et Cie.

Sadji, Abdoulaye. 1947–1948. "Nini." *Présence Africaine* 3: 89–110, 276–298, 458–504, 647–666.

Sartre, Jean-Paul. 1946. *Réflexions sur la question juive*. Paris: Paul Morihein.

Sartre, Jean-Paul. 1948. "Orphée Noir." In *Anthologie de la nouvelle poésie nègre et malgache de langue française*, edited by Léopold Sédar Senghor, Paris: Presses Universitaires de France, ix–xliv.

Sartre, Jean-Paul. 1976. *Anti-Semite and Jew*. Translated by George J. Beker. New York: Schocken.

Sartre, Jean-Paul. 2001. "Black Orpheus," translated by John MacCombie. In *Race*, edited by Robert Bernasconi. Oxford: Blackwell, 116–142.

3

AMERICAN CULTURAL SYMBOLISM OF RAGE AND RESISTANCE IN COLLECTIVE TRAUMA

Racially-Influenced Political Myths, Counter-Myths, Projective Identification, and the Evocation of Transcendent Humanity

Nahanni Freeman

Cultural projections and sociopolitical binaries of exclusion and social categorization can provoke pro-social resistance or annihilating aggression, evoking humane engagement with alterity. The awareness of the evocation as a call from the collective unconscious asks us to encounter the refugee, the alien, and the migrant, not as an "it," but as a face.[1] The encounter with the face acknowledges the uniqueness of the political other, perhaps as a counter for objectification, political alterity, and essentialism.[2] The cultural evocation, like the storm and psychic tunneling that often precedes conversion, is a call for the balancing of polarities.[3] This chapter will explore the transcendent function in current American sociopolitical conflict, examining the role of symbols, myths, anxiety, and nothingness in the teleological movement towards integration of opposites that may ultimately lead to a reduction in dehumanization of the political, racial, and gendered other and the elicitation of pro-social civic engagement.[4]

Internal and external worlds, culture and the individual, participate in reciprocal influence in the midst of political polarization. Cultural projections, ostentatious social identity ownership, and penance may be expressed in the political void that precedes restoration, democratic rebirth, creativity, and a form of pro-social resistance that embodies courage and personal sacrifice; which is ultimately moved not through acausal forces, but through the numinous and mysterium tremendum that guides synchronicitous events in culture.[5] Through the encounter with the alien within the self and within the diversity of shared cultures, America may move towards a phenotype of social intersubjectivity and perspective-taking.[6] The pro-social conversion following the storm may yet promote unity within cultural and intrapsychic microcosms, as aggression is transformed into ethical and compassionate agency, reason, and increased participation as a citizen in the collective cause of democracy.

Projection and the reductive as a hindrance to ethical engagement with the other

The notion of the face of the other implies movement from projection into reception—from racial or political classification into ambiguity—for as Levinas points out, the non-representational elements are the point of ethical encounter.[7] Hand explores how, in Levinas' work, *Totality and Infinity*, the face "denotes the way in which the presentation of the other to me exceeds all idea of the other in me," and simplifying distillations lose their potency, for "the proximity of this face-to-face relation cannot be subsumed into a totality."[8] The face of the *political* other is often obscured in the aggression that emerges from myths and counter-myths. Yet it is also possible that the unfertile wasteland of political rhetoric, megalomania, and exclusion evokes a call; for as Levinas writes in *Beyond Intentionality*, "the face signifies in the fact of summoning, of *summoning me*—in its nudity or its destitution, in everything that is precarious in questioning, in all the hazards of mortality—to the unresolved alternative between Being and Nothingness."[9] The aesthetic emptiness, ambiguity, and intellectual impoverishment that precedes political compassion may be a renunciation of ego, perceived moral superiority, and control. While Levinas indicates that mankind can never be absolved from the responsibility towards all others, he warns that "there's a direct contradiction between ethics and politics, if both these demands are taken to the extreme…(for) politics has its own justification."[10]

In the context of political and racial alterity, animalistic dehumanization may be rooted in the construction of a social identity perceived to be morally distant from the political or racial opponent.[11] Dehumanization of the outgroup may connect to attributions of reduced human uniqueness traits in the other.[12] The devaluation of the other can include mechanization, objectification, and demonization,[13] where the political or racial Lucifer is lodged not only in the outgroup, but also in the neurotic guilt and introjected shame of the individual, embedded in an alienated community. The rhetoric of narcissism sustains the political figure whose attitudes, as described by Kaufmann, convey that "the lord of every sentence is no man but I."[14] This projection may yield the conclusion for disempowered members of society that "you are not found interesting or fascinating at all: you are not recognized as an object any more than as a subject…(for) when you are spoken of, the lord of every story will be I."[15] In the penumbra of the shadow of narcissistic rhetoric, aliens are created within communities, families, and the divisions of the self, promoting moral disengagement and the degradation of social interest. The alien, the traveler, and the confounded observer are contained by sociopolitical boundaries and the dissonance they produce. In contrast, Levinas' analysis of the beginning of Genesis Chapter 18 concludes that the three travelers wandering in the desert, and their welcome with prostration by Abraham, illustrate "the idea of a God inseparable from the face of the other man, and from the summons that this face signifies."[16] All are travelers seeking refuge.

In a discussion of social and ethnic alterity in the United States, Philogéne explores the dehumanization linked to comprehensive and systematic attitude crystallization that increases the salience of differences between social groups.[17] Philogéne identifies the state of exclusion and unfamiliarity that govern alterity in the sense of non-belonging, and identifies its possible origins in self-definition, fear, and boundary-construction. Non-belonging and non-being erase the feeling of being seen, as one becomes submerged in constellations of inter-community and inter-familial hostilities evoked by political difference.

Alterity is heightened by irresponsible and well-funded pseudo-journalism, as well as the politician's avoidance of responsibility and construction of a new political ontology through self-serving speculations of "fake news." Issues with veracity in culture resonate with Kaufmann's caution: "Not all simplicity is wise…the world wants to be deceived…but there is a hierarchy of deceptions. Near the bottom of the ladder is journalism: a steady stream of irresponsible distortions."[18] The televised rhetoric of constant catastrophe fosters anxiety, yet a Heideggerian view may cause one to conclude that this anxiety evokes the nothingness that actually animates existence and produces a sense of significance, for the *Being-Toward-Death* illuminates life.[19]

Nothingness as precedent for developmental shift

Cultural and economic anxiety, as well as the void of inspiring statesmanship, may yield a range of outcomes. Jung, in his review of the *Tao Te Ching* and Wilhelm's *Chinesische Lebensweisheit*, concludes that "'nothing' is evidently 'meaning' or 'purpose,' and it is only called Nothing because it does not appear in the world of the senses, but is only its organizer."[20] If suffering is teleological and impermanence vivifies, how might exclusion, or the authoritarian containment of the unacceptable within the self, enlist greater meaning, emboldening and driving both resistance and counter-resistance? How might nothingness of the intellectual void in culture provide the needed contrast for new energy? The nothingness is to feel invisible, helpless, isolated and unloved, and to thus seek solace in the conformist act.[21] Fromm describes the deepest human need as the solution to the problem of separateness, and the question of "how to achieve union, how to transcend one's own individual life," for "the awareness of human separation, without reunion by love—is the source of shame."[22] Carmelite mystics and desert monastics sought a transcendent Unio Christo and Apophatic non-representation as movement from shame and separation.[23] For America, the tension between diversity and unity tends to heighten separation, as isolationist perspectives grow.

What is the nature of political ontology? If one adopts the phenomenological view that truth is constructed through experience, it may be useful to apply such malleability to alleged political truths, which can emerge independently from ontology. Perhaps we should conclude with Levinas that ethics supersede ontology.[24] Yet, if Levinas is correct in his assertion that the Infinite does not approach us with indifference, what do the binaries and injustices of society evoke in the conscious citizenry, and are such evocations purposive and somehow simultaneously exterior and interior?[25] There is the hidden and the manifest in evocations, the potential for overexpression and silencing, as in the relation between genotype and phenotype. Like the Greek Phaino, the political potential for the community and the self is only a possibility yet to be revealed, non-determined by the democratic gene. [26] The political phenotype, the manifest traits, reveal the subjectivity of political discourse, its rootlessness in ontology, and yet the remarkable lack of intersubjectivity among polarized encampments.

Political perspective-taking and reduction of racism in culture, as signs of developmental progression beyond egocentrism, shows astonishing absence in many informational sources that bear a responsibility to the individual and collective other. When subjectivity defeats ethics, binaries thrive. Yet, perhaps it is through these very irrationalities that creative responses emerge.[27] Perspective-taking conveys a form of empathy that requires a prior attachment to a person over a political idea. In contrasting empathy with caring, Mitchell adopts the view of Kohut that empathy is a form of "vicarious introspection."[28] Perhaps the contemporary American culture, conflicted by a division between the conscious and unconscious drives, must secure insight into herself to drive the needed creativity and intelligence that is possible for regeneration of collectively beneficial forms.

In a review of the neural basis of intersubjectivity, Gallese argues that it is a strong sense of mutual identity that prompts understanding of others and theory of mind, rather than an exclusive capacity for language or cognitive development.[29] In a discussion of mirror neurons, Gallese points out that "to perceive an action is equivalent to internally simulate it. This implicit, automatic, and unconscious process of embodied simulation enables the observer to use his/her own resources to penetrate the world of the other without the need of explicitly theorizing about it."[30] This seems to imply a form of introjection of the other, and Gallese posits that before we can assume another's intentions, we must first "entertain a series of 'implicit certainties' about the individuals we are confronting with."[31] Applied to the political venue of binaries, it could be hypothesized that egocentric certitude, for all of its irrationality, may be a developmental step towards the form of introjection that is necessary for authentic intersubjectivity.[32]

In an analysis of Shaefer's "action language" meta-theory, Mitchell extracts the elements of complexity, intention, and defining power in the idea that emotions are actions, claiming that "keeping hate alive, enemies worth despising, requires effort."[33] At the same time, Mitchell examines the potential for growth in aggression.[34] While he also describes self-destructive forms of aggression, Mitchell describes the transformation of hatred as a point of active movement that can sustain for a long period. While irresponsible hatred may prompt insight in an environment of psychoanalysis, the danger for society to openly explore these impulses underscores the importance of ego control, insight, emotional regulation, and an intentionality for a reasonable society in the effort to use aggressive impulses to fuel pro-social action.

Synchronicity in Culture and the Rebirth of American Democracy

The evocation of a call to transcendent humanity, pro-social resistance, and non-representational, authentic availability to the other may present itself through synchronicitous events, which serve as signposts of change. The source of the evocation may be perceived variously across religious and cultural traditions, yet the manifestations of synchronicitous principles were interpreted as acausal Jung, despite his acknowledgement of Schopenhauer's notion of transcendental will.[35] Evidence of transcendental will may include the perennial theme of rebirth, which Jung alludes to in his analysis of a patient's dream of a golden scarab.[36] Potentially, through the anxiety-provoking challenges that populism offers to American democracy, rebirth of a Platonic Form of democracy may someday find expression, shaped by the collective archetypes of freedom, reason, beneficence, and human rights.[37] These collective archetypes are contained in the conscience of Americans, both those who resist and those who champion existing regimes.

In *Archetypes and the Collective Unconscious,* Jung describes several forms of archetypal rebirth, including resurrection, renovatio, and participation in the process of transformation.[38] The latter concerns an indirect form of rebirth, often accessed through a ritual or rite, such as transmutation of bread and wine in the communion mass or the reception of grace for the Eleusinian mysteries. Symbolic rituals are likewise often employed for transformation in therapeutic acts involving release of attachment to resentment, grief, obsession, or social deviance,[39] and the impact of acts of forgiveness on mental health has been empirically supported.[40] Which forms of symbol production in America are needed for the sort of transformation that replaces aggression and political alterity with superordinate goals and social responsibility?

In Jung's description of renovatio, forms of renewal may affect components of personality through strengthening or curative movement, without changing the essential quality or being of the self, and this may be achieved through means that are unknown, undefined, or external to the person.[41] Jung describes resurrection in the traditional sense of the term, adding that "a new element enters here: that of the change, transmutation or transformation of one's being."[42] While Jung describes resurrection in the sense of a "re-establishment of human existence after death," one might ponder the notion of a return to humanity following the many forms of death that are seen in dehumanizing language, behavior, and fascist or authoritarian trends in society. [43] As change shuttles between the individual and the collective, there is an increased insight that whispers more of a return—a resurrection of the best and most enlightened forms seen in human history as a counter to devolution. This idea of recycling may be embedded in the very notion of the archetypes of the collective unconscious, as articulated by Jung.

The transcendent function as emergent from polarities within the self and the culture

Miller examines the transcendent function within a historical context, considering the roots of the notion in the works of Jung principally, but also exploring connections to the work of Winnocott, Klein, Kohut, and Freud, among others. Miller posits that the transcendent function is the core of Jung's theory, arguing with Jung that a new frame of reference emerges when unconscious material is synthesized with that of consciousness.[44] Miller summarizes the transcendent function well: "Jung believed that the conscious and unconscious contain opposite, compensatory, or complementary material and that psyche's natural tendency is to strive to bring the conscious and unconscious positions together for the purpose of integrating them."[45] In his primer for the transcendent function, Miller goes on to identify this synthesis as a means to maturity, wholeness, and individuation. Miller provides a useful connection to boundary tensions within the self when he states,

> The concepts of a psychic struggle between polarized segments of consciousness, mechanisms that mediate such antithesis, transformation through the liminal spaces between such opposing forces, and the "third" emerging from the struggle of the "two" are all ideas that recur in the field of depth psychology. Indeed, the transcendent function may be an expression of the larger human urge to reconcile ontological quandaries such as spirit and matter, subject and object, inner and outer, idea and thing, form and substance, thought and feeling.[46]

If applied to sociopolitical binaries, one might conclude from these notions that there is something necessary and ultimately reconstructive that occurs with contrast and clash, resistance and counter-resistance, myth and counter-myth. These sociopolitical binaries are inherently interwoven with racial trauma, ethnicity, intergenerational memory, language, and culture. In *Modern Man in Search of a Soul*, Jung argues that complexes may produce guilt and horror, developing in response to something that seems too awful to accept.[47] The feeling of being appalled, activated often in contemporary American society, has produced constellations of sociopolitical complexes. It remains to be seen whether these will prompt creative transformation.

Environmental stewardship and nature as an other: evocation of a call to ethics and transcendent culture in the midst of microcosms in America and within the self

The evocation and call is not only for an ethical and humane society, but also for environmental stewardship. In "Gaia Rising," Elizabeth Ryland examines the gap between knowledge and action with respect to environmental consciousness, suggesting that the Mother Earth archetype may be expressed in both environmental angst and the symbol of Gaia, seen as a view of the fully sunlit earth from outside of the earth, with the notion that life energy sustains and informs the climate.[48] For the symbol of Gaia, earth is alive, which evokes an empathy for her vulnerability. For Jung, archetypes such as Gaia contain an energy that attracts conscious ideas, and "Its passing over into consciousness is felt as an illumination, a revelation, or a 'saving idea'."[49]

Is the source of transformation acausal or teleological and intelligent? While Jung argues for the acausal essence of synchronicitous events, he acknowledges the intentionality identified by Avicenna and Albertus Magnus, quoting the latter's remark that "I discovered…in Avicenna's Liber sextus naturalium…that a certain power to alter things indwells the human soul and subordinates the other things to her."[50] This power is described as containing an affective primary source. The evocation of political change may likewise posit a source embedded in human emotionality, intentions, and intuition. While Jung states that synchronicitous events are acausal, he also identifies the forerunners of his principle in a way that directly implies agentic causation for the events that precipitate evolutionary changes in the psyche or society.[51]

Political commentary often reflects the goal of faction unity within majority diversity, a state that can also be examined within the communication between polarized dimensions of personhood. In speaking of humanity's mediating participation in both noetic and material planes, Ware states that man "is an image or mirror of the whole creation, imago mundi, a 'little universe' or microcosm."[52] The notion of microcosm also appears in Trinitarian theology that seeks to distinguish essence from hypostasis, as shown by the words of Gregory of Nyssa: "Using riddles, as it were, we envisage a strange and paradoxical unity in diversity."[53] Philosophers have also considered the notion of microcosms in the cosmos and subatomic worlds. Jung identifies the monads of Leibniz as "little worlds" or "microcosms," causing one to question the underlying laws that govern such universes. Such questions prompt musings regarding political microcosms, governed by hidden principles, with unknown causation in a myriad of moderator variables that elude true sociopolitical measurement. Leibniz' monadology posed the idea that perception is both unconscious and comprised of pluralities contained within unity.[54] For 21st-century America, it seems that the unity that holds the possibility of containment of microcosm plurality has been compromised. Yet perhaps it is through this very engagement with the disgust that emerges in polarization, and the acknowledgement of shadow, that we gain the proximity to find "the relationship-to-God-in-me" which Levinas speaks to in "Beyond Intentionality."

Prosocial resistance or pacifism? Two responses to our responsibility to the other

The Christian Humanism and ecumenical perspective of Bonhoeffer demonstrates the tension between pacifism and pro-social resistance that is embedded in the question of our responsibility to the other in a politically polarized culture.[55] For Bonhoeffer, murdered by the SS troops in Flossenberg, this ultimate sacrifice came after Buchenwald, and only a few days before the liberation by the Allied Forces. The summon and the evocation came to Bonhoeffer with the words, "When Christ calls a man, he bids him come and die."[56] Bonhoeffer saw the corrupting and immoral force of politics on the church, the clear demarcation that politics is "*of-the world*" and non-transcendent, and his position originated from the rational and historical foundation that religion must be sharply distinguished and separated from politics; this traditional Lutheran view submerged into oblivion in modern America, as branches of the church have become a tool for political agendas.[57] Yet, as Leibholtz points out, "For Bonhoeffer, Hitler was the Antichrist, the arch-destroyer of the world and its basic values…(and) Bonhoeffer was firmly…convinced that it is …a Christian duty towards God to oppose tyranny."[58] Bonhoeffer saw divisions between the world and the church, appearance and reality, the confessor and the doer, judgment and grace, and ultimately concluded that the path to champion for human rights was narrow indeed. This was not the path of corrupting symbiosis between political funding, hidden agendas, and the life of faith.

Polarities and boundaries within the self as co-creators of alterity

Conflicts between cultural and intrapsychic polarities elicit awareness of relationships between matter and spirit, and boundaries between self and other in the context of malleable self-reference, which is not fixed only in the body.[59] Transcendence arises from the contrasts between states of being, for "inquiring into the relationship between body and spirit deepens and enlivens one's experience of living as a body," and even ruminations of death sharpen life.[60] Transcendence can be prompted through a dialectic process "in which each of two opposing concepts creates, informs, preserves, and negates the other."[61] Yet, one must disidentify with the impermanence of the material in the quest for liberty.[62] In an analysis of Patristic writings within Orthodox Christianity, Bishop Kallistos Ware explores the view that manifestations of separation are temporary and unnatural, describing humanity as synthesis when he states "man spiritualizes the creation first of all by spiritualizing his own body and offering it to God…but in 'spiritualizing' the body, man does not thereby dematerialize it: on the contrary, it is the human vocation to manifest the spiritual in and through the material."[63] The evolution of civilization would require the disintegration of racism and materialistic dehumanization of the other, with movement towards a form of racial integration that preserves, values, and explores the spiritual and cultural traditions that emerge from rich engagement with inter-cultural art forms.

Divisions between spiritual and carnal birth, as observed in Christian narratives, highlight the alterity that exists within dimensions of the self, but which can be outwardly projected in a quest to sort the clean from the unclean—in the grasping for personal power and omniscience that guides the attempt to distinguish the authentic from inauthentic believers, as seen in self-legitimizing myths. These myths may serve to distance racial groups as well. Jung describes the desire to become immortal like the sun, which corresponds with the longing to return to the womb and become reborn. Jung describes this longing for the "higher city," citing Galatians 4:26 and 5:1: "But Jerusalem which is above is free, which is the mother of us all. For it is written, Rejoice, thou barren that bearest not; break forth and cry, though thou travailest not: for the desolate hath many more children…"[64] Jung goes on to speak of the liberty from the bondwoman, and the marriage supper of the bride of the lamb in Revelations as expressions of regeneration following the fall of Babylon, including the words from Revelation 22:1: "And he showed me a pure river of the water of life, clear as crystal, proceeding out of the throne of God and the lamb." The water, as an image of the unconscious for some analytic views, connects to rebirth, restoration, and commitment to the baptism. Themes of restoration of relationship, personhood, and community remain central to Christian narratives, yet have not ethically or responsibly informed the religious-political symbiosis in America on a regular basis.

Sources and effects of myths and counter-myths: The need for the numinous in the development towards cultural transcendence

Like the personal myth, cultural and political myths may spring from the biological, personal, communitarian, or numinous. Just as John of the Cross discussed the transformation wrought in the void of the *Dark Night of the Soul*, "personal conflicts—both of one's inner life and external circumstances—are natural markers of these times of transition."[65] There are shades of night that imply a non-busy activity, as well as a passive night of spirit, and emptiness, a sort of spiritual nakedness where deprivation of contemplation occurs such that "God has set a cloud before it through which its prayer cannot pass."[66] It is after this agony of suffering, isolation, and absence that the divine union is enkindled. In his analysis of desert monasticism, Burton-Christie asserts that, in the tradition of Abba Anthony, a life of poverty and detachment from "all misguided, egocentric desires and thought…bore fruit in compassion toward others."[67] In accepting the alien other, the divided self must also work towards integration; for according to

Ware, "modern man has for the most part lost touch with the truest and highest aspect of himself; and the result of this inward alienation can be seen all too plainly in his restlessness, his lack of identity and his loss of hope."[68]

Religion, often a source of intergroup hostility, may also balance reason and intuition, for while east and west may experience transcendent unity differently in the context of ego,[69] both traditions connect the unconscious with the numinous.[70] For the Christian, to unite with Christ is to join in the suffering not only of him, but also of his refugees, witnessing that each face is not a mere representation, but a spiritual, embodied being. The experience of *suffering-with* may require a level of detachment from self and representational knowledge,[71] resembling the divine union expressed by Dionysius the Areopagite in *Pseudo: Dionysius: The Complete Works and Mystical Theology I*. He states:

> Through unknowing reach out ... towards oneness with him who is beyond all being and knowledge ... through ... pure detachment from yourself and from all things, transcending all things and released from all, you will be led upwards towards that radiance of divine darkness which is beyond all being. Entering the darkness that surpasses understanding ... emptied of all knowledge, man is joined in the highest part of himself ... with the One who is altogether unknowable.[72]

Pathological meta-projections

Like the joining of soul and body within a spiritual being, the atomism of the empirical microcosm may inform and receive from the theoretical. Kteily and Bruneau discuss empirical findings regarding meta-dehumanization within the context of the 2016 primaries in America.[73] Using the stimuli of an image of the Ascent of Man, the investigators found that animalistic dehumanization was predicted by candidate and policy support patterns, echoing former researcher's findings that racial resentment served as a foundation for some recent political regimes.[74] In a prior investigation, Kteily, Bruneay, Waytz, and Cotteril found that participants rated some religious and ethnic groups as less evolved and more animalistic than their own group, perhaps driven in part by threats to social identity.[75] The transformation from person to "it" occurs on many levels in culture, and especially as amnesia for history and scholarship afflicts the course of populism. In the second part of *I and Thou*, Buber remarks, "however the history of the individual and that of the human race may diverge in other respects, they agree in this at least: both signify a progressive increase of the It-world," where "causality holds unlimited sway."[76] The rise of American populism and resurgence of racism are no exceptions.

Political binaries and racism are often nourished by pathological meta-projections, which arise from the individual as much as the collective. Projective identification, as first identified and described by Melanie Klein in 1946, is typically a construct thought to exist in therapeutic relationships or other interpersonal contexts with high connectivity.[77] Nevertheless, Bion felt that the process of projective identification also emerged in groups.[78] When extending the idea to cultural meta-narratives, the constant barrage of catastrophic news fosters cathexis and a projective process.

According to Ogden, projective identification can be defined in various ways, but he provides the suggestion that it refers to "a group of fantasies and accompanying object relations having to the do with the ridding of the self of unwanted aspects...the depositing of those unwanted 'parts' into another person...and...the 'recovery' of a modified version of what was extruded."[79] The desire to extricate unwanted parts of the self is elicited from the destructive threat produced by these parts; and as boundaries between the self and the self-object lose clarity, the projector experiences a sense of unity with the object. In the sense of the internalization of the fantasy on a cultural level, one manifestation may be stereotype threat, and yet another may be the form of reactive prejudice where the target digests the negative attitudes held by the exclusionary group. During the construction of meta-projective identification in culture, psychological distance, conveyed as perceived moral-distance from the other, reinforces the notion that the other must become only what is perceived and expected. Binaries presented in journalism- are maintained via outgroup homogeneity, whereby the individuals in the opposing camp or racially-other group are viewed as non-diverse and morally inferior.[80]

If dehumanization is a feature of political binaries and racism, this may form an analog of Ogden's description of the projective identification induction phase. The child's failure to behave in ways guided by the mother's pathology resembles the alien's refusal to internalize the prejudicial meta-position, yet psychological and cultural non-existence emerges with the words, "If you are not what I need you to be, you don't exist for me...I can only see in you what I put there, and so if I don't see that in you, I see nothing."[81] With political outgroup projection, the alien exists only behind a wall; the corruption of a politician exists as caricature of the worst within the self; and members of the opposing political party are just a little closer to primates than oneself. There is non-existence there, as the one subject to projection swallows and is consumed—enacting the fantasy in self-destructive, narcissistic, and self-fulfilling prophecies. Yet, the meta-projective identification, when responded to with an ethical and compassionate society, may result in a transformative containment. Jung describes this in his analysis of Plato's world-soul, which "contains the world in itself like a body, an image which cannot fail to remind us of the mother...this utter inactivity and desirelessness, symbolized by the idea of self-containment, amounts to divine bliss. Man in this state is contained as if in his own vessel."[82]

Non-fundamentalist religion, apophatic mystery and myth in the service of prosocial transformation of language and culture during movement from the reductive

In *Symbols of Transformation*, Jung explores the connections between ancient religious myths surrounding the theme of rebirth in a cross-religious synthesis that considers the significance of images of water, maternal union, containment, and the tree of life. His analytic interpretation of crucifixion would be considered unusual in Reformed theological circles, for he lodges the central story of salvation from sin through propitiation in the analytic notion of "subjugation of instinct."[83] Jung writes of the crucified God:

> The hero suspends himself in the branches of the maternal tree by allowing his arms to be nailed to the cross. We can say that he unites himself with the mother in death and at the same time negates the act of union, paying for his guilt with deadly torment. This act of supreme courage and supreme renunciation is a crushing defeat for man's animal nature, and it is also an earnest of supreme salvation, because such a deed alone seems adequate to expiate Adam's sin of unbridled instinctuality. The sacrifice is the very reverse of regression—it is a successful canalization of libido into the symbolic equivalent of the mother, and hence a spiritualization of it.[84]

The subjugation of aggressive and fear-based instincts may be requisite for the transition from populism to authentic democracy.

Felt responsibility to others, culture, and the environment can be elicited through the irreducible numinous state of mind, as described by Rudolf Otto in *The Idea of the Holy.* [85] Like the sense of isolation in the universe that comes with the Gaia symbol and earth, the creature-feeling aspects of the numinous produce increasing awareness and awe at our ultimate dependence, which is "overwhelming by its own nothingness in contrast to that which is supreme."[86] He describes the Mysterium Tremendum as tranquility or even strange excitement, when presented with a "mystery inexpressible and above all creatures."[87] The Mysterium is fear, yet distinct from fear, and presents that which is unfamiliar and hidden, including a sense of uncanny dread. Otto identifies the inward shuddering that connects to the sense of setting something apart as sacred, where one is submerged by the object of awe. Within the unknowing is the possibility of an *I-You* bond, as expressed by Martin Buber: "Spirit in its human manifestation is man's response to his You. Man speaks in many tongues—tongues of language, of art, of action—but the spirit is one; it is response to the You that appears from the mystery and addresses us from the mystery. Spirit is word."[88] It is within the context of "never-fully-perceiving" that Jung describes the spontaneous production of symbols on both unconscious and conscious levels, which emerges at the "edge of certainty."[89]

The collective nature of cultural narratives serves a function of reducing isolation, and in a context of growth such stories may promote humanitarian political movements. This group-ness that is essential to the formation of myth and counter-myth may prompt social contagion, hysteria, mass aggression, and conformity, or it may instead yield a rushing wind, a Pneuma,[90] and a Great Awakening.[91] If it is possible to harness aggression not as exclusion and outrage of the political other, but rather as a source of dynamic energy for integration, this form of sociopolitical sublimation may sustain and nourish the greatest ideals of the Enlightenment.[92]

Defensive counter-myths and religious pathology

The warring binaries in American sociopolitical culture are not new, and some of the existing polarities have been building for decades. In 1985, Heinz examined some of these polarities in his article "Clashing Symbols: The New Christian Right as Counter-mythology."[93] Heinz identified the New Christian Right as "an emerging coalition of social movements engaged in a contest over the meaning of America's story. The American story refers to how Americans choose to understand and interpret their beginnings, their historical experience, their cultural and spiritual meaning and identity, and their calling and destiny. Crucial to this story is how the American enterprise is legitimized."[94] Using an interpretive frame of Emile Durkheim's concept of "the symbolization of society as the sacred," and Max Weber's "Staende," Heinz considers public symbols to be vessels of meaning-creation where "symbolic universes are constructed, maintained, and enforced."[95] Heinz presents Norman Lear's People for the American Way as a counter-myth for the Moral Majority's dominant narrative, and considers how Weber's notion of status groups (Staende) in conflict over the control of symbols may provide a useful interpretive framework for these cultural phenomena. Heinz' words from 1985 could have been written by a political commentator in 2017:

> They perceive that their values, their story, their interpretation of America are not shared by status elites in government, the media, and higher education. These elites are, however, in control of the socialization process, primarily through control of public symbol production. Thus the politics of lifestyle becomes the politics of counter-mythology.[96]

Heinz discusses how the New Christian Right castigated the members of liberal Christianity from mainline Protestantism, as well as the supporters of secular humanism, as the primary enemy in a "contest over opposing American stories," which engage in the "rhetorical and political use of symbols."[97] As part of this counter-myth production process, ecumenical perspectives within Christendom were denounced. The merging of several sociopolitical ideologies into an entirely new worldview is implied in Heinz' remark that "liberalism married the faith to an aesthetic and scientific culture and conservatism marries it to a nationalistic culture."[98] He points out that single issues can become "symbolic of a larger lost world now to be regained,"[99] thus pointing to the much deeper layers of narrative and meaning attached to seemingly explicit symbols. Heinz concludes his article by pointing out the limitations of many analyses of the New Christian

Right, which are built on an assertion that religious experience is maladaptive, regressive, or naïve, and which label the movement as a form of scapegoating in response to widespread anomie. In contrast, Heinz seeks to deeply understand the symbols, historical significance, and meaning-based associations of the movement and to avoid reductionism of the movement "through an attempt to enter into its own intentionality."[100]

Narrative polarities as energy

A central thesis in this chapter is that individual psychic events may have representation in larger cultural and sociopolitical events of the collective, through shared cultural narratives driven by the energy of polarity and even aggression. This energy from the clash of opposites often includes a projective process that has destructive potential. In projective identification, the fantasy is kept alive in the recipient, who becomes something other than what he/she formerly was. Jung discusses the Babylonian mother of the book of Revelation, described as "the mother of all abominations,"[101] pointing out that she has become "the hold of every foul spirit, and a cage of every unclean and hateful bird...the mother becomes the underworld, the City of the Damned."[102] In this assimilation of darkness, this holding, womblike place, the water of a new birth is made possible. Perhaps it is through the provocation of aggressive political fantasies that restoration and purification can issue.

Symptoms of rage in society may represent creative attempts to symbolize the tension between the Apollonian and Dionysian[103] dimensions of self, other, and community, just as the healing integration of music and ritual interface with personal psychiatric symptoms.[104] Both reason and chaos can provoke creative response. Symbolic experiences may come to serve a transcendent function,[105] while transcendent empathy allows the other to become rather than to freeze.[106] Transcendence fosters engaged, active tolerance *for*, rather than apathetic tolerance *of.* [107] While projective identification of cultural rage and victimization maintain self-estrangement or disintegration of consciousness,[108] recognition of our embeddedness in the world[109] and acknowledgement of the transformative power of both mystical and psychotic phenomena[110] may allow us to move from a worldview that favors sameness[111] to embracing of the alien and a return to justice.

Notes

1   Carl Jung, *The Archetypes and the Collective Unconscious,* ed. Herbert Read, Michael Fordham, Gerhard Adler, William McGuire, trans. R.F.C. Hull, Second Edition, Vol. 9, Bollingen Series XX (1959, New York: Bollingen Foundation Inc.; Princeton: Princeton University Press, 1990), 42, citations refer to the Princeton version. Jung's theory implies that the collective unconscious has adaptive capacities for creative responses. I argue that the call for actions of civic engagement in response to injustice or disgust may have an evolutionary element connected to collective

consciousness; Martin Buber, *I and Thou, a New Translation, with a Prologue and Notes by Walter Kaufmann* (*Ich und Du,* Lepizig: Insel, 1923; English trans. New York: Charles Scribner's Sons, 1970; New York: Simon and Schuster, 1996), 56, citations refer to Touchstone edition; Emmanuel Levinas, "Ethics as First Philosophy," in *The Levinas Reader* (Oxford: Blackwell, 1998), 85.

2 Emmanuel Levinas, "Ethics as First Philosophy," 85; Jonathan Skalski, "The Historical Evolution of Tolerance," *The Humanistic Psychologist* (2017), 8.

3 William James, *Varieties of Religious Experience, Writings 1902–1910* (New York: Longmans Green & Co., 1902; New York: The Library of America, 1987), 140, citations refer to the Library of America version. James describes the neurasthenia and distress that often precedes sudden forms of religious conversion, and contrasts these with other forms of religious experience; Carl Jung, "The Transcendent Function," ed. Herbert Read, Michael Fordham, Gerhard Adler, and William McGuire, trans. by R.F.C. Hull, 2nd ed., in *The Structure and Dynamics of the Psyche, Vol. 8, The Collected Works of C.G. Jung,* Bollingen Series XX (New York: Bollingen Foundation, 1960; Princeton, N.J.: Princeton University Press, 1981), 90.

4 Iain Thomson, "Death and Demise in Being and Time," in *The Cambridge Companion to Heidegger's Being and Time,* ed. Mark A. Wrathall (New York: Cambridge University Press, 2013), 268. Thompson argues that Heidegger proposes the value of confronting anxiety, which allows the release of possibility and return to resoluteness and the world, suggesting the influence of Kierkegaard on this view of movement towards authenticity.

5 Daryl J. Bem, "Self Perception Theory," in *Advances in Experimental Social Psychology,* Vol. 6, ed. Leonard Berkowitz (New York: Academic Press, 1972), 40–41. With respect to cultural projections, we might consider Bem's discussion of difficulties with perceptions of others, including the insider-vs-outsider difference linked to privacy of thought / sensation, and the intimate vs stranger distinction; Rudolf Otto, *The Idea of the Holy, An Inquiry into the Non-Rational Factor in the Idea of the Divine and its Relation to the Rational,* trans. by John W. Harvey (London: Oxford, 1923; Repr. London: Oxford, 1958), 6–10, 12. Otto defines the Mysterium Tremendum as a mystical state comprised of elements of awefulness or holy dread, feeling overpowered (majestas), including completeness, and a sense of energy or urgency, encountering the Divine in a non-rational sense. Numinosum is defined by Otto as a state of mind that cannot be reduced to any other state, nor can it be exactly defined, but has a flavor of absolute dependence and creatureliness; Jeffrey McDonough, "Berkeley, Human Agency and Divine Concurrentism," *Journal of the History of Philosophy* 46, no. 4 (2008), 569. McDonough explores a concurrentist view of Berkeley, claiming that, while creatures exert active and passive power, divine concurrence wills the ongoing existence of these powers.

6 Barnett and Thompson, "The Role of Perspective Taking and Empathy in Children's Machiavellianism," *The Journal of Genetic Psychology* 146, no. 3 (2001): 303. Children showing higher levels of perspective taking and empathy also engaged in more prosocial actions. Perspective taking, a developmental construct identified by Robert Selman, implies a movement from egocentrism. I argue that perspective taking is essential to positive changes in political polarization; Alessandro Duranti, "Husserl, Intersubjectivity and Anthropology," *Anthropological Theory* 10, no. 1 (2010): 9. Duranti makes four principle claims regarding Husserl's intersubjectivity, including the notion that it is a precondition for interaction and even for existence; Levinas states that, "the egological reduction, can only be a first step toward phenomenology. We must also discover 'others' and the intersubjective world."; Emmanuel Levinas, *The Theory of Intuition in Husserl's Phenomenology,* eds. James M. Edie and John McCumber, 2nd ed., trans. André Orianne (Evanston, Ill:

Northwestern University Press, 1995; first pub. *Théorie de l'intuition dans la Phénoménologie die Husserl*, Paris: Librarie Philosophique J. Vrin, 1963), 150. Citations refer to 2nd ed.

7   Levinas points out that, "The face is present in its refusal to be contained. In this sense it cannot be comprehended, that is, encompassed." Speaking on intelligibility as "the very occurrence of representation," Levinas points out that "It is the disappearance, within the same, of the I opposed to the non-I." Emmanuel Levinas, *Totality and Infinity, an Essay on Exteriority*, trans. by Alphonso Lingis (*Totaite et Infini*, The Hague, Netherlands: Martinus Nijhoff, 1961; English trans. Pittsburgh: Dusquesne University, 1969: Pittsburgh: Duquesne University Press, 1998), 1:194, 124. Citations refer to 1998 reprint. Levinas points out that, "Our contact with reality has the structure of a representation." However the representations that we use are limited in scope, for "Thought cannot by itself posit the object's existence." Levinas, *The Theory of Intuition in Husserl's Phenomenology*, 65.

8   Seán Hand, "Introduction," *The Levinas Reader* (Oxford: Blackwell, 1998), 5; Levinas states, "The intention of a word does not necessarily cause the object to be directly seen as it is in imagination or perception," Signifying acts are not reached, but merely aimed at, Levinas, *The Theory of Intuition*, 66.

9   Emmanuel Levinas, "Beyond Intentionality," ed. Alan Montefiore, in *Philosophy in France Today* (Cambridge, UK: Cambridge University Press, 1983), 113, 112.

10 Emmanuel Levinas, "*Ethics and Politics*," in *The Levinas Reader*, 290, 292.

11 Maria Pacilli, Michele Roccato, Stefano Pagliaro, and Silvia Russo, "From Political Opponents to Enemies? The Role of Perceived Moral Distance in the Animalistic Dehumanization of the Political Outgroup," *Group Processes & Intergroup Relations* 19, no. 3 (2016): 369.

12 Jarret Crawford, Sean Modri, and Matt Motyl, "Bleeding-heart Liberals and Hard-hearted Conservatives: Subtle Political Dehumanization through Differential Attributions of Human Nature and Human Uniqueness Traits," *Journal of Social and Political Psychology* 1, no. 1, (2013): 87.

13 Pacilli, Roccato, Pagliaro, and Russo. "From Political Opponents to Enemies?".

14 Walter Kaufmann, "I and You, A Prologue," in *I and Thou, A New Translation, with a Prologue and Notes* (New York: Charles Scriber & Sons, 1970; New York: Simon and Schuster, 1996), 11, 9.

15 Ibid, 11.

16 Levinas, *Beyond Intentionality*, 114.

17 Gina Philogéne, "Social Representations and Alterity in the United States," ed. G. Maloney and I. Walker, in *Representations and Identity: Content, Process and Power* (New York: Palgrave MacMillon, 2007), 33. Philogéne reiterates the Cartledge definition of alterity as, "a condition of difference and exclusion suffered by an outgroup against which a dominant group and its individual members define themselves negatively in ideally polarized opposition."

18 Kaufmann, "I and You, A Prologue," 9.

19 Hand, *The Levinas Reader*, 3. Hand points to the interview of Levinas with Philippe Nemo, in which the influence of phenomenology on the former's work was evidenced. *Ethics and Infinity*, 39–41, Levinas points out that, for Heidegger, "existence itself...is animated by a meaning, by the primordial ontological meaning of nothingness." Emmanual Levinas, *Ethics and Infinity*, Conversations with Philippe Nemo, trans. Richard Cohen (*Ethique et Infini* Paris: Librarie Artheme Fayard et Radio France, 1982; Pittsburgh: Dusquesne University Press, 2004), 40–41, citations refer to the Dusquesne version. Levinas points out that the sense of 'being without object" is significant. Levinas points out that, in Heidegger's view, one would access nothingness through anxiety. Levinas states, "existence itself...is animated...by the primordial ontological meaning of nothingness." Heidegger writes, "When, by

anticipation, one becomes free for one's own death, one is liberated from one's lostness in…possibilities." He goes on to state that, "anticipation discloses to existence that its uttermost possibility lies in giving itself up." Martin Heidegger, *Being and Time,* div. II, part I, trans. John Macquarrie and Edward Robinson (New York: Harper Perennial Modern Thought, 2008), 308.

20 Carl Jung, "Synchronicity, An Acausal Connecting Principle, with a New Forward by Sonu Shamdasani," ed. Herbert Read, Michael Fordham, Gerhard Adler, and William McGuire, trans. R.F.C. Hull, in *The Collected Works of Carl Jung, Vol. 8,* Bollingen Series XX (New York: Bollingen Foundation, 1960; Princeton: Princeton University Press, 2010), 71, citations refer to Princeton edition. Jung points out that Wilhelm argues that cause and effect cannot fully explain how meaning connects to what exists in reality.

21 Erich Fromm, *The Art of Loving, Fiftieth Anniversary Edition* (New York: Harper and Brothers, 1956; New York: Harper Perennial Modern Classics, 2006), 9; Heidegger states "Dasein…in this distinctive possibility of its own self…has been wrenched away from the 'they'." Heidegger states that death individualizes Dasein. Heidegger, *Being and Time,* 307–308, para. 263.

22 Ibid, 9.

23 Luis M. Girón-Negrón, "Dionysian thought in 16th Century Spanish Mystical Theology," *Modern Theology* 24, no. 4, (2008): 696. The Unio Christo is the Union with God, which is discovered through the pursuit of unknowing, as seen in Apophatic traditions, such as both the Carmelite mystics of Teresa of Avila and John of the Cross, and their predecessors; Maureen Flynn, "The Spiritual Uses of Pain in Spanish Mysticism," *Journal of the American Academy of Religion* LXIV, no. 2 (1996): 270. Flynn describes the language of the void used by John of the Cross to attempt to express the ineffable divine communion that occurs in contemplation of emptiness.

24 Hand, *Introduction to The Levinas Reader,* 8.

25 Levinas, "Beyond Intentionality," 113.

26 Faina Rokhlina and Gennadiy Novik, "Phenotypes of Juvenile Idiopathic Arthritis," *Pediatric Rheumatology Online Journal* 12, no. 1, (2014): 161. The authors identify the general significance of the phaino with the words, "The term "phenotype" comes from the Greek word "phaino" representing the mix of characteristics and properties of the body, formed in the process of individual development. In medicine phenotype has traditionally been viewed as the result of the interaction between the phenotype and the genotype (genetic characteristics of the organism to the conditions of external environment). By applying the term phenotype, I mean to imply the plasticity of political outcomes in a sociocultural context, and the sense of unknown potentials. The term Phaino literally means shining forth.

27 B. R. Hergenhahn and Tracy B. Henley, *An Introduction to the History of Psychology,* 7th ed. (Belmont, CA: Wadsworth Cengage Learning, 2014), 196–197, 204. The authors describe the emphasis placed by Romantic authors, such as Rousseau, on irrational components of human nature, the value of seeing the person holistically, the importance of trusting natural instincts, and the limitations of rationalism for truth-seeking. The authors also identify the utility of phenomenology as a behavioral guide for existential philosophers.

28 Stephen Mitchell, *Relationality: From Attachment to Intersubjectivity, vol. 20, Relational Perspectives Book Series* (Hillsdale, NJ: The Analytic Press, Library of Congress, 2003), 135.

29 Vittorio Gallese, "The Roots of Empathy: The Shared Manifold Hypothesis and the Neural Basis of Intersubjectivity," *Psychopathology* 36, no. 4 (2003): 171.

30 Ibid, 174.

31 Ibid, 172.
32 McDonough claims that Berkeley's Principles suggest that, "we know other spirits by means of our own soul, which in that sense is the image of idea of them," McDonough, "Berkeley, Human Agency and Divine Concurrentism," 578.
33 Mitchell, *Relationality: From Attachment to Intersubjectivity*, 130.
34 Ibid, 139. Mitchell argues ironically of the psychoanalytic environment that, "the kind of aggression that is often useful is an irresponsible hate, a hate without regard for the impact on the other, the kind of all-out hatred that is sometimes associated with Winnocott's phrase 'the use of the object.'"
35 Jung, *Synchronicity, An Acausal Connecting Principle*, 11. Historical predecessors to Jung's notion of synchronicity include Schopenhauer's work, *On the Apparent Design in the Fate of the Individual*. Jung argues that Schopenhauer's view posits that causal sequences are first caused by a transcendental will, which prompts meaningful and simultaneous relationships.
36 Ibid, 23. Jung states that, "Any essential change of attitude signifies a psychic renewal which is usually accompanied by symbols of rebirth in the patient's dreams and fantasies."
37 Lawrence Cunningham and John Reich, *Culture and Values*, vol. 1, 5th Edition (Australia, Wadsworth Thompson Learning, 2002), 80. The authors point out that Plato's Theory of the Forms is relevant to political theory because it posits that, "in a higher dimension of existence there are perfect forms of which all the phenomena we perceive in the world around us represent pale reflections." This quest for an ideal society is essential to the theory of the Forms. Arguably, it may also be essential to the notion of natural law, which was influential to Enlightenment political theory. Perhaps this ideal democratic vision is not something to return to, for it has never yet existed but in the mind, yet such visions can motivate and create goals; Maureen Flynn, "The Spiritual Uses of Pain in Spanish Mysticism," 273. Flynn discusses the value that Teresa of Avila placed upon her own suffering as "the passage to psychic purity because it suggested that she was nearing her destination to an immaterial presence." Within Spanish mysticism, the notion of pain as a route to purification connotes a sort of rebirth, which is implied in the current chapter's discussion of the evocative effects of current cultural trauma in America.
38 Carl Jung, *The Archetypes and the Collective Unconscious*, 113–115.
39 Salvadore Minuchin, *Families and Family Therapy* (Cambridge, MA: Harvard University Press, 1974), 233. The enactment in structural family therapy can include paradoxical interventions, such as rituals or tasks prescribed ironically, as shown with the request of the client to set a fire as part of the reorganization of the family subsystems. Minuchin is known for his therapeutic work with Anorectic patients.
40 Charlotte Witvliet, Thomas Ludwig, David Bauer, "Please Forgive Me: Transgressors' Emotions and Physiology During Imagery of Seeking Forgiveness and Victim Responses," in ed. Daryl Stevenson, Brian Eck, and Peter Hill, *Psychology and Christianity Integration, Seminal Works that Shaped the Movement* (Illinois, Christian Association for Psychological Studies, Inc, 2007), 352.
41 Jung, *The Archetypes and the Collective Unconscious*, 114.
42 Ibid.
43 Ibid.
44 Jeffrey Miller, *The Transcendent Function, Jung's Model of Psychological Growth through Dialogue with the Unconscious* (New York, State University of New York Press, 2004), 3.
45 Ibid, 4.
46 Ibid, 5.
47 Carl Jung, *Modern Man in Search of a Soul*, trans. W.S. Dell and Cary F. Baynes (Orlando: Harcourt Inc., 1933), 202. Jung speaks of psychic energy that "flows back

to its source; the inner man wants something which the visible man does not want, and we are at war with ourselves."

48 Elisabeth Ryland, "Gaia Rising, A Jungian Look at Environmental Consciousness and Sustainable Organizations," *Organization and Environment 13*, no. 4. (2000): 381.

49 Carl Jung, *Symbols of Transformation*, ed. Herbert Read, Michael Fordham, Gerhard Adler, William McGuire, trans. R.F.C. Hull, 2nd ed., in *The Collected Works of C.G. Jung*, vol. 5, Second, Bollingen Series XX (*Symbole der Wandlung*, 4th ed. Zurich: Rascher Verlag, 1952; New York: Bollingen Foundation, 1956; Princeton, Princeton University Press, 1976), 294, citations refer to the Princeton version.

50 Jung, *Synchronicity*, 20, 29, 32. Jung suggests that space and time are "essentially psychic in origin…created by the intellectual needs of the observer." He goes on to posit that, "experience has shown that under certain conditions space and time can be reduced almost to zero," which leads to the disappearance of causality. Furthermore, Jung argues against the notion of transcendent causation, for that which is transcendental cannot be demonstrated.

51 Jung, *Synchronicity*, 69–83. Jung refers to precursors to his theory in the bond of community mentioned by Theophrastus (371–288 B.C.), Pico della Mirandola's Threefold Unity, Agrippa von Nettesheim's (1651) inborn knowledge and soul of the world, Jakob Böhme's Signature of All Things, and Leibniz' (1646–1716) pre-established harmony, among many other predecessors. Jung also identifies the assertion of Johannes Kepler that geometrical principles contain a spiritual nature (*Tertius Interveniens*, 1610). The conclusion that synchronicitous events are acausal seems to deviate from the trajectory of almost all of the forerunners to the basic premise.

52 Kallistos Ware, *The Orthodox Way* (London: A.R. Mowbray and Co., 1979; repr. New York, St. Vladimir's Seminary Press, 2003), 49.

53 Ibid, 31. Ware cites Basil's Letter 38. For Christians, unity is represented by the indwelling of the Holy Spirit, which Ware describes as "a gift of diversity: the tongues of fire are 'cloven' or 'divided' (Acts 2:3)," yet he also identifies the Spirit as a gift of unity, 95.

54 The authors contend that, for Leibniz, "everything was living. The universe consisted of an infinite number of life units." They also stated that Leibniz proposed that, "organisms are aggregates of monads representing different levels of conscious awareness." Hergenhahn and Henley, *An Introduction to the History of Psychology*, 174–175.

55 Dietrich Bonhoeffer, *The Cost of Discipleship*, trans. from *Nachfolde* by Reginald.H. Fuller, rev. Irmgard Booth (Munich: Chr. Kaiser Verlag Müchen, 1937; London: SCM Press, 1959; New York, Simon and Schuster, 1995), 22.

56 Ibid, 11.

57 Ibid. In his consideration of the suffering of messengers, Bonhoeffer quotes the warning in the gospel which states, "behold, I send you forth as sheep in the midst of wolves…but beware of men: for they will deliver you up." Matt. 6:10. He concludes the chapter with a reminder of regeneration in the promise of Christ's imminent return. Bonhoeffer's harbinger of division and sacrifice is also seen in his discussion of the Great Divide, where he once again quotes Matthew, "Beware of false prophets, which come to you in sheep's clothing, but inwardly are ravening wolves," Matt 7:14.

58 G. Liebholz, "Memoir," in *The Cost of Discipleship* (New York: Simon and Schuster, 1992), 30.

59 Vipassana Esbjorn-Hargens, "Union of Flesh and Spirit in Women Mystics." *The Humanistic Psychologist* 32 (2004): 409.

60 Ibid, 414.

61 Thomas H. Ogden, *The Matrix of the Mind* (Northvale, NJ: Jason Aronson Inc., 1990), 208.

62 In a study of female mystics, physical changes were reported, including "a movement from density to light or spaciousness." Esbjorn-Hargens, "Union of Flesh and Spirit" in *Women Mystics*, 414.

63 Ware, *The Orthodox Way*, 50. The Imago Dei, according to Ware, includes the notion that, "man is a finite expression of God's infinite self-expression," and exists simultaneously in the noetic, intellectual, and material states, 49.

64 Jung, *Symbols of Transformation*, 212.

65 Ross Collings, *John of the Cross*, ed. Noel Dermot O'Donoghue, *The Way of the Christian Mystics*, Vol 10 (Collegeville, MN: The Liturgical Press, 1990), 61–84. Collings' work reviews *The Complete Works of St. John of the Cross*, trans. and ed. E. Allison Peers and trans. Keiran Kavanaugh and Otilio Rodriguez, and the *Poems of St. John of the Cross*, trans. Roy Campbell; David Feinstein and Stanley Krippner, "Reconciling Transcendent Experiences," *The Humanistic Psychologist* 22 (1994): 212; Thompson, "Death and Demise in Being and Time," 267. Thompson argues that Heidegger sought to secularize Kierkegaard's notion of spiritual birth as following death to the material.

66 Collings, John of the Cross, 75. The author cites D.N. 11, 8, 1; "Authentic being-towards-death cannot evade its own-most non-relational possibility, or cover up this possibility by thus fleeing from it..." Heidegger, *Being and Time*, 304.

67 Douglas Burton-Christie, *The Word in the Desert: Scripture and the Quest for Holiness in Early Christian Monasticism* (New York: Oxford University Press, 1993), 214.

68 Ware, *The Orthodox Way*, 49; Bem, "Self Perception Theory," 2, 4. In empirical support for Self-Perception Theory, Bem articulates the view that individuals will rely on observation of external behaviors when internal cues are ambiguous, in order to ascertain internal states. He also points out that individuals can hold erroneous self-attributions, and builds his theory on the Skinnerian view that individuals do not have direct knowledge of internal states. This could be taken to infer a sort of alienation from internal experience, although Bem does not directly posit this.

69 Jung points out that, to the Western point of view, "consciousness is inconceivable without an ego." In contrast, "The Eastern mind...has no difficulty in conceiving of consciousness without an ego." Carl Jung, *Psychology and Religion: East and West*, ed. Herbert Read, Michael Fordham, Gerhard Adler, and William McGuire, trans. R.F. C. Hull, 2nd ed., in *The Collected Works of C.G. Jung*, Vol. 11, Bollingen Series XX (New Haven, CT: Yale University Press, 1938; Princeton: Princeton University Press, 1969), 484

70 According to Coward, Jung, in *Psychology and Religion*, stated that mystical revelations often first appear in dreams, when the symbol "reaches the level of the personal subconscious." The cross as symbol moves away from egoistic manipulation, and "is now sensed as being numinous—as having a power and meaning about it which causes the conscious ego to pale." Coward argues that, while Jung identified differences in mystical experiences reported by Western and Eastern perspectives, "the psychological processes involved seemed very similar." Harold Coward, "Jung's Conception of the Role of Religion," *The Humanistic Psychologist* 17 (1989): 271–272.

71 McDonough, "Berkeley, Human Agency," 578. McDonough's account favors the idea that Berkeley proposed that ideas cannot represent one who is volitional, perceives or has cognition—a spirit. We can only try to represent others based on an appraisal of our own actions.

72 Ware, *The Orthodox Way*, 24.

73 Nour Kteily and Emile Bruneau, "Backlash: The Politics and Real-World Consequences of Minority Group Dehumanization," *Personality and Social Psychology Bulletin* 14, no. 1 (2017): 99–103.

74 Ibid, the authors cite the investigations of Cohn, 2015 and McElwee & McDaniel, 2016, 87.

75 Nour Kteily, Emile Bruneau, Adam Waytz, and Sarah Cotteril. "The Ascent of Man: Theoretical and Empirical Evidence for Blatant Dehumanization," *Journal of Personality and Social Psychology* 109, no. 5 (2015): 901, 923–926.

76 Buber, *I and Thou,* 87, 100.

77 Giovanna Goretti, "Projective identification: A Theoretical Investigation of the Concept." *International Journal of Psychoanalysis* 88 (2007): 389–391,387. Using Klein's *Notes from Some Schizoid Processes* (1946), Goretti explores the various range of readings of the defining features of Klein's projective identification, contrasted with Rosenfeld's, concluding that a broader interpretation and application appears warranted, and that projective identification may in some cases distort perceptual realities. She discusses Klein's notion of expulsion in the aggressive relation, as the object is, "'harmed, occupied and controlled' with rejected, despised and hated parts of the self." Furthermore, Goretti highlights one view of identification as "a way for managing otherness and the separateness of the object;" Ogden points out that, "The projector feels that the recipient experiences his feeling...his own feeling has been transplanted into the recipient." Ogden quotes a personal communication with Schafer, 1974, stating that the person projecting feels 'at one with.'" Thomas Ogden, "On Projective Identification," International Journal of Psycho-Analysis 60 (1979): 358. Roy Schafer, "The Psychoanalyst's Empathic Activity," in The Analytic Attitude, (New York: Routledge, 2018), 29. Schafer refers to transient identifications that arise through projections and introjections, "or imagined merging of self and object." Schafer argues that transient identifications influence cognitive aspects of analytic empathy.

78 Bion states that, when the group analyst is enlisted in projective identification, "The analyst feels he is being manipulated so as to be playing a part, no matter how difficult to recognize, in somebody's else's phantasy...there is a sense of being a particular kind of person." W.R. Bion, *Experiences in Groups and Other Papers* (New York: Basic Books Inc., 1959), 149.

79 Ogden, "On Projective Identification," 357.

80 Mark Brauer, "Intergroup Perception in the Social Context: The Effects of Social Status and Group Membership on Perceived Out-group Homogeneity and Ethnocentrism," *Journal of Experimental Social Psychology* 37 (2001): 15–31. Outgroup homogeneity posits that, when examining a group to which one does not hold membership, there is a tendency to reduce the perception of difference among members of the excluded group. These authors did not find support for the notion that higher status groups are more likely to demonstrate the effect.

81 Thomas H. Ogden, "On Projective Identification," *International Journal of Psycho-Analysis* 60 (1979): 359.

82 Jung, *Symbols of Transformation,* 266.

83 Ibid, 263.

84 Ibid.

85 Otto, *The Idea of the Holy,* 7. Otto states that the numinous state of mind is unique, primary, irreducible to other experiences or states, and is entirely other than "the good."

86 Ibid, 10.

87 Ibid, 13.

88 Buber, *I and Thou,* 89.

89 Carl G. Jung, M.L. Von Franz, Joseph L. Henderson, Jolande Jacobi, and Aniela Jaffé, *Man and His Symbols,* eds. Carl Jung and M.-L. von Franz (New York: Dell Publishing, 1964), 4.

90 Peter Hill, Kenneth Pargament, Ralph Hood, Jr., Michael McCullough, James Swyers, David Larson, and Brian Zinnbauer, "Conceptualizing Religion and Spirituality," *Journal for the Theory of Social Behaviour* 30, no. 1 (2000): 57. The pneuma is

a Greek term for the religious spirit, which is also connoted by the Latin root Spiritus, meaning breath or life, and is referred to in the Hebrew of the Old Testament as ruach.

91 The Great Awakening in America, ushered in by Jonathan Edwards, may evoke sensory consciousness, as shown by the words of Miller, "In Edwards' 'sense of the heart' there is nothing transcendental; it is rather a sensuous apprehension of the total situation." I use the reference to also evoke the sense of a communal response or contagion effect. Perry Miller, "Jonathan Edwards on the Sense of the Heart," *Harvard Theological Review* 41, no. 2. (1948): 127.

92 The Enlightenment ideals referred to include the foundations of Jefferson's *Declaration of Independence*, such that, "We hold these truths to be self-evident, that all men are created equal, that they are endowed by their Creator with certain unalienable Rights, that among these are Life, Liberty and the Pursuit of Happiness." Other Enlightenment ideals referred to include the universal right to "liberty, property, security, and resistance to oppression," as stated in the *Declaration of the Rights to Man*. Lastly, important ideals of American democracy are alluded to, such as freedom of speech, a free press, and a balance of powers. Cunningham and Reich, *Culture and Values*, 243–245.

93 Donald Heinz, "The New Christian Right as Counter-Mythology," *Archives de Sciences Sociales Des Religions* 59, no. 1 (1985): 153–173.

94 Ibid, 155.

95 Ibid. Heinz uses Berger's (1969) description of public symbols.

96 Ibid, 156.

97 Ibid, 159.

98 Ibid.

99 Ibid, 168.

100 Ibid, 169.

101 Jung, *Symbols of Transformation*, 214–215.

102 Ibid. Rev. 18:2.

103 Jaci Maraschin, Culture, Spirit and Worship, *Anglican Theological Review* LXXXIL, no. 1 (2000): 48, 50, 58. The author argues of an Anglican context in Brazil that, "the first cultural drive is Apollonian. It depends on reason, measure, correction and symmetry." She also states that, "In the traditional and apollonian culture of Brazil, spirit means that which opposes matter." This is contrasted with the Dionysian focus on the body and the emotions. Both are necessary for holistic numinous experience, for, "Immanence and transcendence are to be related as contextualization and globalization, Apollonian culture and Dionysian culture in order to produce a new spiritual quality in our worship." These distinctions were earlier identified by Nietzsche in *The Birth of Tragedy in the Spirit of Music*, 1871.

104 McClary states, "That a person can be healed by music is a reminder of the connection between music therapy and the myth of Orpheus. For in using the Orphic tool of music, one can chart the unconscious...in order to be reborn into one's truer, fuller nature. This process allows one to transcend, through the symbol-making process." Rebecca McClary, "Healing the Psyche through Music, Myth and Ritual," *Psychology of Aesthetics, Creativity and the Arts* 1, no. 3, (2007): 159.

105 Jung, "The Structure and Dynamics of the Psyche," in eds. Herbert Read, Michael Fordham, Gerhard Adler, and William McGuire, trans. R.F.C. Hull, Second Edition, *The Structure and Dynamics of the Psyche*, vol. 8, *The Collected Works of C. G. Jung*, Bollingen Series XX (New York: Bollingen Foundation, 1960), 77. Jung points out that the unconscious material which yields the transcendent function is most easily accessed by dreams, which in Jung's theory, contain archetypal symbols.

106 John Riker, "Empathy, Otherness and Ethical Life," *Journal of Theoretical and Philosophical Psychology* 32, no. 4 (2012): 246. Riker cites Kohut's 1985 notion of

transcendent empathy and its relation to personality evolution; Flynn, "The Spiritual Uses of Pain in Spanish Mysticism," 268, Flynn discusses how John of the Cross developed his own theory to modify the classical and scholastic models in which he had been trained, which "meant destroying impressions rooted in the mental faculties of the will, memory and reason." Such a transcendence, born in the second night of spiritual transformation, could be extrapolated to allow the release of limiting and static projections of the Other.

107   Skalski, "The Historical Evolution of Tolerance," 1–8, esp. 1 and 7. Skalski provides an historical context for tolerance, noting the inadequacies of several views of tolerance, including the more contemporary notion of tolerance as "the act of enduring." He poses the question, "As we consider ourselves tolerant, we would do well to regard the question 'What am I intolerant of?'"

108   Hunt states of mystical poverty in Christian mysticism and Buddhist meditation that, "the sustained direct experience of ongoing consciousness…entails a felt dissolution of the ordinary social-personal sense of self." The felt absence of self and God can "lead to a sense of utter loss—and to an unexpected inner crisis of nihilism." Harry Hunt, "Dark Night of the Soul: Phenomenology and Neurocognition," *Review of General Psychology* 11, no. 3 (2007): 213, 209–234.

109   Paul Cammell, "Relationality and Existence," The Humanistic Psychologist 43, (2015): 240. Cammell refers to Heidegger's (1928) notion of Being-in-the World, he states that Dasein and throwness include relational elements of Mitwelt and Mitsein.

110   Hunt, "Dark Night of the Soul: Phenomenology and Neurocognition, 227–228. Hunt discusses the dark night of the soul as experienced in Schizophrenic crisis, yet also highlights the human penchant for symbolic representation, novelty, and satisfaction of the quest for meaning in the individual and culture, which can also be mediated through psychotic and mystical experience. He adds the absence and alienation in contemporary life is connected to spiritual nihilism.

111   Cammell, "Relationality and Existence," 245. Cammell points out the work of Jacques Derrida and Emmanuel Levinas in their critique of "the ontology of sameness," which privileges the former over Otherness. He points out that Otherness, "represents anything that surpasses our capacity to understand, interpret, to represent, and differs or is alien."

References

Barnett, Mark, and Shannon Thompson. "The Role of Perspective Taking and Empathy in Children's Machiavellianism, Prosocial Behavior and Motive for Helping." *Journal of Genetic Psychology* 146, no. 3(2001): 295–305. doi:10.1080/00221325.1985.9914459.

Bem, Daryl. "Self-Perception Theory." In *Advances in Experimental Social Psychology* 6, New York: Academic Press Inc., 1957.

Bion, Wilfred. *Experiences in Groups.* New York: Basic Books, 1959.

Bonhoeffer, Dietrich. *The Cost of Discipleship.* Translated from Nachfolde by Reginald H. Fuller, revised by Irmgard Booth. Munich: Chr. Kaiser Verlag Müchen, 1937. London: SCM Press, 1959. Touchstone Edition New York: Simon and Schuster, 1995. Page references are to the 1995 edition.

Buber, Martin. *I and Thou, A New Translation, with a Prologue and Notes by Walter Kaufmann. Ich Und Du,* Leipzig: 1923. English Translation New York: Charles Scribner's Sons, 1970. Touchstone Edition New York: Simon & Schuster, 1996. Page references refer to the 1996 edition.

Brauer, Markus. "Intergroup Perception in the Social Context: The Effects of Social Status and Group Membership on Perceived Out-group Homogeneity and Ethnocentrism." *Journal of Experimental Social Psychology* 37(2001): 15–31. doi:10.1006/jesp.2000.1432.

Burton-Christie, David. *The Word in the Desert.* New York: Oxford University Press, 1993.

Cammell, Pat. "Relationality and Existence: Hermeneutic and Deconstructive Approaches Emerging from Heidegger's Philosophy." *The Humanistic Psychologist* 43(2015): 235–249. doi:10.1080/08873267.2014.996808.

Collings, Ross. *John of the Cross,* edited by Noel Dermot O'Donoghue, Vol. 10, The Way of the Christian Mystics, A Micahel Glazier Book. Collegeville, Minnesota: The Liturgical Press, 1990.

Coward, Harold. "Jung's Conception of the Role of Religion in Psychological Transformation". *Humanistic psychologist* 17, no. 3(1989): 265–273. doi:10.1080/08873267.1989.9976858.

Crawford, Jarrett, Sean Modri, and Matt Motyl. "Bleeding-heart liberals and hard-hearted Conservatives: Subtle Political Dehumanization through Differential Attributions of Human Nature and Human Uniqueness Traits." *Journal of Social and Political Psychology* 1, no. 1(2013): 86–104. doi:10.5964/jspp.v1i1.184.

Csordas, Thomas. "Asymptote of the Ineffable." *Current Anthropology* 45, no. 2(2004): 163–185. https://ezproxy.ccu.edu:2529/login.aspx?direct=true&db=sch&AN=12941784&site=ehost-live.

Cunningham, Lawrence and John Reich. *Culture and Values, A Survey of the Humanities.* Australia: Thompson Wadsworth Learning, 2002.

Duranti, Alessandro. "Husserl, Intersubjectivity and Anthropology." *Anthropological Theory* 10, no. 1(2010): 1–20. doi:10.1177/1463499610370517.

Esbjorn-Hargens, Vipassana. "Union of Flesh and Spirit in Women Mystics." *The Humanistic Psychologist* 32 (2004): 401–425. doi:10.1080/08873267.2004.9961762.

Feinstein, David and Stanley Krippner. "Reconciling Transcendent Experiences with the Individual's Evolving Mythology." *Humanistic Psychologist* 22 (1994): 203–227. doi:10.1080/08873267.1994.9976947.

Flynn, Maureen. "The Spiritual Uses of Pain in Spanish Mysticism." *Journal of the American Academy of Religion* LXIV, no. 2(1996): 257–278. https://doi.org/10.1093/jaarel/LXIV.2.257.

Fromm, Erich. *The Art of Loving, Fiftieth Anniversary Edition,* New York: Harper and Brothers, 1956. Reprinted New York: Harper Perennial Modern Classics, 2006. .

Gallese, Vittorio."The Roots of Empathy: The Shared Manifold Hypothesis and the Neural Basis of Intersubjectivity." *Psychopathology* 36 no. 4(2003): 171–180. doi:10.1159/000072786.

Giron-Negron, Luis. "Dionysian thought in Sixteenth-Century Spanish Mystical Theology." *Modern Theology* 24, no. 4(October 2008): 693–706. doi:10.1111/j.1468-0025.2008.00494.x.

Goretti, Giovanna. "Projective Identification: A Theoretical Investigation of the Concept Starting from 'Notes on Some Schizoid Mechanisms.'" *International Journal of Psychoanalysis* 88(2007): 387–405. https://doi.org/10.1516/4V21-4KV7-46G2-M8Q3.

Hand, Seán. "Introduction," in *The Levinas Reader.* 1–8. Malden, MA: Blackwell Publishers, 1989.

Hill, Peter, Kenneth Pargament, Ralph Hood, Jr., Michael McCullough, James Swyers, David Larson, and Brian Zinnbauer. "Conceptualizing Religion and Spirituality: Points of Commonality, Points of Departure." *Journal for the Theory of Social Behaviour* 30, no. 1(2001): 51–77https://ezproxy.ccu.edu:2529/login.aspx?direct=true&db=aph&AN=4374064&site=ehost-live.

Heidegger, Martin, "Dasein's Possibility of Being-a-Whole, and Being-Towards Death," in *Being and Time,* Translated from *Sein und Zeit,* 7th Edition, by John Macquarrie and Edward Robinson, 279–304. Tübingen: Noemarius Verlag, 1926. Reprint New York: Harper Perennial Modern Thought, 2008.

Heinz, Donald. "Clashing Symbols: The New Christian Right as Counter-mythology." *Archives de Sciences Sociales des Religions* 59 no. 1(1985): 153–173. https://www.jstor.org/stable/30116084.

Hergenhahn, B.R. and Tracey Henley. *An Introduction to the History of Psychology*, 7th Edition. Belmont, CA: Wadsworth-Cengage, 2014.

Hunt, Harry. "'Dark night of the soul': Phenomenology and Neurocognition of Spiritual Suffering in Mysticism and Psychosis." *Review of General Psychology* 11 no. 3(2007): 209–234. doi:10.1037/1089-2680.11.3.209.

James, William. *The Varieties of Religious Experience: A Study in Human Nature, 1902–1910 Writings*, the Gifford Lectures on natural religion delivered at Edinburgh in 1901–1902. New York: Longmans Green, 1902. Reprinted New York: The Library of America, 1987. Citations refer to the Library of America version.

Jung, Carl, M.-L. von Franz, Joseph L. Henderson, Jolande Jacobi, and Aneila Jaffé, *Man and His Symbols*, eds. Carl Jung and M.-L. von Franz. New York: Dell Publishing, 1964.

Jung, Carl. *Modern Man in Search of a Soul*. Orlando: Harcourt Inc., 1933.

Jung, Carl. *Symbols of Transformation*, Edited by Herbert Read, Michael Fordham, Gerhard Adler, William McGuire, Translated by R.F.C. Hull, Second Edition, in *The Collected Works of C.G. Jung*, vol. 5, Bollingen Series XX. *Symbole der Wandlung*, 4th edition. Zurich: Rascher Verlag, 1952. New York: Bollingen Foundation, 1956. Reprinted Princeton: Princeton University Press, 1976. Citations refer to the Princeton version.

Jung, Carl. *Synchronicity: An Acausal Connecting Principle with a New Forward by Sonu Shamdasani*, eds. Herbert Read, Michael Fordham, Gerhard Adler, and William McGuire,. Translated by RFC Hull. In *The Collected Works of C.G. Jung, Volume 8*, Bollingen Series XX. New York: Bollingen Foundation, 1960. Reprinted Princeton, N.J.: Princeton University Press, 2010. Citations refer to Princeton edition.

Jung, Carl. "Approaching the Unconscious." In *Man and his Symbols*, eds. Carl Jung, and M.L. von France, Joseph L. Henderson, Jolande Jacobi, and Aniela Jaffé. London: Aldus Books, 1964. Reprinted New York: Dell Publishing Company, 1968.

Jung, Carl. "The Archetypes and the Collective Unconscious." In *The Collected Works of C. G. Jung* 9. eds. Herbert Read, Michael Fordham, Gerhard Adler, and William McGuire. Translated by R.F.C. Hull, 2nd Edition, Vol. 9, pt. 1, Bollingen Series XX. New York: Bolingen Foundation, 1959. Reprinted Princeton, N.J.: Princeton University Press, 1990. Citations refer to Princeton edition.

Jung, Carl. "Psychology and Religion: East and West." In *The Collected Works of C.G. Jung*, Vol. 11, eds. Herbert Read, Michael Fordham, Gerhard Adler, and William McGuire. Translated by R.F.C. Hull, 2nd Edition, Bollingen Series XX. New Haven, CT: Yale University Press, 1938. Reprinted Princeton: Princeton University Press, 1969. Citations refer to Princeton edition.

Jung, Carl. "The Transcendent Function." In *The Structure and Dynamics of the Psyche*, Vol. 8, *The Collected Works of C.G. Jung*, eds. Herbert Read, Michael Fordham, Gerhard Adler, and William McGuire, Translated by R.F.C. Hull, 2nd Edition, Bollingen Series XX. New York: Bollingen Foundation, 1960. Reprint Princeton, N.J.: Princeton University Press, 1981. Citations refer to the Princeton edition.

Kaufmann, Walter. "Prologue." In *I and Thou* by Martin Buber: A New Translation, With a Prologue and Notes. Translated by Walter Kaufmann. New York: Touchstone, 1989.

Kteily, Nour and Emile Bruneau. "Backlash: The Politics and Real-World Consequences of Minority Group Dehumanization." *Personality and Social Psychology Bulletin* 43, no. 1 (2016): 87–104. doi:10.1177/0146167216675334.

Kteily, Nour, Emile Bruneau, Adam Waytz, and Sarah Cotterill. "The Ascent of Man: Theoretical and Empirical Evidence for Blatant Dehumanization." *Journal of Personality and Social Psychology* 109, no. 5(2015): 901–931.

Levinas, Emmanuel. "Ethics as First Philosophy." In *The Levinas Reader,* eds. Seán Hand. Translated by S. Hand and M. Temple, 75–87. Oxford, UK: Blackwell Publishers, 1989. Reprinted Oxford: Blackwell Publishers, 1998.

Levinas, Emmanuel. *The Theory of Intuition in Husserl's Phenomenology,* eds. James M. Edit and John McCumber, 2nd Edition. Translated by A. Orianne. Evanston, I.L.: Northwestern University Press, 1995. First published 1963 as *Théorie de l'intuition dans la Phénoménologie die Husserl,* Paris: Librarie Philosophique J. Vrin,

Levinas, Emmanuel. *Totality and Infinity: An Essay on Exteriority.* Translated by Alphonso Lingis. *Totaite et Infini* The Hague, Netherlands: Martinus Nijhoff, 1961. English translation Pittsburgh: Dusquesne University, 1969. Reprinted Pittsburgh: Dusquesne University Press, 1998. Citations refer to the 1998 edition.

Levinas, Emmanuel. "Ethics and Infinity." Conversations with Philippe Nemo. Translated by Richard Cohen. 1982. Pittsburgh: Dusquesne University Press, 2004. First published Ethique et Infini in Paris: Librarie Artheme Fayard et Radio France, 1982. Citations refer to the 2004 edition.

Levinas, Emmanuel. "Ethics and Politics." In *Les Nouveaux Cahiers,* ed. Sean Hand. 18. Translated by Sean Hand and M. Temple. In *The Levinas Reader,* 75–87. Oxford, UK: Blackwell Publishers, 1981.

Levinas, Emmanuel. "Beyond Intentionality." In *Philosophy in France Today,* ed. Alan Montefiore. Cambridge, U.K.: Cambridge University Press, 1983.

Liebholz, G. "Memoir to Dietrich Bonhoeffer," in *The Cost of Discipleship.* 1937. Translated by H. Fuller. 13–39. Reprint,New York: Touchstone, 1959.

Maraschin, Jaci. "Culture, Spirit and Worship." *Anglican Theological Review* LXXXIL, no. 1 (2000): 47–63. https://ezproxy.ccu.edu:2529/login.aspx?direct=true&db=aph&AN=2913144&site=ehost-live.

McClary, Rebecca. "Healing the Psyche through Music, Myth and Ritual." *Psychology of Aesthetics, Creativity and the Arts* 1, no. 3(2007): 155–159. doi:10.1037/1931-3896.1.3.155.

McDonough, Jeffrey. "Berkeley, Human Agency and Divine Concurrentism." *Journal of the History of Philosophy* 46, no. 4(2008): 567–590. doi:10.1353/hph.0.0056.

Minuchin, Salvadore. *Families and Family Therapy.* Cambridge, MA: Harvard University Press, 1974.

Mitchell, Stephen. *Relationality: From Attachment to Intersubjectivity, Vol. 20, Relational Perspectives Book Series.* Hillsdale, N.J.: The Analytic Press, Library of Congress, 2003.

Ogden, Thomas. "On Projective Identification." *International Journal of Psycho-Analysis* 60 (1979): 357–373.

Ogden, Thomas. *The Matrix of the Mind: Object Relations and the Psychoanalytic Dialogue.* Northvale, NF: Jason Aronson, 1990.

Otto, Rudolf. *The Idea of the Holy,* 2nd Edition. Translated by John Harvey from the 9th German edition of Das Heilige – Über das Irrationale *in* der Idee des Göttlichen und Sein Verhältnis zum Rationalen, Marburg: 1917. Reprinted London: Oxford University Press, 1958.

Pacilli, Maria, Michele, Roccato, Silvia Pagliaro, and Stefano Russo. "From Political Opponents to Enemies? The Role of Perceived Moral Distance in the Animalistic Dehumanization of the Political Outgroup." *Group Processes & Intergroup Relations* 19, no. 3(2016): 360–373. doi:10.1177/1368430215590490.

Miller, Jeffrey. *The Transcendent Function: Jung's Model of Psychological Growth through Dialogue with the Unconscious.* New York: State University of New York Press, 2004.

Miller, Perry. "Jonathan Edwards on the Sense of the Heart." *Harvard Theological Review* 41, no. 2(1948): 124–145. https://doi.org/10.1017/S0017816000019416.

Philogéne, Gina. "Social Representations and Alterity in the United States." In *Representations and Identity: Content, Process and Power*, eds. G. Maloney and I. Walker. New York: Palgrave, MacMillan, 2007.

Riker, John. "Empathy, Otherness, and Ethical Life: A Response to Frank Summers." *Journal of Theoretical and Philosophical Psychology* 32, no. 4(2012): 246–250. doi:10.1037/a0030218.

Rokhlina, Faina and Gennadiy Novik. "Phenotypes of Juvenile Idiopathic Arthritis." *Pediatric Rheumatology Online Journal* 12, no. 1(2014): 161. doi:10.1186/1546–0096–12-S1-P161.

Ryland, Elizabeth. "Gaia Rising: A Jungian Look at Environmental Consciousness and Sustainable Organizations." *Organization & Environment* 13 no. 4(2000): 381–402. doi:10.1177/1086026600134001.

Schafer, Roy. "The Psychoanalyst's Empathic Activity," in *The Analytic Attitude*, New York: Routledge, 2018, 29.

Skalski, Jonathan. "The Historical Evolution of Tolerance, the Experience of Tolerating, and the Face of the Other." *The Humanistic Psychologist* (2017): 1–9. doi:10.1037/hum0000050.

Stevenson, Daryl, Brian Eck, and Peter Hill. *Psychology and Christianity Integration: Seminal Works that Shaped the Movement.* Bavaria, Illinois: CAPS International, 2007.

Thomson, Iain. "Death and Demise in Being and Time," in *The Cambridge Companion to Heidegger's Being and Time*, ed. Mark A. Wrathall, 260–290. New York: Cambridge University Press, 2013,

Ware, Kallistos. *The Orthodox Way, Revised Edition.* London: A.R. Mowbry & Co. Ltd, 1979. Reprinted Crestwood, N.Y.: St. Vladimir's Seminary Press, 2003.

Witvliet, Charlotte, Thomas Ludwig, and David Bauer, "Please Forgive Me: Transgressors' Emotions and Physiology During Imagery of Seeking Forgiveness and Victim Responses," in *Psychology and Christianity Integration, Seminal Works that Shaped the Movement*, eds. Daryl Stevenson, Brian Eck, and Peter Hill. Illinois: Christian Association for Psychological Studies, Inc., 2007.

4

NEOLIBERALISM AND THE ETHICS OF PSYCHOLOGY[12]

Jeff Sugarman

In recent years, my attention has turned to the political. I have come to appreciate that "the personal is political." I hope my appropriation of the slogan will be forgiven. My meaning is that the forms of the personal, or personhood, what I believe is the appropriate and distinctive subject matter of psychology, has become inextricably political. Personhood takes its form from the kinds of relations in which human beings are immersed, and politics—the organized influence and control of others, or what Foucault referred to as governmentality—is a constitutive feature of both collective and individual psychological life. For this reason, psychologists cannot ignore the political—neither in their explanations of psychologically capable human personhood, nor in the conduct of their professional practices. Failing to take into account the constitutive influence of sociopolitical institutions leads mistakenly to fixing features of persons to human nature rather than to characteristics of the institutions within which we become persons. Neglecting the political also perpetuates scientistic mythology, such as the ideals of disciplinary and professional neutrality and objectivity—that psychologists can operate without presuppositions, without moral and ethical commitments, outside the particularities of history, and immune to the effects of politics. In the absence of concern for the political dimensions of personhood, I believe psychology and psychotherapy are susceptible to being deficient, misguided, and potentially damaging to humankind, despite most psychologists' well-intentioned aspirations to be a force for good.

I wish to sketch some of the psychological effects of the current neoliberal political order and the implications for psychological ethics. Neoliberalism has proliferated rapidly throughout the globe.[3] Yet it's hard to find someone who admits to being a neoliberal. Neoliberalism has managed to make itself invisible by becoming common sense. Common sense permeates our everyday thinking by providing an orientation with which to make sense of the world, of others, and of ourselves; and, by living our lives in the terms it sets, it strikes us as intuitively valid.

Neoliberalism is a political doctrine founded during the closing decades of the 20th century by the Chicago School of political economy. It began as a set of monetary and fiscal policies in response to the economic turmoil of the 1970s and the rise of the social welfare state that many thought was to blame. Multinational corporations, whose profits were threatened by soaring inflation and the growing power of labor in developed nations, together with the World Bank and the International Monetary Fund, abetted a seismic shift in governmental policy from "interventionism" to the "liberalization" of trade, financial transactions, business, and industry. The key features of neoliberalism are a radically free market in which competition is maximized, free trade achieved through economic deregulation, privatization of public assets, vastly diminished state responsibility over areas of social welfare, the corporatization of human services, and monetary and social policies congenial to corporations and disregardful of the consequences: poverty, rapid depletion of resources, irreparable damage to the biosphere, destruction of cultures, and the erosion of liberal democratic institutions. However, the reach of neoliberalism is even more extensive. Neoliberalism is reformulating personhood, psychological life, moral and ethical responsibility, and what it means to have selfhood and identity.

Neoliberalism should be of great concern to psychologists. Yet, while it is commanding considerable attention among scholars in disciplines such as sociology and economics, there is comparatively little discussion of neoliberalism and its consequences among psychologists. My intention is to cast some light on psychological ethics in the context of neoliberalism—what we do to others and how we justify our actions—in the name of psychology. The thrust of my discussion is that psychologists need to be ideologically aware if they are to comprehend more fully their disciplinary and ethical practices. Equipped with such awareness, it is plain that currently dominant trends of psychological theorizing, research, and professional practice are contributing to a neoliberal ideological climate in which persons are not obliged to consider, let alone take responsibility for, the welfare of others. To allege this contravenes psychological codes of professional conduct is to belittle the point. It also seems to me that recent revelations regarding the American Psychological Association's condoning torture and the institutional structures that made unethical practices possible are connected to our contemporary political predicament.

The neoliberal turn was revealed by Michel Foucault.[4] Foucault saw a link between neoliberal styles of government and subjectivity. By government or "governmentality," his invented term, Foucault meant features and functions of sociopolitical institutions that regulate the attitudes and conduct of individuals. Foucault identified the governmentality at work in neoliberal political structures that arose in the 1970s and 1980s in the U.S. and the U.K. Foucault saw "enterprise" as a form and function of governmentality that not only was structuring sociopolitical and economic institutions, but also was shaping personhood and individual life.

In neoliberalism, the technologies of the market work as mechanisms through which persons are constituted as free, enterprising individuals who govern themselves and, consequently, require only limited direct control by the state. According to Foucault, the language of enterprise articulates a relation between the economic well-being of the state and individual fulfillment: the economy is optimized through the entrepreneurial activity of individuals and if individuals are free to direct their lives as entrepreneurs, they can achieve their potential.

It is important to distinguish neoliberalism from classical liberalism. In classical liberalism, people owned themselves as though they were property and could sell their capacity for labor in the market. By contrast, in neoliberalism, people own themselves as if they are entrepreneurs of a business. They conceive of themselves as a set of assets—skills and attributes—to be managed, maintained, developed, and treated as ventures in which to invest. However, the major distinction between classical and neoliberalism is that in neoliberalism, individuals are not only obliged to be engaged in economic activity, they are expected to create it.

In neoliberalism, governing is said to occur by providing individuals with choices and holding them accountable for the choices they make. However, many of the life choices with which individuals are now faced are the result of reduced government services that, in effect, transfer risk from the state to individuals. Risk and uncertainty are nothing new. But there is less and less separating those who pursue risk intentionally from the rest of us for whom it is being woven ideologically into the fabric of everyday life—whether it is matters of personal health, the care and education of our children, the increasing unpredictability of employment, or dignity in old age. Along with increased risk, the current emphasis on choice and self-reliance insinuates failure as self-failure, for which one is expected to bear sole responsibility. There is diminishing appreciation that the predicaments of individuals are a product of more than simply their individual choice and have to do with access to opportunities, how resources are made available, the capacity to take advantage of what is offered, and a host of factors regarding personal histories and the exigencies of lives.

Another feature of choice in neoliberal governmentality is that despite endless proliferation of matters over which choice can be exercised and options made available, many of our choices are preconfigured to preclude more fundamental choices. For example, there is an enormous variety of credit cards from which one may choose. However, possessing a credit card is not subject to choice if one wishes to purchase an airline ticket, make hotel reservations, or rent a car. In neoliberal societies, choosing not to possess a credit card, own a bank account, use computer technology, compete for employment, or choosing "not to choose," imposes severe limitations. Choices are made between predetermined possibilities, and the structural reasons for those limitations are overlooked.

The idea of choice is connected intimately to our understanding of ourselves as free, autonomous actors, capable of choosing rationally in ways that will bring about our self-chosen ends. We have become enraptured by the idea that more choice means more individual freedom. These days, it is hard to see how our choices are determined by anything other than our own self-initiated desires and deliberations. However, we always are embedded in practices that are mutually constitutive and so much a part of the warp and woof of daily life as to render them imperceptible. To the extent that enterprising subjects understand themselves as free in this way, it is seen as inherent in human nature, normal, vital, even virtuous, and commonsensical, and the apparatus of neoliberal governmentality remains concealed.

Foucault argued that neoliberal governmentality harnesses individual choice and freedom as a form of power.[5] It operates not through coercion, but rather inconspicuously through social practices within which persons are reconfigured through a conception of enterprise and by acting on them through their capacity for agency. But neoliberalism is not just something outside of us. The language and practices of neoliberalism are revising how, as self-interpreting beings, we see ourselves and others, inevitably transforming what we are. How are we changing?

Prior to the late 20th century, a job furnished not only security, but also an identity. The original meaning of the word "career" was a carriage road and, as it came to be applied to vocations, a clear way ahead—a prepared path. This is no longer the case. Career counseling clients are now told to expect eleven job changes over their working lives. The neoliberal context of employment is perpetually transitional. It exploits a workforce that is global, disembedded, mobile, and flexible. Life-long vocations are being replaced by job portfolios composed of short-term projects and contracts.

Richard Sennett argues that this shift can be traced to a change in the tactics of big money from owning companies to trading in them.[6] The result was not only how companies were seen and managed, but also how workers were seen and managed. The strategies of short-term investment and companies retooling quickly to take advantage of rapid changes in consumer demand were translated and imposed on the labor force. In the new neoliberal regime—what Sennett calls "flexible capitalism"—workers are "asked to behave nimbly, to be open to change on short notice, [and] to take risks continually".[7] They are expected to be good at "multi-skilling," and to embrace flextime, re-engineering, de-layering, teamwork, constant performance appraisals, ongoing change in working conditions, and exceeding the job description in ways that profit the company. Proponents claim that the new emphasis on flexibility provides people with greater freedom. But, as Sennett deciphers, the new regime simply replaces old controls with new ones.

According to Sennett, the social and psychological costs of these changes are profound. We now live in a contracting society. Traditional values are undermined as we rely increasingly on the letter of legalistic contracts and less on trust, promises, and long-term covenants, such as those that once existed between employers and employees. In a context of work built on short-term contracts, flexibility, and mobility, it becomes difficult to preserve the value and viability of long-term commitments and relationships. A society of individuals frequently switching jobs, relocating, and preoccupied with personal risk and self-interest is conducive neither to stable families nor to cohesive communities.

Sennett sees these changes as an assault on character. Character refers to the enduring personal characteristics we value in ourselves and for which we want to be valued by others. Character is social and long term. It finds expression in loyalty and mutual commitment, and in the sustained pursuit of goals over time. But, as Sennett asks, "How do we decide what is of lasting value in ourselves in a society which is impatient, which focuses on the immediate moment? How can long-term goals be pursued in an economy devoted to the short-term? How can mutual loyalties and commitments be sustained in institutions which are constantly breaking apart or continually being redesigned?"[8]

Character unfolds through the coherence of our lived experience of time and space. But, as Sennett observes, a hazard of flexible capitalism is experience that drifts in time, from place to place, job to job, and contract to contract. In lives composed of fragments, episodes, chameleon values, and where career is no longer a meaningful concept, how does one make and maintain the long-term commitments required of people to form their characters into sustained narratives? Life narratives are not merely registers of events. They bestow temporal logic and coherence—ordering the progress of life in time. As Mark Freeman's work instructs, life narratives furnish hindsight, foresight, and insight, rendering explanations for why things happen, and providing for the integrity of self and identity.[9]

Psychoanalyst and social critic Susie Orbach says that the life narratives of neoliberal selves are fragmented and more resemble a checklist of capacities than a coherent life story.[10] Such checklists aren't psychologically nourishing and are inadequate for a deeply meaningful experience of self and identity. Orbach also detects that the convenient corporate solution to the neoliberal fragmenting of time, loss of place, and overwhelming sense of personal insignificance is branding. The buying and wearing of brands has become our way to belong and find our place. Our personal commitments and orientations are defined not through discovering and defending communal values and civic virtues, but rather by donning Nike, drinking Starbucks, buying iPhones, and driving hybrids. Perhaps the hardest disease to cure is the medicine one takes.

Fifteen years ago, Philip Cushman and Peter Gilford astutely described the kind of personhood condensing in the neoliberal atmosphere of the early 1990s.[11] Most notably was a transformation in self-understanding. As Cushman and Gilford explain, the shift was from a self that "had a deeply felt yearning to experience an interior essential change, to a self that yearns to have many exteriors to change into".[12] Gone was the ideal of authentic selfhood—a self richly furnished and unified by its intuitions of depth and inner life, compelled and steered by its own moral and aesthetic convictions, and indifferent to, if not disdainful of, conformity and consumer appetites fed by fashion, fame, and wealth. In its place, a new "multiple self" was finding form. This new self dispensed with self-discovery and the search for authenticity, depth, and cohesion. The goal of self-development was not to become what you truly are, but rather, to make oneself as flexible and adaptable as possible in order to take advantage of whatever opportunities came one's way. Selves were no longer singular and unified. They were multiple and decentered, composed of a cluster of pliable identities identified with, but peripheral to the individual. Identities were now cultivated instrumentally and selected or refashioned to present oneself as an attractive package given the marketing needs of the moment. The multiple self is like a Swiss army knife, a multi tool readied with a set of manipulable appearances that can be projected to help one adapt or get a competitive edge as circumstances require. It's not that authenticity has disappeared. But it no longer connotes being free-spirited, spontaneous, and true to one self. It now means being or having something sufficiently unique that it can be exploited. As Rob Horning writes, "if your personality can't be leveraged—then authenticity is not really available to you. You can't afford to be yourself".[13]

Multiple selves, by comparison with their predecessor, are less complex and conflicted—untroubled by authenticity and mysteries of personal depth. But what does concern them is visibility and recognition. Generation Y (the Millennials) don't aspire to see the world's great religious shrines to witness the awe or reverence inspired by worship of the divine; instead, they build shrines to themselves on Facebook or other social media sites in acts of self-worship, so that an audience of nameless others can know of them—know that I exist, know that my life matters—as if posting a selfie with my freshly purchased grande triple skinny vanilla soy latte is freighted with existential or spiritual significance. Visibility and recognition once implied privileged status bestowed by inheritance or earned by achievement. Now visibility and recognition are rights and entitlements to be claimed and conferred by everyone. We are now all visibility and recognition entrepreneurs. As Stephen Marche assesses, as our on-line communities become the engine of visibility and self-image, visibility and self-image become the engine of community.[14] But social media create networks, not communities. A network is not a community, in the same way a connection is not a bond, something Facebook and other social media make painfully apparent. Electronic connectivity is broad, but shallow. It lacks loyalty and commitment. Thus, according to Marche, while we are generating and proliferating ever more novel electronic platforms for socializing, we have less and less actual society and less and less of value to say to one another.

Neoliberal selves are primed for opportunities, at least to recognize them. But they find committing to them or to what is required to capitalize on them difficult, whether it is relationships, jobs, financial obligations, or planned social engagements. For some, the issue is being fickle or easily bored; for others, it's fear of missing out on that something better waiting just around the corner. In fact, there's now a term for this: FOMO (Fear of Missing Out), which, no doubt, will become a diagnostic classification in the next edition of the DSM.

Neoliberalism has redefined our notions of identity and personal fulfillment—what matters to us, what we care about, what guides our sense of right and wrong, better and worse, appropriate and inappropriate. But how is psychology implicated in neoliberalism? Psychologists' extensive participation in branding and marketing provides ample illustration of collusion with neoliberal governmentality. However, I wish to focus briefly on three other examples that illustrate psychologists' complicity in the neoliberal agenda: social anxiety disorder, positive psychology, and educational psychology.[15]

Social anxiety is now the third most common psychological disorder after depression and alcoholism,[16] deemed "a public health danger ... heading toward epidemic proportions".[17] The rapid rise in social anxiety disorder is striking given it did not become a diagnostic category until 1987 and its predecessor, social phobia, was rare, found in less that 3% of the population.[18] Neoliberalism has been influential in shaping a space of possibility in what was once simply called "shyness" could become an object of expert psychological knowledge and intervention.

In a 2013 paper in *Theory & Psychology*, Sarah Hickinbottom-Brawn identifies two important sources that brought heightened attention to social anxiety.[19] One is the specific role played by SmithKlein Beecham, makers of the pharmaceutical Paxil, the preferred treatment. A timely removal of advertising restrictions permitted the company to market the drug directly to consumers. What is more significant is that the company's multibillion-dollar marketing campaign was highly effective in linking the disorder to all manner of interpersonal and job-related problems in a way that refashioned all social discomfort as dis-ease. The second source of attention, on which the first depended, is an enterprise culture that places a premium on social prowess, confidence, exuberance, and initiative—characteristics needed for effective networking and self-presentation that, in turn, are believed necessary for success in a competitive marketplace. Given such a setting, it is easy to see how shyness and social discomfort can be made to stand out as problematic.

By pathologizing and medicalizing shyness, and locating the source of the problem within individuals, psychologists operate behind a veil of science and value neutrality. Ideological complicity is rarely addressed. In cognitive-behavioral therapy, the second most common form of treatment, the therapist is the authoritative expert who conducts sessions with rigorous supervision, instructing clients how to interpret their experiences while teaching them techniques of self-control. The aim of therapy is the "transfer of control" by which clients are directed to manage themselves. However, it is recommended that therapists act "paternally" and client compliance is considered the single most important factor for therapeutic efficacy. The assumptions perpetrated by psychologists are that social anxiety is a pathological disorder internal to individuals, that individuals bear sole responsibility for their condition, and that expert treatment is required for ameliorating the disorder. Such expert treatment consists in methods of self-surveillance and self-management—methods that encourage conformity to neoliberal ideals and may in fact exacerbate clients' difficulties. Never are the predicaments, contradictions, and risks wrought by the institutions of neoliberalism, and in which individuals are compelled to participate, considered.

As remarked by Hickinbottom-Brawn, social anxiety may be a highly individual and private experience.[20] But it doesn't follow that the origins or causes of such experience are located within individuals. Hickinbottom-Brawn submits that the conception of social anxiety as an individual disorder deters us from looking at the broader sociopolitical context in which it is manifest, "where previous ideals of citizenship and commitment to others have been supplanted by a vision of social relations as a matter of interaction between economic units for the purpose of personal fulfillment and attainment of instrumental ends".[21] Hickinbottom-Brawn asserts that in their conceptualization and treatment of social anxiety, psychologists thus promote an instrumental orientation to social and personal life, contribute to naturalizing and normalizing neoliberalism, and maintain the neoliberal status quo.

In his book, *Happiness as Enterprise: An Essay on Neoliberal Life*, Sam Binkley marshals evidence to show how happiness is being recast by neoliberalism as an entrepreneurial project. In what Binkley dubs "the new discourse on happiness," individuals are not only encouraged to cultivate their attributes, assets, potentials, and purposes for the sake of their personal success, but also to exploit happiness itself as an attribute, asset, potential, and purpose that can be harnessed in aid of such success.[22] In this way, happiness becomes both goal and means. It is an effect of success, yet also a resource for further success, occasioned by life interpreted as an endless array of emerging opportunities and resources, including one's own emotional states, to be engaged, deployed, and even risked toward the overarching goal of making oneself as competitive and effective as possible. Happiness, as ends and means, is that of an autonomous agent who regards the world not as defined by social norms and responsibilities to which one must adjust, but rather as a store of resources to be used in the service of self-optimization. The new discourse on happiness reflects a fundamental transformation in how we see life and our relation to it, from the social and mutual to the entrepreneurial and opportunistic.

According to Binkley, much of what is propelling the new discourse on happiness is the positive psychology movement. Binkley details how positive psychologists have taken a vital role in shaping this new understanding of happiness and purveying it to the public. Positive psychology is a multibillion-dollar field of research and intervention commanding enormous attention both within and outside of psychology. The reach of its influence extends far beyond counseling and psychotherapy to education, economic analyses, business, management, marketing, sports coaching, life coaching, law enforcement, corrections, and military training.

As understood by positive psychologists, happiness is a product of individual effort. Only you can you make yourself happy. The valence of emotions directly reflects optimistic and pessimistic thoughts. Thoughts are within one's control and can be manipulated to effect desired emotional states. Consequently, not only are individuals capable of changing their emotions, but they are also ultimately responsible for their emotional experience. According to positive psychologists, when we accept responsibility for how we feel and learn to wield our thoughts in the service of bettering our lives, positive emotions and happiness result. It is this exercise of agency forged by a sense of self-responsible freedom that is the substance of happiness. By the same token, we are to blame for our unhappiness. If we are unhappy, it is because we have failed to accept responsibility for our circumstances and take action. Abdicating responsibility for our state of being and inaction derive from succumbing to pessimism bred from docility, resignation, dependency, and believing falsely that our futures are determined by traumas and other psychological injuries sustained in our pasts.

Positive psychology is radically transforming the nature of therapy and the goals of intervention. As Binkley discusses, psychotherapies styled on deep exploration of past relationships and reflection on the suffering incurred are being displaced by life coaching, which not only eschews reflective examination of individuals' histories, but also the very assumption that clients need healing. The task of the life coach is assisting clients in building visions of their future happiness, setting self-enterprising life goals, strategizing about available means, and motivating them to act in ways to achieve their purposes. Using a mixture of techniques adopted from counseling, business consulting, and the human potential movement, coaching is eclectic, pragmatic, forward-looking, results oriented, and aimed at efficient and productive living. It typically consists of short-term, focused consultations that address highly circumscribed personal issues and challenges most often related to career and business concerns. Most such concerns often can be traced to the highly competitive climate of life in a neoliberal global economy. However, in the paradigm of coaching, such concerns become private individual shortcomings to be remedied by strengthening individuals' psychological resources. Tracing the well-established link between coaching and positive psychology, Binkley reveals how positive psychology lends coaching scientific legitimacy, while positive psychology benefits from coaching through increased dissemination of its psychological platform.

What is perhaps most disconcerting in Binkley's analysis is the way in which positive psychology and coaching are reformulating our understanding of relationships in the context of enterprise culture. Relationships are reduced to means-ends calculations, and pursued solely for self-interest and emotional self-optimization. Acts of love, friendship, benevolence, and generosity are valued to the extent they increase individuals' social capital. Even our most intimate relationships are interpreted as assets and liabilities. And, in the competitive social market where flexibility and mobility are prized, relationships are best engaged as short-term contracts in which we might even withhold our deepest feelings for fear of their being used against us. Flexible capitalism demands a high degree of mobility, and a willingness to exit relationships that are no longer profitable. The context of neoliberalism seems to dissolve the capacity to respect and cherish others, especially with the kind of loyalty and commitment that Sennett insists is disappearing from the list of human virtues.[23] What becomes clear from Binkley's account is that the new discourse on happiness delivered by positive psychology strongly reflects and sustains neoliberalism and enterprise culture.

In another compelling book, *The Education of Selves*, Jack Martin and Ann-Marie McLellan illuminate how, over the latter half of the 20th century, psychological expertise served in shifting the goals of education from traditional functions of preparing citizens to concern with the psychological needs of individual learners.[24] By the late 1970s, psychologists had declared that by enhancing self-esteem, self-concept, self-regulation, and self-efficacy, students could acquire the psychological capabilities required to become enterprising, life-long learners. According to Martin and McLellan, the psychologized image of the successful student has three key features. First, students act and experience in ways that are expressive of their pre-sumed, uniquely-individual psychological interiors. Second, they are strategically enterprising in pursuit of self-defined goals. Third, these features of self-expression and self-enterprise are entitlements, basic rights students can presume and demand from teachers, school administrators, and peers. The expressive, enterprising, and entitled student is a unique individual who is active, self-disciplined, self-directed, self-assured, who bears the responsibility for learning, and who is equipped with strategic tools for goal-setting, progress monitoring, performance evaluation, and problem solving. Martin and McLellan assert that these characteristics align with a very specific form of self-governance, one especially well suited to the govern-mentality required of neoliberalism.

In detailing the historical influence of psychologists on views of learners and curricula, Martin and McLellan show how the idea of expressive, enterprising selves became linked to the terminology, technologies, and authority of psy-chologists. Under psychology's influence, children increasingly became under-stood as autonomous individual learners who needed to be taught to recognize, value, and express their unique perspectives and abilities. This was promoted by psychologists under the banners of self-esteem and self-concept, while self-regulation and self-efficacy were used to elevate the self's hypothesized capacities as a strategic manager to monitor and direct itself in pursuit of its own self-interests. What is now referred to explicitly as "enterprise education" and incorporated in many American, Canadian, and European school policies and practices, not only relies on this psychologized conception of the learner, but also teaches and encourages risk-taking, initiative, self-esteem, self-appraisal, management and orga-nizational skills, flexibility, team building, and how to market skills and abilities in the same way as one would a business. It should be noted that behind enterprise education is ideological adherence to meritocratic notions of individual success and responsibility. Insensitive to matters of race, class privilege, and gender, enterprise education presupposes that educational outcomes are simply a matter of effort and ability, and inequalities can be attributed to insufficient sources of personal control.[25]

Martin and McLellan argue that the expressive, enterprising, and entitled learner advanced by psychology is ill suited to the purposes of education.[26] Whereas psychology is focused on enhancing the interior experience, self-governing capacities, self-concern, and self-serving instrumental expression of individuals, education has the broader mandate of preparing citizens to be capable not only of developing themselves, but also of contributing to their communities for the collective good. Martin and McLellan worry that educational aims concerned with the values of committed citizenship, civic virtue, and the greater collective good are being undermined by the mission of psychologists to help learners acquire skills, abilities, and dispositions that make them adaptive workers equipped psychologically to meet the ever-changing demands of neoliberal flexible capitalism.

Neoliberal economic policies have had dramatic global consequences. However, neoliberalism is no longer just a set of economic policies. It has disseminated and imposed market values at every corner of human life. At the nexus of these values are entrepreneurialism and market rationality. By institutionalizing these values, neoliberalism has had not only normative consequences, but also ontological ones, extending to the very psychological constitution of persons. Societies require people to do and be certain kinds of things and are structured sociopolitically to produce persons, selves, and contexts that elicit and regulate actions of these kinds. Neoliberal governmentality requires individuals who are responsible for themselves and reflexively manage their skills, abilities, and relationships such that they can be deployed as marketable assets. Neoliberalism succeeds in producing such individuals and the prescribed economic activity through the extension of market conditions to every aspect of human endeavor. Market rationality configures human life as enterprise. Individuals are made responsible to provide for their own needs, aspirations, and happiness. In order to do so under market conditions, they are encouraged to conceive of themselves as autonomous entrepreneurial actors who must steer themselves strategically through a competitive field of opportunities, alliances, and obstacles. As evidence of the ubiquity of market rationality applied to everyday life, witness how it is displayed blatantly as the common plot of a hoard of reality television shows proliferating globally,[27] such as Afghan Idol, Fear Factor India, Serbian Survivor, Turkish Project Runway, or the Ukrainian version of The Voice.

Neoliberal individuals, as autonomous self-concerned strategists locked in competition with others, are preoccupied with choosing for themselves. They have little impetus to engage cooperatively with others to organize or revise the options over which choice can be exercised, especially for the collective good. The hyper-self-sufficiency of neoliberalism denies and prevents social relatedness. As Brown surmises, the consummate neoliberal public could hardly be said to exist as a public: "The body politic ceases to be a body, but is, rather, a group of individual entrepreneurs and consumers".[28] However, the hypertrophied indivi-dualism of the neoliberal order does not simply undermine social relatedness. It also cements unequal power relations among economically defined individuals who may consider themselves as autonomous agents, but who ostensibly are segmented by race and class. Theories of the market are formulated in terms of inputs of labor, not human beings and, thus, are not conspicuously racialized. Nevertheless, the contemporary global economy is the product of an ongoing history of practices of racial and class division and exploitation. The market always has functioned by dominance and subjugation, and the perpetuation of inequality for the purposes of profit remains a strategy of the global elite. Under neoliber-alism, belief in the "maleness" and "whiteness" of power is an undercurrent of neoliberal common sense, prescribing which societies exemplify approved wes-tern values and who is authorized to intervene in international matters.[29]

A vital function of governmentality is not only to produce and regulate forms of subjectivity, but also to legitimize the status quo regarding ordinary life and what is deemed "natural" about it. Perhaps the most powerful penetration of governmentality is to be found in what passes for common sense. This is why neoliberalism is so pervasive and, at the same time, often so difficult to detect. However, neoliberalism is not a natural phenomenon or an inevitable historical development. I may not be an economist, but there is nothing natural biophysi-cally, sociologically, or psychologically about market rationality. Market trading is neither structurally necessary for the organization of societies nor to be found in our genes. Yet, despite the contingency of our sociopolitical and economic cir-cumstances, we sense little control over them. We are inundated with endless choices, but so implicated in a seemingly monolithic neoliberal order there appears little choice as to living outside it. Most are so seized by the social ima-ginary of neoliberalism that alternative sociopolitical and economic arrangements and how they might be achieved seem inconceivable, especially for those born after 1970. But there are alternatives. For example, some feminist economic the-orists propose an economy of care and human development.[30] After all, most of what is involved in the preservation and reproduction of individual and collective life depends not on financial transactions, but rather on other more fundamental kinds of relations—care, trust, respect, responsibility, teaching, and learning.

Human beings enter the world utterly helpless and would perish quickly without care. We depend on others for our lives. It is not our flexibility and ability to adapt effectively to our environments that is key to our survival. Quite conversely, it is a complete absence of ability to do so that creates a relation of dependence inscribed at birth, necessary to securing human life. All infant and childhood development is instigated by others on whom we depend to equip us, not just to become surviving organisms, but, moreover, psychologically capable persons who can function in the myriad relational contexts comprising human life. It is well-established knowledge in psychology that the quality of early rela-tionships can have vital and lasting consequences for further development and well-being. As the world of the child expands to school, peer relationships, and a host of new material and social needs, there are more dependencies on others. But not only do we require the care and support of others at the beginning of our lives and, as we grow, to enculturate and educate us, but we also are vulnerable during the course of our lives to illness and, eventually, to the ravages of age. Many of you have had the experience of caring for aging parents and the complex of dependencies involved. I lost my mother to Alzheimer's after a protracted, gradual diminishment of the person I knew, an experience now so prevalent it's commonly called "the long goodbye." It was a goodbye that entailed endless deliberations over care and its costs, the disposition of her property, and navigating, on her behalf, institutional rules and requirements that demanded strategizing instrumentally. But to reduce what my sister and I were doing to that—to occlude the overarching concern we had to insure her quality of life and accord her the respect and dignity she clearly was owed morally and ethically—is to lose sight of the significances of personhood and the profound depth of our relationship. Under neoliberalism, our social relationality is being monetized. The human meaning and significance of our social relations are being lost as they disappear behind their characterization in terms of market rationality and are replaced by electronic facades.

All of what Vygotsky called our higher order psychological capacities—the dimensions of thinking that we are taught to bring under linguistic control—any freedom and ability to choose that we possess, the reflexive understanding of ourselves as individuals or as agentive authors of our actions, are developmental accomplishments facilitated by a multitude of dependencies and complex, morally-saturated social relations and interactions.[31] Neoliberalism assumes that the human world is an aggregate of individuals who should be free to advance their own interests and made responsible for their choices within the constraints of a market economy. As I have suggested, whether the self-interested, enterprising individual is the fundamental structural unit on which politics and economics should be based is a matter for debate. It could be argued that this assumption is undermining the very social conditions within which personhood is realized—not only social conditions, but also the biophysical conditions on which human life depends. An economy of care and psychological development extends to the ecological realm. Marketing dangerous products and polluting the environment are efficient and lucrative practices in the short term. Conservation only becomes a consideration when it is made profitable as shown by companies attempting to convince consumers that they are "green" irrespective of the real environmental impact of their products. But without breathable air, arable land, nutritive food, and potable water, we cannot survive. Economy is embedded in ecology. In fact, the words "economy" and "ecology" both find their origins in the Greek "oikos" meaning dwelling place. The environment is the foundation of, and limit on, economics, and the peril of our environmental situation poses an urgent challenge to the market rationality of neoliberalism. But sadly, I am not telling you anything we don't already know.

Whether or not an economy of care and psychological development is a viable replacement for neoliberalism is also debatable. It could be argued that it would require a return to the kind of welfarist policies, interventionism, and bloated government to which banks and corporations are opposed. But I am not of the opinion that an economy governed by market logic and the best interests of banks and corporations will make for a better world.

As I have discussed, there is ample evidence that many psychologists sustain and promote the globally-dominant neoliberal agenda. In some ways, this should not be surprising. Psychology is wedded to the social, cultural, political, and economic conditions of its times.[32] However, as some have long noted,[33] psychologists have been unwilling to admit their complicity with specific sociopolitical arrangements. For to do so would undermine a credibility forged on value neutrality presumed to be ensured by scientific objectivity and moral indifference to its subject matter. Consequently, as the historical record attests, in the main, psychologists have served primarily as "architects of adjustment" in preserving the status quo and not as agents of sociopolitical change.[34] However, if psychologists are to act ethically, we cannot continue "hiding behind a veneer of scientism".[35] We are compelled not only to admit that psychology is ideologically laden, but also to ask ourselves whether we are acting ethically in preserving the neoliberal status quo. This entails interrogating neoliberalism, our relationship to it, how it affects what persons are and might become, and whether it is good for human well-being. It is only by such examination that we might comprehend the ethics of our disciplinary and professional practices in the context of a neoliberal political order.

Notes

1 A portion of the material in this chapter was adapted from Jeff Sugarman, "Neoliberalism and Psychological Ethics," *Journal of Theoretical and Philosophical Psychology* 35, no. 2 (2015): 103–116 with permission from the publisher (Copyright © 2015 by the American Psychological Association).
2 An earlier version of this paper was presented at the Psychology and the Other Biennial Conference (2015, Cambridge, MA).
3 Bronwyn Davies and Peter Bansel, "Neoliberalism and Education," *International Journal of Qualitative Studies in Education* 20 (2007).
4 Michel Foucault, *The Birth of Biopolitics: Lectures at the Collège De France, 1978–1979*, eds. Michel Senellart, François Ewald, and Alessandro Fontana (Basingstoke: Palgrave Macmillan UK, 2008).
5 Ibid.
6 Richard Sennett, *The Corrosion of Character: The Personal Consequences of Work in the New Capitalism* (New York: WW Norton & Company, 1998).
7 Ibid., 9.
8 Ibid., 10.
9 Mark Freeman, *Hindsight: The Promise and Peril of Looking Backward* (New York: Oxford University Press, 2010).
10 Susie Orbach, "The Payoff: Susie Orbach on How the Market Induced Our Moral Panic," *The Guardian*, March 19, 2001, http://theguardian.com/society/2001/mar/20/26.

11 Philp Cushman and Peter Gilford, "From Emptiness to Multiplicity: The Self at the Year 2000," *The Psychohistory Review* 27 (1999).

12 Ibid., 17.

13 Rob Horning. "Do the Robot," *The New Inquiry*, August 12, 2015, https://thenewinquiry.com/blog/do-the-robot/, paragraph 3.

14 Stephen Marche, "Is Facebook Making Us Lonely," *The Atlantic* 309 (2012).

15 Kim Su Rasmussen, "Foucault's Genealogy of Racism," *Theory, Culture & Society* 28 (2011).

16 Allan V Horwitz, *Creating Mental Illness* (Chicago: University of Chicago Press, 2002).

17 Lynne Henderson and Philip Zimbardo. "Shyness," in *Encyclopedia of Mental Health*, ed. Howard Friedman (San Diego: Academic Press, 1998).

18 Kevin Aho, "The Psychopathology of American Shyness: A Hermeneutic Reading," *Journal for the Theory of Social Behaviour* 40 (2010).

19 Sarah Hickinbottom-Brawn, "Brand 'You': The Emergence of Social Anxiety Disorder in the Age of Enterprise," *Theory & Psychology* 23 (2013).

20 Ibid.

21 Ibid., 746.

22 Sam Binkley, *Happiness as Enterprise: An Essay on Neoliberal Life* (Albany: State University of New York Press, 2013).

23 Sennett, *The Corrosion of Character: The Personal Consequences of Work in the New Capitalism*.

24 Jack Martin and Ann-Marie McLellan, *The Education of Selves: How Psychology Transformed Students* (New York: Oxford University Press, 2013).

25 Stephen Vassallo, *Critical Educational Psychology* (Baltimore: Johns Hopkins University Press, 2017).

26 Martin and McLellan, *The Education of Selves: How Psychology Transformed Students*.

27 Nick Couldry, "Reality TV, or the Secret Theater of Neoliberalism," *The Review of Education, Pedagogy, and Cultural Studies* 30 (2008).

28 Wendy Brown, "Neo-Liberalism and the End of Liberal Democracy," *Theory & Event* 7 (2003): paragraph 15.

29 Sally Davison and George Shire, "Race, Migration and Neoliberalism," *Soundings* 59 (2015); Randolph Hohle, *Race and the Origins of American Neoliberalism* (New York: Routledge, 2015).

30 Paula England, "Separative and Soluble Selves: Dichotomous Thinking in Economics," in *Feminist Economics Today: Beyond Economic Man*, ed. Julie A Nelson and Marianne A Ferber (Chicago: University of Chicago Press, 2003); Julie A Nelson, "Feminism and Economics," *Journal of Economic Perspectives* 9 (1995); Sabine O'Hara, "Everything Needs Care: Toward a Context-Based Economy," in *Counting on Marilyn Waring: New Advances in Feminist Economics*, eds. Margunn Bjømholt and Ailsa McKay (Bradford, Canada: Demeter Press, 2013).

31 Lev Semenovich Vygotsky, *Mind in Society: The Development of Higher Psychological Processes* (Cambridge, MA: Harvard University Press, 1978).

32 Kurt Danziger, *Naming the Mind* (London: Sage Publications, 1997).

33 Isaac Prilleltensky, "Psychology and Social Ethics," *American Psychologist* 49 (1994); Isaac Prilleltensky and Richard Walsh-Bowers, "Psychology and the Moral Imperative," *Journal of Theoretical and Philosophical Psychology* 13 (1993).

34 Richard Walsh-Bowers, "Taking the Ethical Principle of Social Responsibility Seriously: A Socio-Political Perspective on Psychologists' Social Practices" (paper presented at the Annual Meeting of the Canadian Psychological Association, Ottawa, Ontario, Canada, 2007).

35 Prilleltensky, "Psychology and Social Ethics," 967.

References

Aho, Kevin. "The Psychopathology of American Shyness: A Hermeneutic Reading." *Journal for the Theory of Social Behaviour* 40(2010): 190–206.

Binkley, Sam. *Happiness as Enterprise: An Essay on Neoliberal Life*. Albany: State University of New York Press, 2013.

Brown, Wendy. "Neo-Liberalism and the End of Liberal Democracy." *Theory & Event* 7 (2003).

Couldry, Nick. "Reality TV, or the Secret Theater of Neoliberalism." *The Review of Education, Pedagogy, and Cultural Studies* 30(2008): 3–13.

Cushman, Philp and Peter Gilford. "From Emptiness to Multiplicity: The Self at the Year 2000." *The Psychohistory Review* 27(1999): 15–31.

Danziger, Kurt. *Naming the Mind*. London: Sage Publications, 1997.

Davies, Bronwyn and Peter Bansel. "Neoliberalism and Education." *International Journal of Qualitative Studies in Education* 20(2007): 247–259.

Davison, Sally and George Shire. "Race, Migration and Neoliberalism." *Soundings* 59 (2015): 81–95.

England, Paula. "Separative and Soluble Selves: Dichotomous Thinking in Economics." In *Feminist Economics Today: Beyond Economic Man*, edited by Julie A Nelson and Marianne A Ferber, 33–59. Chicago: University of Chicago Press, 2003.

Foucault, Michel. *The Birth of Biopolitics: Lectures at the Collège De France, 1978–1979*. Edited by Michel Senellart, François Ewald and Alessandro Fontana. Basingstoke: Palgrave Macmillan UK, 2008. doi:10.1057/9780230594180.

Freeman, Mark. *Hindsight: The Promise and Peril of Looking Backward*. New York: Oxford University Press, 2010.

Henderson, Lynne, and Philip Zimbardo. "Shyness." In *Encyclopedia of Mental Health*, edited by Howard Friedman, 497–505. San Diego: Academic Press, 1998.

Hickinbottom-Brawn, Sarah. "Brand 'You': The Emergence of Social Anxiety Disorder in the Age of Enterprise." *Theory & Psychology* 23(2013): 732–751.

Hohle, Randolph. *Race and the Origins of American Neoliberalism*. New York: Routledge, 2015.

Horning, Rob. "Do the Robot." *The New Inquiry*, August 12, 2015, https://thenewinquiry.com/blog/do-the-robot/.

Horwitz, Allan V. *Creating Mental Illness*. Chicago: University of Chicago Press, 2002.

Marche, Stephen. "Is Facebook Making Us Lonely." *The Atlantic* 309(2012): 60–69.

Martin, Jack and Ann-Marie McLellan. *The Education of Selves: How Psychology Transformed Students*. New York: Oxford University Press, 2013.

Nelson, Julie A. "Feminism and Economics." *Journal of Economic Perspectives* 9(1995): 131–148.

O'Hara, Sabine. "Everything Needs Care: Toward a Context-Based Economy." In *Counting on Marilyn Waring: New Advances in Feminist Economics*, edited by Margunn Bjømholt and Ailsa McKay. Bradford, Canada: Demeter Press, 2013.

Orbach, Susie. "The Payoff: Susie Orbach on How the Market Induced Our Moral Panic." *The Guardian*, March 19, 2001, http://theguardian.com/society/2001/mar/20/26.

Prilleltensky, Isaac. "Psychology and Social Ethics." *American Psychologist* 49(1994): 966–967.

Prilleltensky, Isaac and Richard Walsh-Bowers. "Psychology and the Moral Imperative." *Journal of Theoretical and Philosophical Psychology* 13(1993): 90–102.

Sennett, Richard. *The Corrosion of Character: The Personal Consequences of Work in the New Capitalism*. New York: WW Norton & Company, 1998.

Su Rasmussen, Kim. "Foucault's Genealogy of Racism." *Theory, Culture & Society* 28 (2011): 34–51.

Sugarman, Jeff. "Neoliberalism and Psychological Ethics." *Journal of Theoretical and Philosophical Psychology* 35(2015): 103–116.

Vassallo, Stephen. *Critical Educational Psychology*. Baltimore: Johns Hopkins University Press, 2017.

Vygotsky, Lev Semenovich. *Mind in Society: The Development of Higher Psychological Processes*. Cambridge, MA: Harvard University Press, 1978.

Walsh-Bowers, Richard. "Taking the Ethical Principle of Social Responsibility Seriously: A Socio-Political Perspective on Psychologists' Social Practices." Paper presented at the Annual Meeting of the Canadian Psychological Association, Ottawa, Ontario, Canada, 2007.

5

BLACK RAGE AND WHITE LISTENING

On the Psychologization of Racial Emotionality

Sam Binkley

That conversations around race evoke powerful emotions is a fact widely acknowledged across a range of civic, institutional, cultural, and popular spaces. It is believed that participants in such conversations must display a special sensitivity to each other's feelings if they are to overcome deeply entrenched attitudes and habits of thought. Indeed, on an organizational level, tremendous value is attached to the sensitivities demanded of conversations on race: "It has been shown," argues Derald Wing Sue, in his influential book *Race Talk and the Conspiracy of Silence: Understanding and Facilitating Difficult Dialogues on Race*, "that honest race talk is one of the most powerful means to dispel stereotypes and biases, to increase racial literacy and critical consciousness about race issues, to decrease fear of differences, to broaden one's horizons, to increase compassion and empathy, to increase appreciation of all colors and cultures, and to enhance a greater sense of belonging and connectedness."[1] Such is the currency organizations place on the capacity to manage and interpret emotions, one's own and others, that surrounds the problem of race.

What is proposed here is a somewhat different view of the imperative to manifest sensitivity to the emotional character of race. While it is accepted that such sensitivities are morally and politically laudable and that such emotions are often the genuine response to real social conditions, it is proposed here that the summoning of such sensitivities on the institutional level often occurs within a set of managerial rationalities whose end result is the reproduction of those very racial attitudes and subject-positions that they purport to transform.[2] Such a display of sensitivity is a form of management that operates not through the suppression or obstruction of emotions, but precisely through efforts to acknowledge and produce them, to apprehend the inner content of emotions and to dignify and legitimize their public display.[3] This is particularly true when we consider such emotions in terms of the multiple configurations, or the interlocking ensembles they assume in such displays, which often link expressions of anger, guilt, hostility, fear, and shame into complex affective economies.[4] In what follows, one such configuration will be considered for the ways in which seemingly oppositional emotional styles achieve a sort of balancing act: rage, often expressed by people of color at conditions in institutional settings, and the posture of empathic listening, practiced by whites in response to such displays of rage. While originating in organic affective responses to real social conditions, this emotional ensemble incorporates and directs such affects into a certain functional equilibrium, a delicate stability in which racialized positions are reproduced and managed, even as they are ostensibly being challenged. Moreover, this equilibrium is accomplished through a discourse on emotion and racial sensitivity originating in the history of psychological thought. It is not an exaggeration to claim that many eruptions of racialized rage and listening are powerfully strengthened by a long history of psychological speculation on race and its emotional terrain—a conversation that has given a certain reality to these emotional styles as reified, organizational types. Thus, my concern is not just with emotional expressions themselves, but also with the position and authority allocated certain emotional ensembles, or paired emotional performances. The encounter between black rage and white listening tells us a lot about racial experiences and racial emotionality on an experiential level, but it also tells us something about how these emotions are regulated, psychologized, and eventually corralled into manageable forms, and how the social arrangements that produced them are ultimately conserved and reproduced within even the most benevolent institutions.

Toward this end, what follows is an effort to trace the history of these two emotional figures, the raging black and the listening white, and the apparatus of incorporation they compose, through a short archaeology of the psychologization of racial emotion. The aim is to try to capture the gradual elaboration, the professional coding and the ultimate embedding of these two figures in contemporary managerial practices, and the slow formation over the course of the last half of the 20th century of their unique functional symbiosis. For this purpose, an inquiry analogous to Michel Foucault's genealogical method will be used, not just because Foucault so well understood how the sciences of the human were woven into processes of historical and institutional development, but because Foucault also understood how these sciences had the effect of producing certain kinds of subjects, of making up people in particular ways.[5]

Situating Black rage and white listening

First, a brief anecdote: on an afternoon in April, the faculty of a small liberal arts college gathered for the monthly ritual of their Faculty Assembly meeting. Amid the exchange of salutations and the sampling of humus and pita slices from a buffet at the back of an auditorium, bodies distributed themselves amongst the chairs laid out for the occasion, awaiting the signal from the Assembly Chair that the meeting was ready to begin. But as business got underway, it soon became apparent that something unusual was taking place. The angry sound of protest chanting could be heard in the distance—What do we want? Fair education! When do we want it? Now!—growing louder and building in intensity. Soon students began to fill the auditorium, chanting slogans and shouting out demands at the faculty as they filled the space, gathering in clusters, dropping their book bags on the floor and taking up spots along the wall and in the aisles, forming an enormous circle around their besieged professors, who began awkwardly fingering their pens and cellphones under the noise of protest. The students' voices grew thunderous and angry: as faculty sat motionless, chants gave way to charges and testimonies—Open your eyes! This environment is killing me! We pay your salaries! Converging on the Chair's microphone, their voices called out a college culture they experienced as racist and chauvinistic, their time here a daily slog barbed with tiny insults and slurs, whose effect was toxic and even lethal to their very wellbeing. The faculty sat motionless as the intensity of student testimonies increased, their voices openly challenging the captive faculty with accusations of racism and demands that the College take action against a culture of bias and insensitivity. I sat with my colleagues, motionless.

Several things struck me during the time that it took for this encounter to unfold, which prompted a train of thought leading ultimately to the writing of this chapter, foremost being my own response to these events, which was one of conflict and ambivalence. While initially supportive of the students for their energy and conviction, in a short time my mood changed. I took it personally: I was put off by the shouting and finger-pointing, at the impingement on what I thought was the respect I was entitled to as a college professor. Mixed with this was no doubt some element of the indignation expressed by many liberal whites at the charge of racism: as good guy in the politics of race, certainly I didn't deserve this abuse. I was overcome by a strong desire to leave the room—which I did, for a few minutes, but then only to return again, for reasons I could not quite understand, and then to leave once again a little later on. I was confused by my own behavior. But I also found puzzling the behavior of my colleagues, whose stoic, nodding, hands-folded-across-their-laps response in the midst of such an outpouring struck me as uniquely disturbing. How were they able to absorb such a harangue without any evidence of strain? Why didn't they feel the need to leave, as I did, or to defend themselves or to speak back? What shield did they employ to deflect the charges of the students? Where was their vulnerability?

Reflecting on my ambivalence in the days that followed, I mulled over the obvious interpretation of my reticence as one of white fragility—a response of defensive hostility at a disruption to my own white comfort zone. There is certainly validity to this claim as I have, over the years, become quite habituated to the unearned presumption of civility, intelligence and competence that constitute one of the benefits of my whiteness. But it seemed to me that, in an odd way, much of what I took to be the problem of whiteness was actually being reinforced in this confrontation, where it was somehow assumed that, if I wanted to, I could still emotionally escape the students' rage by retreating to that invulnerable and lofty place to which white people take flight when the going gets tough. It seemed that the silence and reserve which I was invited to join actually operated so as to reproduce a certain white security and thoughtful distance—an elsewhere which the mere act of listening seemed to produce. This was an operation whose function was fundamentally conservative, serving to constrain or dilute some other more powerful and unsettling potential, a force that might have transformed this white comfort zone in more provocative ways. The shouting of the students and the reticence of the faculty seemed to me an odd and unhealthy symbiosis of practices, a living enactment of two psychological types well-worn into the fabric of American race relations—that of black rage and its correlate, white listening—whose combined effect was to maintain whiteness intact. It wasn't so much my objection to either one that drove me from that room and brought me back again, but the way in which rage and listening folded so neatly, sustaining and enriching each other, wedded in a conspiracy to keep me where and who I was, and to suppress any possibilities for an overturning of things as they were, or imagining things as they might be. Raging and listening seemed, for me, in that moment, bound in an unholy contract to which I did not wish to add my name.

Further reflection led me through a series of exploratory encounters leading to the following assertions: perhaps these particular forms of listening and raging were things that had been evolved and codified long before we took them up and put them into effect on that day. Each had developed from separate conversations and practices rooted in a cultural preoccupation with the racial, the emotional, the moral, and the epistemological that draws heavily from psychological thought and practice. On the one hand, the performances in that auditorium were deeply rooted in a folk psychological belief in the truthfulness of psychic tension, cathartic discharge, and rage; and on the other in a profound commitment to the therapeutic effect of empathic co-presence and listening—two beliefs that have become fixtures of our contemporary therapeutic public culture.[6] In a general sense, this culture has expanded in recent years to reshape the politics of racial inequality around its emotional dimensions, and to pose a specifically psychologistic approach to the combating of racism in our personal and public lives.[7] Where once the politics of race might have been about conflicting ideas, structural analyses, and moral commitments, today it is about empathic sensibilities, emotional states, and the capacity to sense and respond to what others around you are feeling.

Put differently, today, we have come to think of the problem of racial justice, at least from the standpoint of those who enjoy the privileges of contemporary racial arrangements, through the lens of a unique form of emotional competence. This awareness, we believe, is very hard to come by and requires a journey from one's own comfortable state of ignorance through an emotional catharsis brought on by the rage of the other. To encounter and experience the rage of black people is, for the organizational white liberal, a developmental milestone toward overcoming the pathologies of one's own unacknowledged racism, but it is also an encounter with a fundamental truth of oneself that a white person must undergo. Moreover, this journey, for those with the courage to undertake it, is tied to the acquisition of a certain therapeutic acumen, the capacity to hear this rage, to listen for its subtle messages and decipher its inner content.[8] White privilege is blind, not just to the lives of others, but also to its own existence. It is a mode of somnambulism—a life lived unaware, even of its own existence, to which the cultivated capacity to listen to black rage brings a jolt of awakening, and a moment of insight into one's authentic identity. As such, a hermeneutics of black rage plugs in to a deeply rooted yearning for self-authenticity and transformation that has taken varied forms throughout our cultural history, from the Great Awakening of the 18th century to the counter culture of the 1960s.[9] Black rage, so psychologized, is fitted with something of an oracular authority: it functions as a wake-up call, the satori of a listening, white sleep—a discharge of force and a shock that white people need if they are to wake up from what Ta-Nehisi Coates calls "the Dream" of white privilege.[10] In other words, empathic co-presence and listening, and the kinds of people we have to make ourselves into in order that we might successfully carry out our responsibilities as listeners, has become the medium through which self knowledge is gained and racism is unlearned, and the open ended project of the emotionally competent citizen of a pluralistic society—or the well-managed employee of a pluralistic institution.

An excavation of the psychologization of these two emotional styles, and their shaping into a durable emotional ensemble, is not just an exercise in the deconstruction of something we had previously taken as natural. Nor is it a critical debunking in any conventional sense. It allows us to reflect on the promise implied by this listening, on the specific relationship this listening develops with that object of its excited attention, the rage of black people. My question is one that goes beyond the critique of white, liberal anti-racism, whose pretense to listening, to acquiescence, and appeasement, is so often revealed as a clever evasion of one's own ultimate racism.[11] My argument is not about individuals or even groups and their intentions. It is about arrangements among people and things, organizations and the discourses that serve to regulate their members, and about how certain arrangements embed their own intentions, unbeknownst to actors themselves. Inevitably, this is an argument that poses an ideal type—a rage-listening doublet—which, as is the case with all ideal types, works very well for a small number of cases, very badly for some other number, but contains shades of truth for the large number in between. It fits best with raging/listening episodes and arrangements, particularly those observed in highly circumscribed organizational settings in which liberal whiteness is the norm, such as in American universities and at progressive political gatherings. This is not a general characterization of raging or listening as separate political strategies in their own right, and does not endeavor to describe those situations where, for example,

Black rage erupts spontaneously, as in the case of confrontations with police or political groups that are more openly racist.

Racial feeling as abnormality

That psychological types (the idiot, the hysterical woman, the sexual pervert, the masturbating child etcetera) can be traced to the criminological and psychological conversations through which they were shaped is a claim familiar to readers of Michel Foucault. More recently, with the translation of some of his more obscure lectures, this project, so well applied to the subjects of sexuality, criminology, and madness, has expanded to address that of race. Like the homosexual and the lunatic, the history of the raced subject is bound up with a form of power that Foucault elaborates in his 1974–5 lecture course, published in English as *Abnormal,* and which he terms "normalization." Normalization operates through the authority of psychiatry and the human sciences in the targeting of marginal individuals (particularly madmen, sexual minorities, women and other "deviants"). Traces of hereditary development, variation and degeneracy apparent within the body of the subject herself are assessed as abnormalities constitutive of distinct behavioral types.[12] Taking up a series of morbid cases from French criminal history from the 17th to the 20th century, Foucault traces normalization to a coordinated division of labor between criminal justice and psychiatry, law and medicine, around a specific juridical question: what is the proper legal response to monstrous criminal acts, acts of such a horrific nature as to defy traditional assessment of criminal intentionality, and thus any measure of the proper degree of punishment? Through the lens of psychiatric criminology, there is an effective doubling of the criminal body: to the sovereign body of intention and interest that stands before the law and takes responsibility for its actions is added a second body, a biological, potentially abnormal body whose behaviors are transmitted through inherited physiological and psychological deviations from the norm. This second body is one that acts *through* the sovereign body, although it is only visible through the lens of medical science.

> This gives rise to the need to discover the background body, so to speak, that by its own causality confirms and explains the appearance of an individual who is the victim, subject, and bearer of this dysfunctional state... What is the background-body, this body behind the abnormal body? It is the parents' body, the ancestors' body, the body of the family, the body of heredity.[13]

The consequence is that the criminal act itself is effectively doubled: the offense against the law is traced to a range of genetic and hereditarily transmitted psychological abnormalities that afflict human life, shaping behaviors and sensibilities. Take, for example, the strange, motiveless crimes of Henriette Cornier, a despondent young woman who stole away her neighbor's children to bludgeon them to death in her room. Showing no trace of criminal intention, when asked why she took the children's lives she attributed her actions to "an idea," that came to her, and that was all she said.[14] Where traditionally, malevolent motives could be assigned only to the first body, the sovereign body of law, such "motiveless" acts confounded the legal establishment as they were carried out without any single malicious interest, and could thus only be attributed to the effects of a behavioral tendency induced by a hereditary, psychological variation. Such aberrant psychological subjects as the idiot, the socio-path, the homosexual, and the imbecile could all be explained and understood as the effect of a movement of this second body that lurked behind and within the criminal act itself. This was a shadow body that was visible from the standpoint of the "doctor-judge"—a view that combines, as Foucault puts it, "the sordid business of punishing [with] the fine profession of curing."[15]

The abnormal subject is thus two bodies: a sovereign subject of law and reciprocity and the "subject-to-subject cycle," but also another body, a deeper presence against which it is necessary to read through to more profound and determining source. The doctor-judge must see (or hear, if listening is what's at stake) the abnormal movements of this hereditary, second body, through and against the more clear iterations of the sovereign body—a predilection upon which psychology and the therapeutic arts are based, and upon which today's heightened states of emotional sensitivity are styled. Indeed, as Foucault shows, from this discussion of criminal psychiatry, it is a short, but surprising leap to an account of the origin of the modern concept of race itself. The second body of a hereditary, psychiatric abnormality, evidenced by the case of Henriette Cornier, provides the conceptual architecture that later supports the racial variant. Race, like psychology, derives from those genetic and hereditary chains that form the basis of abnormal human life—a notion summarized by Foucault with his assertion that psychiatry is "racism against the abnormal."[16]

Thus, when we think racially, we do so against the backdrop of a psychological doubling of the body. Racism itself involves a reading through of subjectivity, both our own and others', for the subtle movements of this second body, the body of abnormality. As racialized subjects, we have all become doctor-judges, not just in our reading of the subjectivities of others, but in the way we seek to grasp our own subjective lives. In other words, racism is a kind of hermeneutic, if a paranoid one: it undertakes a "reading through" of a manifest subject, a first body of civility and law, to the second body of genetic and hereditary abnormality.

Listening is, or can be, one manifestation of this hermeneutic. It is a way of detecting this second body, of interpreting its movements and predicting its behaviors, with the effect of reducing all the body's possibilities back to this original object. Listening for race's second body frames otherness in terms of the problem of an implicit background agency, an object of cryptic, abnormal and inscrutable intentionality. The knowledge that the other is listening for or speaking to this second body thus functions in the very formation of a racialized subject itself: it maps a relation and a technique by which we listen for and interpret this body within ourselves, adopt and commit to its existence, and reduce our

own freedom back to the inevitability of the second body. This is an effect identified by phenomenologists of race as one in which the subject "finds oneself in
the world ahead of oneself, the space one occupies as already occupied."[17] To the
extent that we invest in this body, we surrender our possibilities to it. We tie
ourselves to it and invest in its imperative. It becomes our truth, our soul, and
ultimately our prison, denying us the possibility of becoming otherwise. Moreover,
the deployment of a specific set of racialized emotions, whose ultimate origins and
whose mysterious movements can only be grasped through the lens of a racialized
psychology mediated by managerial professionals, serves as a powerful instrument
for the inscription and sustaining of this second body. It is to this deployment that
we now turn.

The emotionalization of race

What are the origins of this second body in the biological and psychological sciences, and what are its current mutations? Since the inception of scientific racism,
racial variety has been described in terms of a notion of abnormality, of a variation from an organic, biological norm.[18] Herbert Spencer furnished the view of
the differentiated capacities of the primitive brain that, while biologically human,
had developed through its adaptation to primitive rather than modern conditions
a sensory acuity that could not compensate for the deficiencies of its higher cognitive capacities. Stanley Hall popularized the more liberal view of non-European
races as, while essentially human, still languishing in a state of evolutionary under-
development, and Gustav LeBon introduced the notion of atavism into the developmental image of racial differences. In different ways, these theories understood
racial variety in terms of a developmental variation on an essential human type,
whose potentials were best expressed in white, European stock.[19]

Moreover, this variation has for a long time been linked with problems of
diagnosis and detection, of its visibility and audibility. The architects of physiog-
nomy and phrenology labored over the correct methods by which biological
variation might be observed and measured in the contours of the face and skull,
and Galton himself would attempt to visualize statistical variations across a population in his famous composite photographic overlays. In a technique of photographic double exposures, Galton transposed sets of forensic portraits to compose
statistically average photographs of criminals, paupers, mental patients, and
syphilitics, whose transposed facial features combined to form a single, blended
face of abnormal physiognomic characteristics, a ghostly depiction of deviance
itself.[20] In a sense, Galton's was a gaze that would shape the racism of the 20th
century as others would learn to read the bodies around them in terms of the
generalized variations, the abnormalities that loomed up behind them like
phantom second bodies. Within the field of psychology, from the intelligence
testing of race psychologists to eugenics and ultimately the race policies of
Nazism, the capacity to trace mental and emotional expressions to abnormal

hereditary dispositions would shape a mode of social perception that would take root across the world.

Of course, Galton's gaze would undergo significant renovation over the course of many years. In the decades leading up to the Second World War and with the subsequent collapse of National Socialism and the emergence of a global anti-racist consensus, the field of psychology would renounce the program of scientific racism as an effort to link racial differences to biological variations. The abandonment of the project of race psychology in the 1930s and 1940s would come with more liberal social or environmental psychological explanations.[21] Psychologists would turn from the study of the deficiencies of minority racial groups to the ways in which these groups were shaped by societal and environmental conditions, and specifically by the prejudicial attitudes of the majority themselves. In other words, the relations around racism, and not race itself, became the problem for psychological understanding. The focus was on the effects of prejudicial attitudes on minority groups, whose emotional lives were thought to be singularly shaped by their encounter with white racism. Nonetheless, while environmental psychology and emotional biography were substituted for the older arguments concerning biological heredity, the same assumptions concerning the radical alterity of the emotional and psychological lives of racial minorities remained intact. Even amid this reversal, racism's second bodies would persist as emotional, racialized subjects were again abnormal, again characterized by a double body, split between one part that was answerable before the law, and another that exerted effects from some deeper, darker place. But now this abnormality was a cultural, not a biological problem: one of a differentiated emotional state brought on by the specific moral failings of those members of the majority, unknowingly motivated by the irrationalism of prejudice and discrimination.

This is a shift of emphasis that carries a broad significance, not only for how we think of race and racism, but for how we understand racism's critique, and the increasingly hegemonic status that has been ascribed to anti-racism since state racism's demise.[22] The turn to a psychology of the environmental causes of racism does not signify a clean break with the past: it represents a new organization of old racial categories that carries over many of the assumptions and basic structures from racism's older, biologically-grounded view. It signals the beginning of a transition into what Etienne Balibar has described as "neo-racism"—a racial ideology largely disengaged from the explicit ideology of biology and blood characteristic of scientific racism, which substitutes instead cultural, social and environmental attributes as ways of understanding racialized differences.[23] Racial otherness, once a problem of heredity, has become a problem of sensibilities, cultures and emotions, understood as ways of living and perceiving the world.

While this transition, as Balibar argues, did not overturn racism itself, it did create the conditions for new racial agencies and a new focus on environmental racial emotionality that would later emerge as a powerful political force. While the belief in a distinct black emotionality advanced an already deeply entrenched criminalization of black conduct, particularly through the policing of public sexuality, this same racial emotionality, in a different guise, became the touchstone of a broad popular resistance. By the 1960s, black rage and anger had developed into uniquely black emotional states bearing the force of critique and the power to tell truths that could force the contradictions of a racist society to the forefront of public consciousness, even if these emotional states could not be readily interpreted. With the civil rights movements and race riots, the emotional and psychological states of African Americans became the cipher through which new anxieties over public order could be expressed, as reflected in the pages of the Kerner Commission report: what do blacks want? Why are they so angry and what are they feeling? How might it be possible to restore them to orderly subordination by understanding their anger, by listening, or making them feel that we are listening to their emotional expressions?[24] And how might we discover the truth of ourselves as white people by listening to these emotional expressions? These were questions that demanded new competencies of emotional interpretation from whites if public order was to be preserved. And this was a program for which psychology, even in its most radical versions, lent valuable legitimacy. A prominent African American psychiatrist, Kenneth Clark, attributed the causes of black rioting to what he termed "community suicide," an impulsive destructiveness rooted in Black self-hatred, low self-image, and a generalized sense of cultural castration to which white people should become sensitive.[25] Alvin Poussaint, in a 1967 article in the *New York Times Magazine* titled "A Negro Psychiatrist Explains the Negro Psyche," attributes the wave of racial violence not just to self-hatred, but to pent up anger and rage:

> Through systematic oppression aimed at extinguishing his aggressive drive, the black American has been effectively castrated and rendered abjectly compliant by white America. Since appropriate rage at such emasculation could be expressed directly only at great risk, the negro repressed and suppressed it, but only at the great cost to his psychic development. Today this "aggression-rage" constellation, rather than self-hatred, appears to be at the core of the Negro's social and psychological difficulties.[26]

What became known as the "damaged negro" thesis invited studies of the accumulated consequences of racism on the psyches of black people, afflicted with low self-esteem, castration anxiety, and a neurotic sense of split consciousness. This other emotional life was defined by anger and rage: employing a Freudian psycho-dynamic model, Poussaint understood not just the neurotic effects of repression but also the cathartic effects of discharge as defining qualities of black emotionality, whose interpretation was the specific responsibility of whites. Whites had to listen: they had to enable black emotional discharge, to facilitate its expression and assume an affirmative and enabling stance with regard to its outpouring, even if only in the interest of sustaining civil order. In other words, white responsiveness to the experiences of black people, as a newly derived empathy for a racialized emotional abnormality, was the extension of a new policing technology; to ensure public order and contain dissent, the normal had to co-emotionalize with and listen to the abnormal—an operation which also involved the exploration of their own habitualized racial prejudices.

So, the psychologization of blackness served the ends of both criminalization and critique: angry blacks had to be policed more vigorously, while their rages had to be sought out for the inner truth of whiteness it revealed. Black rage was both the monster at the gates of the city but also the Sphinx whose riddles granted access to the truth of white subjectivity. There was, however, a third function of this racial emotionality, and the emotional ensemble it composes that I have already tried to describe, one that provided a foothold for another much subtler regime of social control. To delve further into this development, we must consider the origins and function of the new emotional regime's two constituent elements—listening and raging—and trace their migration from strategies of resistance to the imperatives of the smoothly functioning organization.

Listening and neoliberal containment

Where did listening come from? And how did it attain its current status as a feature of contemporary organizational life? One possible answer to this question lies with a broad set of economic, political, and cultural changes that have shaped the character of contemporary institutions, which can be broadly summarized under the notion of neoliberalism. The valorization of listening as an institutional practice represents a response on the part of Western capitalism to the problem of both workplace alienation and to the containment of a variety of social movements that threatened to transform the American social fabric in the wake of the student movements of the 1960s.[27] Among these movements, the movement for racial justice became a prominent and visible feature of this period, and remains a foundational element of contemporary organizational and civic life. The institutional valorization of managerial listening draws from two principal developments: the rise of psychological and therapeutic discourse as focal technologies in the organization of private and public life, and a broad turn in the priorities of capitalist production and labor from a Fordist model of organized, impersonal production to a Post-Fordist emphasis on emotion, inter-personal communication, and affective labor processes. At the center of both of these processes is the emerging and increasing acceptance of psychology and the management of emotions in managerial and economic thought.[28]

From its inception, the field of psychology elaborated a special role for the practice of therapeutic listening—a commitment developed most visibly in the field of psychoanalysis, but also one infused across a whole range of psycho-therapeutic fields and practices. Throughout, listening is described as an active process, one that places the therapist in a specific technical and productive relation, not only with the emotions of others, but with her own psychic and emotional state. Theodore Reik provides an account of this process:

> The analyst, too, must acknowledge the mixed character of the analytic session, he must breathe the same atmosphere as the patient. Only when he is ready to drop all speculation while he analyzes will he be able to catch the emotional undertones in what his patient says. He should not "argue" the case like a lawyer, but face it spontaneously and without preconceived ideas. Only then will the emotional undertones become clearly audible and distinct as if amplified by a microphone of unconscious processes. The analyst must oscillate in the same rhythm with his patient within the realm between fantasy and reality, sometimes approaching one, sometimes the other.[29]

Therapeutic listening found a niche in evolving business practices of the 1980s, which were increasingly distancing themselves from the top-down administrative models of the Fordist firm. Tom Peters' influential manual on management and business planning, *Thriving on Chaos*, promoted the notion of active and skilled listening as an important corporate strategy, particularly in the context of intensifying market competition and the increasing need to foster close understandings of the changing needs of consumers. "The organization prepared to move fast is the listening-intense organization," writes Peters, "not only in sales and marketing, but in engineering and manufacturing."[30] But equally important to the new popularity of therapeutic listening as an organizational and industrial technique were pressures to reform institutional culture itself to accommodate the increasing diversity of the labor force.

By the 1970s, Title VII of the Civil Rights Act prohibiting discrimination in hiring and in other workplace practices had introduced broad change to the American workplace. A host of compliance-oriented, anti-discrimination training programs were developed across corporate and public institutions in response to the threat of discrimination lawsuits, mostly centered in the legal and managerial aspects of discrimination and bias.[31] Soon, however, these policies would shift from legal compliance in hiring and promotion to the fostering of cultural norms and personal sensibilities within workplace environments themselves. Managing diverse institutions became a therapeutic undertaking, addressing a range of interpersonal, emotional and cultural elements of professional life.[32] A report from the Hudson Institute released in 1987, *Workforce 2000*, predicted large numbers of women and minorities entering professional life and the need to create diverse work environments, not just to avoid litigation but for the purposes of enhancing profitability and for business survival itself.[33] In the 1980s and 1990s the focus of diversity training shifted to that of workplace cultures and the interpersonal sensibilities and communicative styles of workers and managers. Listening practices had to be engrained into the very fabric of organizational life itself.

But practices of racialized listening would only acquire institutional urgency as they passed through another specific transformation: the implicitly Freudian emphasis on repressed hostility and its mediation through affirming and empathic co-presence would be reformulated through an encounter with humanistic psychology and the human potential movement that was increasingly taking root in American culture. In their foundational work in Black psychology, Poussaint and Clark would incorporate therapeutic listening with the new black emotionality through a humanistic emphasis on the specificity and validity of individual experience.[34] The "Person Centered" approach of Rogerian psychotherapy sought to bring about personality change through a form of treatment that stressed the authenticity of the therapist and the unconditional positive regard the patient would receive through the relating of experience. The human potential movement sought to tap into deep emotional states through intense and personal group therapeutic sessions, in which participants engaged in the sharing and expressing of pent up feelings, including aggression. Its therapeutic methods—psychodrama, T groups, and consciousness raising—invested heavily in a therapy of catharsis; if one underwent intense emotional experiences, either through the release of one's own feelings or by sharing in the cathartic experiences of others, one would overcome the conditions of emotional repression to which we are typically consigned and arrive at a sort of affective equilibrium, a self-distancing and reflective awareness of one's own emotional patterns, encountered only at a peak experience. Indeed, Price Cobbs, one of the authors of the seminal work of black psychology, *Black Rage*, gave a special place to the cathartic benefits of emotional discharge amongst a circle of skilled, sensitized, sympathetic listeners.[35] Following a period of notoriety as a figure within the black militant circles of the 1960s, Cobbs turned to humanistic psychology following a series of workshops he organized at the Esalen Institute in California, in which racial encounter sessions brought members of the Black Panther Party together with progressive whites to share the emotional burdens of racism and racial difference in sessions that stressed sympathetic listening and the cathartic value of emotional release. He took this idea into the field of business management, where he launched a private firm that carried out a series of workshops meant to raise multi-cultural awareness and diminish workplace racial tensions. Under the rubric of "ethnotherapy," Cobbs' workshops would set the pattern for an emerging industry of diversity experts, trainers and therapists in the 1970s and 1980s, whose method was to invoke the intensity of racialized emotionality in order to absorb its effect into a cathartic experience.[36] Like the encounter sessions at Esalen, the diversity workshops implemented by Cobbs induced emotional release in environments where acceptance had already been secured under the implicit terms of a therapeutic contract. Cobbs' work would provide the blueprint for an immense and expanding industry of diversity experts, trainers, managers and organizers that would become a fixture of corporate life.

Inaccessible rage as catharsis

Psychology has long held an interest in the effect of catharsis. Derived from the Greek word for "cleansing" or "purification," catharsis is deeply tied to notions of psychic discharge, to the expulsion of affect deriving from an original trauma. For Beuer and Freud catharsis is an instinctive body process like crying that might be induced through hypnosis, and which opens up a unique, therapeutic link between inner feelings and outer expressions.[37] Yet as much as the effect of catharsis is thought to be emotional, it also produces a significant cognitive effect, a moment of clarity and wisdom, a transcendence that follows from the expulsion of blinding passions. Sociologist Thomas Scheff has described both the emotional-somatic discharge and the cognitive awareness, which produces a "distancing" effect on mundane experience in which vivid insight is derived, together with a recollection of long forgotten traumas.[38] Through the lens of psychodynamic psychology, the containment of pent up emotions is depicted as the hydraulic function of a censoring external agent, in which catharsis represents an important moment of "venting." The release of pressurized, "bottled up" forces whose discharge from interior to exterior restores an original equilibrium and brings relief. In this way, the catharsis of black rage became linked, through its cognitive component, with insight into the everyday relations of race, or for those whites who experienced this catharsis viscerally, with a new insight to one's own whiteness, one's white emotional biography, lodged in a remote but accessible psychological interior.

The inscription of black rage with this oracular power came as black emotionality was increasingly described as particular to black experience, unique to the irreducible otherness of black identity and ultimately remote from anything white people could ever hope to truly know or understand. The more inaccessible the origin of black rage, the more valorized and sought after it became for its capacity to lay bare the truths of the white subject. This is not to suggest that racial empathy was abandoned: in the years following the civil rights movement, new psychologies developed around the challenge of capturing black emotionality in practices of empathic white listening, though many remained, as illustrated by Daniel Patrick Moynihan's thesis on the black family, firmly within an earlier framework of racial pathologization. But the threshold of this empathy, as it was recorded in the managerial strategies of the new diverse organization, was raised to a level that was by definition and necessity unattainable by whites. Indeed, a central admonition of the discourse on diversity includes warnings against appeals by whites to any common experience that goes beyond the situated and limited experiences of racialized particularity—appeals that are read as expressions of naive liberal color blindness and a denial of one's culpability in an ultimate racism itself.[39] William Grier and Price Cobb's landmark study, *Black Rage* in many ways secured the view of an inaccessible racialized emotionality that operated at the very limits of white empathy.[40]

Cobbs and Grier described black rage as a force that would interrupt a false and stifling civility to which blacks and whites had become accustomed. In their account of the paradigmatically repressed black man, the authors described a character:

> He is passive, non assertive, and nonaggressive. He has made a virtue of identification with the aggressor, and he has adopted an ingratiating and compliant manner. In public his thoughts and feeling are consciously shaped in the direction he thinks white people want them to be... This man renounces gratifications that are available to others. He must figure out "the man" but keep "the man" from deciphering him... The danger he poses to himself and others is great, but only the surface of passivity and compliance is visible. The storm below is hidden.[41]

That this storm may be hidden should be legitimately interpreted, as the authors argue, as a survival strategy for angry blacks in a racist society. But, through the form of its appropriation into a managerial strategy, the remoteness of this emotional realm comes to serve an additional, supplemental function. This inaccessibility, thematized within a program of racial emotionality and inscribed within a managerial rationality responsive to the needs of a diverse organization, serves as an instrument of regulation. Like the second body of racism itself, the hidden storm of black rage becomes the philosopher's stone of post-racist white subjectivity, sought after for its alchemical properties.

Today in popular discussions on race, we seldom speak of white racism as an intelligent evil. Instead we speak of whiteness as a state of denial, or a learned ignorance about itself and its own delusions from which an empathic encounter with black rage promises a path to an epiphanous transcendence. The prospect of becoming "woke" has served as a powerful instrument, both for the disruption of white racial ignorance, and for the summoning, examination and dispelling of that body that follows whiteness around, the second body of an ingrained and inherited white privilege. But the investment in this "hidden storm" of black rage serves an ambiguous purpose. For blacks and whites this rage becomes a core commitment around which a radical racial alterity is proposed, negotiated, and performed, but also studied for deeper significance and listened to for hidden truths. Rage becomes precisely the second body that it seeks to dispel, a body whose movements are barely detectable behind that of the first. This is a second body whose eruptions bring powers of illumination that disrupt but also silently restore that other second body that is necessary for the racial contract to remain in place: the second body that constitutes whiteness itself.[42]

Conclusion: toward a recovery of racial emotion

Racial emotions are potentially very powerful things. They can pry people apart and change them, shatter them and frighten them, make them no longer themselves—a process Michel Foucault describes as "desubjectification." Conversations infused with racial emotions open new horizons for affirming each other's dignity and freedom, but also force us into a painful confrontation with dignities denied, and with our own inability to confer dignity to those who deserve it. This is particularly the case with that emotional state that many contemporary practices of racial dialogue induce. But through the silent linking of rage and listening into a coherent practice of organizational self-understanding, much of the transformative potential that emerges when black and white bodies emotionally confront each other is dissipated. What we undertake today when we seek an institutional conversation on race winds up serving, against our will and often our knowledge, to codify, rationalize and ultimately contain the intensity of shared racial affect, and to reproduce precisely those racial comforts that need to be challenged. Thinking back to the student occupation of a faculty meeting, to the raging-listening doublet performed in that instance, one wonders: without these doubled bodies to which we felt constrained and whose meanings we sought to understand, what might our own emotional bodies have done? What might they be able to do? Foucault, in one of the most striking passages from *Discipline and Punish* describes his inquiry as a "genealogy of the modern soul," an investigation of a secular soul that, unlike its Christian predecessor, "is born rather out of methods of punishment, supervision and constraint." This soul, Foucault warns us, is not the essence of a true subject waiting to be understood, cured and set free, but is in fact the instrument and effect of a power "which is itself a factor in the mastery that power exercises over the body." This soul, Foucault asserts, in a cunningly anti-platonic inversion, is not held captive within the body, but is in fact the very prison of the body itself, that which constrains its possibilities and reduces its effects. "The soul is the prison of the body." Might it be possible, then, to follow Foucault in declaring the racial soul to be the prison of the racial body?[43]

Notes

1 Derald Wing Sue, *Race Talk and the Conspiracy of Silence: Understanding and Facilitating Difficult Dialogues on Race* (Hoboken, NJ: Wiley & Sons, 2015), xii.
2 Arlie Hochschild, *The Managed Heart: Commercialization of Human Feeling* (Berkeley: University of California Press, 1983).
3 Sam Binkley, *Happiness as Enterprise: An Essay on Neoliberal Life* (Albany: State University of New York Press, 2014); "Anti-Racism Beyond Empathy: Transformations in the Knowing and Governing of Racial Difference," *Subjectivity*, Vol. 9, No. 4 (June 2016); "The Emotional Logic of Neoliberalism: Reflexivity and Instrumentality in Three Theoretical Traditions," David Primrose, ed., *Sage Handbook of Neoliberalism* (London: Sage, 2018).
4 Sara Ahmed, "Affective Economies," *Social Text*, Vol. 22, No. 2 (2004). Linda Martin Acroff, "Towards a Phenomenology of Racial Embodiment" *Radical Philosophy*, Vol. 95, No. 1 (May/June 1999).
5 Ian Hacking, "Making up People," in T.C. Heller, M. Sosna and D. E. Wellbery, eds. *Reconstructing Individualism* (Stanford: Stanford University Press, 1986); Michel Foucault, "Nietzsche, Genealogy, History," in *Language, Counter-memory, Practice*, D. F. Bouchard, ed. (Ithaca: Cornell University Press, 1977), 139–164.
6 Frank Furedi, *Therapy Culture: Cultivating Vulnerability in an Uncertain Age* (New York: Routledge 2003).

7 Elizabeth Lasch-Quinn, *Race Experts: How Racial Etiquette, Sensitivity Training, and New Age Therapy Hijacked the Civil Rights Revolution* (New York: Rowman & Littlefield, 2002).

8 Frank Furedi, *Therapy Culture.*

9 Jackson Lears, *No Place of Grace: Antimodernism and the Transformation of American Culture, 1880–1920* (New York: Pantheon Books, 1981).

10 Ta-Nehisi Coates, *Between the World and Me* (New York: Random House, 2015).

11 Shannon Sullivan, *Good White People: The Problem with Middle Class White Anti-Racism* (Albany: State University of New York Press, 2015).

12 Michel Foucault, *Abnormal: Lectures at the Collège de France, 1974–1975*, Valerio Marchetti and Antonella Salomoni, eds., Graham Burchell, trans. (New York: Picador, 2004).

13 Ibid., 313.

14 Ibid., 114.

15 Ibid., 23.

16 Ladelle McWhorter, *Racism and Sexual Oppression in Anglo-America: A Genealogy.* (Indianapolis: Indiana University Press, 2009); David Macey, "Rethinking Biopolitics, Race and Power in the Wake of Foucault," *Theory, Culture & Society* Vol. 26, No. 6 (2009): 186–205; Chloe Taylor, "Race and Racism in Foucault's Collège de France Lectures" *Philosophy Compass* Vol. 6, No. 11(2011): 746–756; Michel Foucault, *Society Must Be Defended: Lectures at the College de France, 1975–76*, trans. David Macey, ed. Mauro Bertani and Alessandro Fontana (New York: St. Martin's Press, 2003), 316–317.

17 Linda Martin Acroff, "Towards a Phenomenology of Racial Embodiment" *Radical Philosophy*, Vol. 95, No. 1 (May/June 1999), 24. https://www.radicalphilosophy.com/article/towards-a-phenomenology-of-racial-embodiment. Accessed January 7 2019.

18 George M. Fredrickson, *Racism: A Short History* (Princeton: Princeton University Press, 2002); Graham Richards, *'Race,' Racism and Psychology: Towards a Reflexive History* (London: Routledge, 2012).

19 Gustav Le Bon, *Psychology of Crowds.* (Southampton UK: Sparkling Books, 2009); Francis Galton, *Hereditary Genius: An Inquiry into its Laws and Consequences* (New York: Macmillan and Company, 1892); Stanley G. Hall, "Adolescence: Its Psychology and its Relations to Physiology, Anthropology, Sociology, Sex, Crime, Religion and Education" *Classics in the History of Psychology 2* (New York: Appleton & Company, 1905).

20 Francis Galton, 1878–1906. Composite Portraiture. http://www.galton.org/composite.htm. Accessed January 7 2019.

21 Franz Samuelson, "From 'Race Psychology' to 'Studies in Prejudice': Some Observations on the Thematic Reversal in Social Psychology" *Journal of the History of the Behavioral Sciences Vol.* 14, No. 3 (1979): 265–278.

22 Thomas, James M. & Sander Gilman, *Are Racists Crazy? How Prejudice, Racism, and Antisemitism Became Markers of Insanity* (New York: NYU Press, 2016).

23 Etienne Balibar, "Is There a 'Neo-Racism'?" in Etienne Balibar and Immanuel Wallerstein, *Race, Nation, Class: Ambiguous Identities* (London: Verso, 1991), 21.

24 Thomas J. Hrach, *The Riot Report and the News: How the Kerner Commission Changed Media Coverage of Black America* (Amherst, MA: University of Massachusetts Press, 2016).

25 Kenneth Clark, *Dark Ghetto* (New York: Harper and Row, 1965).

26 Alvin Poussaint, "A Negro Psychiatrist Explains the Negro Psyche," *New York Times Magazine* (August 20 1967), 53, 98, 316, 318, 319, 321, 334, 336, 337, 339, 341. 53.

27 David Harvey, *A Brief History of Neo-liberalism* (Oxford: Oxford University Press, 2005).

28 Arlie Hochschild, *The Managed Heart: Commercialization of Human Feeling*; Eva Illouz, *Cold Intimacies* (New York: Polity, 2007).

29 Theodore Reik, *Listening with the Third Ear: The Inner Experience of a Psychoanalyst* (New York: Grove Press, 1948), 116.

30 Tom Peters, *Thriving on Chaos: Handbook for a Management Revolution* (New York: Knopf, 1987), 146.

31 Rohini Anand, and Mary-Frances Winters, "A Retrospective View of Corporate Diversity Training From 1964 to the Present," *Academy of Management, Learning & Education*, Vol. 7 No. 3 (2008): 356–372.

32 David A. Thomas & Robin J. Ely "Making Differences Matter: A new Paradigm for Managing Diversity" *Harvard Business Review*, Vol. 74, No. 5 (1996): 79–90.

33 William B. Johnston & Arnold E Packer, *Workforce 2000: Work and Workers for the 21st Century* (Indianapolis: Hudson Institute, 1987).

34 Alvin Poussaint, *Why Blacks Kill Blacks* (New York: Emerson Hall Publishers, 1976); Kenneth Clark, *Dark Ghetto* (New York: Harper and Row, 1965).

35 Price Cobbs, *My American Life: From Rage to Enlightenment* (New York: Atria Books, 2006).

36 Elizabeth Lasch-Quinn, *Race Experts: How Racial Etiquette, Sensitivity Training, and New Age Therapy Hijacked the Civil Rights Revolution*.

37 Joseph Breuer & Freud Sigmund, *Studies on Hysteria* (Harmondsworth: Penguin Books, 1974).

38 Thomas Scheff, *Catharsis in Healing, Ritual, and Drama* (Lincoln, NE: iUniverse.com, 2001).

39 Eduardo Bonilla-Silva, *Racism without Racists: Color-Blind Racism and the Persistence of Racial Inequality in the United States* (Maryland: Rowman & Littlefield, 2006).

40 Price Cobbs and William Grier, *Black Rage* (New York: Basic Books, 1968).

41 Ibid.

42 Charles Mills, *The Racial Contract* (Ithaca: Cornel University Press, 1997).

43 Michel Foucault, *Discipline and Punish*, Alan Sheridan, trans. (New York, Random House, 1977), 30.

6

JOUISSANCE **AND DISCONTENT**

A Meeting of Psychoanalysis, Race, and American Slavery

Sheldon George

Our[1] current political climate has given rise to fears over the future of America. Many find emanating from the political sphere new license to discriminate against racial others, license that they fear will lead to a dissolution of American values, and even, potentially, of the nation itself. I suggest, however, the greater danger may be that this license has little destructive impact upon the broad structure of our civil society. Race and racism hold a fraught relation to what Sigmund Freud called civilization and its discontents. Freud maintained that the decisive step in the development of civilization was replacement of the power of the individual by the power of the community.[2] He saw such communal formations as based on the renunciation of impulse gratification[3] and the curtailing of natural instincts of "aggressiveness and destructiveness."[4] It is in this way, Freud argued, that civilization itself is largely responsible for our misery,[5] frustrating our pursuit of instinctual pleasure.[6] But, foreshadowing contemporary fears, Freud's theory also implies that group and race identity may actively unleash aggressive instincts and lead to regressions in the development of civilization.

Freud observed that, beyond the initial formation of community, the further course of cultural development in civilization "seems to tend towards making the law no longer an expression of the will of a small community [...] or a racial group—which, in its turn, behaves like a violent individual towards other, and perhaps more numerous, collections of people."[7] Suggesting the incommensurability of these group and individual instincts with civilization, Freud argues that, in consequence of the fact that "instinctual passions are stronger than reasonable interests," "civilized society is perpetually threatened with disintegration."[8] However, beginning with slavery, what the history of race and racism in America has shown is the possibility of civilization grounding itself on these very instincts of aggression and destruction whose repression in Freud's theory seem so essential to social progress.

Freud himself remained largely unconcerned with this racist history. After the horrors of the First World War, Freud voiced his astonishment at recognizing the full power that destructive instincts have over civilization. He lamented the unexpected pre-eminence of such instincts in members of the white race now turned in conflict upon each other. As Freud divulges, "we were prepared to find that wars between the primitive and the civilized peoples, between the races who are divided by the colour of their skin [...] would occupy mankind for some time to come," but "we had expected the great world-dominating nations of [the] white race" would find "another way of settling misunderstandings and conflicts of interest."[9] Hampered by what we must recognize as a racism that causes his reluctance to align primitive instincts with civilized white nations, Freud was shocked by the frightening ubiquity of aggressive impulses when they are no longer directed at racial others. As Jacques Lacan specifies in his rereading of Freud's theories, Freud was appalled most specifically by the "horror of the civilized man," whose brutality seems newly unveiled by war.[10] But Lacan's own rearticulation of these instincts as tied to "the frightening core of the *destrudo*" or the death drive—the "unconscious aggression" that *each* subject's desire for pleasure or "jouissance contains"—enables us to imagine slavery as an earlier upsurgence of destructive *jouissance* in American history, one produced by Freud's dominating white race precisely through a structuring of civilization around racial identity.[11]

Slavery, I argue, and the history of racism that proceeds from it, allow us unique insight into the aggressions that plague our subjective psyches. Through a focused effort to articulate these aggressions in relation to race and Lacan's concept of *jouissance*, I will show below that slavery unveiled the psychic condition of alienation that drives subjectivity in its perpetual pursuit of *jouissance*. The American slave's bondage allowed for a striking manifestation of such subjective alienation, pinning this psychic reality exclusively to the slave while generating race itself as a compensatory source of *jouissance*, a Lacanian *object a*. This fantasy *object a*, I suggest, structured the national self around an impossible whiteness that continues to root social progress simultaneously within fantasy and aggression. The means through which African Americans have responded to their social and psychic alienation keenly displays the broader function of both fantasy and religion in reproducing a *jouissance* that, as Lacan specifies, is ever lost to the subject. I will trace the African American pursuit of this religious and fantastical *jouissance* through an analysis of not just slavery itself, but also the work of African American folklorist Zora Neale Hurston, whose writings allow us to track the historical path of the *object a* in its fantasy production first of the slave's religious soul, and later of the African American's racial identity. Troubling this production, I will show, is the basic subjective conflict initially identified by Freud between pursuit of *jouissance* and the racial identities through which subjects situate themselves within broader structures of community.

Jouissance and the modern institution of slavery

Because racialized formations of group and communal identity allowed for unusual expressions of aggression in Antebellum American society, this historical period uniquely facilitates our shift from Freud's focus on the recognized brutality of a civilized man at war to what Lacan calls the evil located in each "man's deepest heart."[12] Through this shift, I wish to suggest both a notion of the psyche as cross racial and an understanding of slavery as not a primitivism germane to the past, but a savagery essential to the modern. Rejecting the stricter separation between primitivism and civilization too often implied in Freud's theories, my reading here aligns with the assertion of thinkers like cultural studies theorist Paul Gilroy that "all simple periodisations of the modern and the postmodern [need] to be drastically rethought"[13] through recognition of slavery as "the natal core of modern society."[14] Not only does slavery provide the economic structure that gives rise to modern America, but, I will suggest, it positions African American slaves as among what we may call the first truly modern subjects, developing within them a unique appreciation for alienation and fragmentation decades before this signature sensibility comes to characterize later historical moments.

Classic definitions of modernism identify a new sense of alienation that emerges in the subject as a direct result of the First World War, describing this alienation as significantly heightened in the postmodernism that would follow the Second World War. The two World Wars are rightly recognized as laying bare to "civilized" society the innate savagery of mankind, manifesting an unacknowledged version of the self whose existence caused this society to call into question the value of its religions and beliefs. Confronted after the First World War with a wasteland of death and destruction, T.S. Eliot voiced a question that would characterize the sense of alienation and uncertainty that plagued the times: "What are the roots that clutch, what branches grow / Out of this stony rubbish?"[15] Eliot articulates a search for substantial meaning that, in some sense, would be supplied by psychoanalysis, in the form of a reified notion of the self as fragmented between consciousness and a now visible unconscious brutality.

Recognizing the deeper implications of subjective alienation from the unconscious through the war's striping off of the "later accretions of civilization,"[16] Freud declared to a modern audience left aghast by the violence of the First World War that "the primitive mind" is in the strictest sense "imperishable,"[17] concluding insistently that humans are nothing but "a gang of murderers."[18] While grounding meaning in a notion of fragmentation and instinctual brutality, Freud further eroded the basis of religious certainty by pronouncing Christianity to be no more than a means of guilty "atonement," through the figured death of the son, for Oedipal desires to kill the father.[19] In so doing, Freud produced for modern subjects an image of themselves as bound to others within civilization by a common "great crime" committed at the psychic level of their desires,[20] a crime that causes mankind to erect civilization and its laws of prohibition out of "guilt" over wishes that ever threaten to drive us toward new patricidal and transgressive acts.[21]

But this modern confrontation with the psyche as split between the drive to destroy and structures of Eros exulted by civilization is already recognizable in the institution of slavery. Enslavement of American blacks within genteel southern society facilitated a social manifestation of the split psyche. For the Southern gentleman, as Eugene Genovese notes, "strength, graciousness, and gentility," the markers of the southern slave master's position within civilized society, came to coexist in the social sphere with his instinctive drive toward aggression, "his impulsiveness, violence, and unsteadiness."[22] In ways made understandable by Lacanian theory, this coexistence of civilization and the master's unrepressed drives meant for the slave that his or her psychic alienation was manifested as a recognizable social reality. We can begin to understand these social dynamics and the psychic drive toward *jouissance* that structures them by returning to Lacan's discussion of what he calls the *vel* of alienation, the forced choice that each subject makes to alienate him/herself from *jouissance* in order to attain subjectivity (see Figure 6.1).

Through the notion of *jouissance*, Lacan's *vel* rethinks Freud's discussion of instincts and resituates the moment in which the subject loses access to the pleasures the instincts promise. Where Freud had linked the sacrifice of instincts to the birth of civilization,[23] Lacan describes *jouissance* as the "pound of flesh" or the "sacrificed" pleasure that all subjects forego through entry into the Symbolic world of meaning.[24] This entry constitutes the subject as split between meaning and what Lacan calls being. Where the Symbolic is structured by the language of the Other, the subject accesses subjectivity through language's ability to organize meaning; but subjectivity simultaneously deprives subjects of access to all parts of

The *Vel* of Alienation

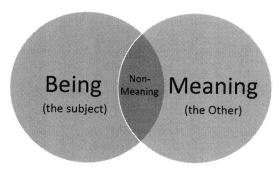

FIGURE 6.1 The *vel* of alienation

the self that escape language. This deprivation constitutes within the psyche a lost part of the self called being that the subject renounces, but which the instincts or, in Lacan's terminology, the drives seek insistently to manifest; what is ultimately lost to the subject is not only being, but also *jouissance*, the pleasure tied to being that subjects ever seek to access through the two modalities of fantasy and transgression of the law, both of which can serve to satisfy the drive's urges toward aggression and destruction.

It is particularly through a melding of fantasy and transgressive aggression, as with racism, that the drive may obliquely pursue *jouissance* in the social sphere. Lacan clearly specifies that the drive is not aimed directly at external objects of pleasure. Instead, the drive is "internal" to subjectivity,[25] manifesting the "irrepressible life" subtracted from the subject,[26] the being that "survives [the] division"[27] of the *vel* by emerging outside of the agency of the signifier only as a "constant force" from within.[28] But this insistent force makes present a psychic loss that, through fantasy, is re-associated with the Symbolic; the drive is "coextensive" with what Lacan describes as a fantastical "remembering" that "historiciz[es]" being as a recoverable source of *jouissance* sacrificed in an identifiable moment in time.[29] Lacan indicates the true temporal status of this lost being in his description of the *vel* as a forced choice that, from the onset, "condemns the subject to appearing only in [a] division," such that "if it appears on one side as meaning, produced by the signifier, it appears on the other as *aphanisis*," or a disappearance of being.[30] Subjectivity, he shows, arises only through this split, producing an absence that specifically constitutes, not precedes, subject formation; but, ever alienated by language, the constituted subject is yet driven by the fantasy of an anterior oneness with lost being, a unified psyche that existed before the spilt of subjective formation. Through what Lacan identifies as this "mirage" of a previously unified self,[31] the subject's pursuits and desires come to be "agitated in the drive."[32] This fantastical lost oneness organizes the subject's drive as fundamentally a death drive, or a "will to destruction," that is violently directed at the Symbolic in the subject's tireless pursuit of "an Other-thing" not "registered in the [Symbolic's] signifying chain"—an absent, lost being that can root the subject in a perpetual state of *jouissance*.[33]

Where the drive aims at manifesting within the Symbolic the *jouissance* that was anterior to the subject's splitting, slavery itself may be identified as a historicizing of *jouissance*, as what we can call after Lacan "a reference point" through which we recognize *jouissance* and "the death drive [as] situated in the historical domain."[34] Lacan's theory makes apparent this historical link between slavery and *jouissance*. Significantly, Lacan calls his subjectifying *vel* the "primary alienation," that "by which man enters into the way of slavery.[35] He explains this *vel* through both the choice that confronts the victim of a robbery—*Your money or your life!*— and the choice that confronts the slave—*Your freedom or your life!*[36] In either case, he conveys, the subject can only retain his life through a constrictive alienation that forces his sacrifice of something valuable, for if he chooses money or freedom over life, he loses both his life and the precious freedom or money he would not sacrifice to the Other. First presenting this reading in *Seminar XI*, Lacan reinforces this association of being with freedom and money years later in *Seminar XVII* through discussions of economics and slavery that provide some of his most cogent articulations of *jouissance*. Here, in a reading that allows us to theorize the interconnection between slavery and capitalism in ways not fully appreciated by Lacan himself, he makes the striking argument that capitalism allowed for access to a quantifiable form of *jouissance*, maintaining that, beginning with some "unknown traffic of ships around Genoa, or in the Mediterranean Sea, or anywhere else," at "a certain point in history," "capital begins" and "*jouissance* became calculable, could be counted, totalized."[37]

Because Lacan's discussion of slavery is focused upon its practice in such societies as classic Greece and Rome, he does not acknowledge the fact that this traffic of ships makes *jouissance* calculable by facilitating not only the transport of goods, but also the transformation of individuals into goods. What Lacan does recognize, however, is that such trafficking is coextensive with a change in the master's discourse at this point in history.[38] Indeed, I suggest that what starts to develop through capitalism and slavery is "a society founded" on the master's discourse,[39] the very purpose of which is to mask the division of the master by presenting the objects of his possession as proof that he does not lack.[40] Lacan has traced this discourse in his repeated critiques of the Cartesian formula *cogito ergo sum*—"I think therefore I am"—as rooting the subject in a fantasy of the self as whole and "univocal."[41] In *Seminar XVII*, Lacan returns to the notion of the *vel* to emphasize that this illusory univocality masks the true condition of the subject; he insists that what the subject is confronted by in the *vel* is most properly expressed in the choice "either I am not thinking or I am not,"[42] elaborating that "there where I am thinking I do not recognize myself" because it is "the unconscious," not the subject, that thinks.[43] Highlighting the unconscious as that zone of nonmeaning already displayed in Figure 6.1, Lacan recognizes the *cogito* as an effort to circumvent lack and the truth of the unconscious through a fantasy of univocality, but he does not acknowledge the *cogito*'s paralleling role in constituting this univocal self as a unified racial self.

Articulated in 1637 when the Atlantic Slave Trade had already been fully established, René Descartes' vision of the human mind as grounded in rationality helped facilitate an existential separation of races that stratified their calculable relation to being, establishing them as quantifiably different gradations of human beings. As Henry Louis Gates Jr. has noted, the Age of Enlightenment, to which Descartes would help give birth, is "famous for establishing its existence upon the human ability to reason," and it "simultaneously used the absence and presence of 'reason' to delimit and circumscribe the very humanity of cultures and people of color which Europeans had been 'discovering' since the Renaissance."[44] This process by which reason was used to tie being to race has its roots, ultimately, in an earlier concept for the ordering of the Symbolic called the Great Chain of

Being, a concept that originates with Plato and Aristotle but extends into and beyond the Renaissance and Enlightenment. This concept established a hierarchical structure for the Symbolic, vertically arranging all levels of being from God, through the various orders of angels, to animate and inanimate earthly objects, so that "by 1750, the chain had become individualized" with a subdivided "human scale"[45] that positioned blacks "as the 'lowest' of the human races, or as first cousin to the ape."[46] Race came to stand as an external sign of internal capacities for reason and sentiment, two differentiating features among beings within the chain that would continue to hold sway in later American constructs of racial identity.

Indeed, so powerful was their sway that these features become articulated by Thomas Jefferson himself, third president of the United States and author of the "Declaration of Independence," with all of its Enlightenment notions of the rights of man. Acknowledging a contemporaneous, fundamental debate over the "unity or plurality of mankind" that saw in race proof of the possible "polygenetic" origins of the species,[47] Jefferson voices both his uncertainty "whether [blacks are] originally a distinct race, or made distinct by time and circumstance" and his "suspicion" that they are "inferior to the whites in endowments both of body and mind."[48] Retaining a focus on the animalistic primitivism of blacks, Jefferson simultaneously asserts that, despite black women's lack of beauty, "the Oranootan" would choose "the black women over those of his own species," and finds that "love seems with [blacks] to be more" an "ardent" and "eager desire, than a tender delicate mixture of sentiment and sensation."[49]

We can already see in Jefferson's reading of blacks' desires the unrestrained impulses Freud would later ascribe to primitives. But such renderings of blacks as insensate and incapable of rational thought also lay the grounds for their emergence in slavery as representatives of subjective, psychic lack. Lacan asserts that "there is no contingency in the slave's position," for the slave's presence is "the necessity" that allows for "something to be produced that functions in knowledge as a master signifier."[50] Operative in slavery is a knowledge of self rooted in the master signifier of whiteness as a univocality or ideal ego achievable by the master:[51] the master's discourse "intervenes in the system of knowledge" that structures the Symbolic, redefining the self that is split in discourse between unconscious and conscious by projecting lack onto the slave.[52] Slavery allowed the master to embody in the slave a condition of lack that seemed to be the slave's exclusive, differentiating characteristic. Significantly, in his reading of subjectivity, Lacan argues that the subject is reduced by the Symbolic to the status of a signifier, forced to emerge as meaning only through his or her semiotic relation to other signifiers. This is what Lacan indicates in his famous articulation that the subject is a signifier "that represents a subject for another signifier,"[53] a notion that highlights the fact that the "*I* comes on the scene as a subject" through "a discourse in which it is death that sustains existence."[54] The subject, Lacan stresses, is "ravaged by the Word,"[55] experiencing through the signifier "the death" that "brings life."[56] It is this death to being that is visibly bound to the slave in order to facilitate recuperation of the master's lost being as a quantifiable *jouissance*.

This psycho-social process of recuperation depended upon what Orland Patterson has called the slave's "social death."[57] In a cross-historical, cross-cultural study of slavery, Patterson determines that what "gave the relation of slavery its peculiar value to the master" was that slavery allowed the slave "no independent social existence" from his master.[58] To the degree that it could establish the slave as insensate and irrational, slavery facilitated the "natal alienation" of slaves, separating families and breaking links of kinship in rejection of all "claims and obligations" to "remote ancestors" or "descendants."[59] Patterson shows that the slave thus "ceased to belong in his own right to any legitimate social order."[60] What we can specify through Lacanian theory is that this alienation is an expression of the slave's relation to the signifier. Slavery attempted to unveil the slave's true psychic condition of lack by making the slave's social positioning mirror his or her psychic reality. It did this by reducing the slave to the status of a signifier, as a mere commodity in an exchange system, a signifier within a chain of meanings. This signifying chain incorporated the hierarchal structure of the Great Chain of Being in an articulation of the slave as a paradoxical nonbeing, whose erasure facilitated his or her redeployment as a signifier for the master's own recuperated being.

Being and *jouissance* are ever lost to the subject, but through slavery, *jouissance* comes "back within the master's reach" in the form of what Lacan describes as "something not unlike jouissance—a surplus."[61] Lacan ties this surplus to fantasy and transgression, suggesting it arises ultimately within the frame of discourse. Discourse, by its very nature, argues Lacan, "is constantly touching on" *jouissance* by "virtue of the fact that this is where it originates," emerging in an effort to name and make present the absence it signifies.[62] Facilitating the white subject's recuperation of an extreme sense of being less available in other discourses, the racism that secured slavery allowed for unusual access to this surplus *jouissance*. Being was actively siphoned from the person of the slave in order to guarantee this surplus and grant the master access to whiteness as the master signifier of being. Lacan clarifies that the "signifier that represents a subject with respect to another signifier" is the very signifier that "articulates the master's discourse."[63] The slave, as signifier, articulated unto whiteness its exultant function as the master signifier that "defines" the "readability" of slavery as a discursively justified social institution.[64]

Through discourse, the master circumscribed the slave himself as the Lacanian *object a*. This *object a* is the fantasy object that promises to return the subject to a *jouissance*-filled state of wholeness, the illusory object that is here given presence in the form of the slave in order to make present the lost *jouissance* and being of the master. Once subjected to the social death described by Patterson, the slave was employed as a signifying emblem of the master's fulsome wealth and being, facilitating a structuring of Southern society that emulated the Great Chain of

Being by placing the master at its pinnacle in a stratification of the levels of being that is accessible to the human subject. Slavery not only allowed for ascension of the master over the slave as representative of a superior being, but it also gave structure to a class-based society subdivided among whites. Owning slaves allowed white Southerners to rise above their none-slaveholding compatriots, establishing themselves as the most genteel, refined members of the citizenry, the quintessential manifestations of an ascendant being attainable to a select few in the Symbolic. The slave was thus the *object a*, the sign that the master possessed an elusive means of self-completion, a source of univocality and wholeness.

Without doubt, in the end the master, like all subjects, was truly split in the *vel* that alienates him from being, constituting within him Lacan's three registers of the psyche: the Symbolic, which emerges through language; the Real, which comprises all that escapes language; and the Imaginary, which is structured by the concepts of wholeness that defy the facticity of the split through fantasies that first emerge in the mirror stage (Figure 6.2). Through a capitalism rooted in slavery, however, slave masters sought to suture the split that lacerates the human psyche.[65] The Lacanian concept of suture describes a "conjunction" or stitching together of "the imaginary and the symbolic" registers of the psyche over the gap of the Real.[66] Using the slave as *object a*, the master sewed his Imaginary fantasies of wholeness into the tapestry of the Symbolic itself, blanketing the Real of his lack with the embellishments of a racist discourse that reinforced his notions of being (Figure 6.3). What thus emerged through slavery's discourse of race was a means of organizing both the American Symbolic and the racialized white psyche.

Far from destabilizing Southern society in the ways Freud predicts, therefore, the master's freedom to exploit the slave as a source of surplus *jouissance* founded

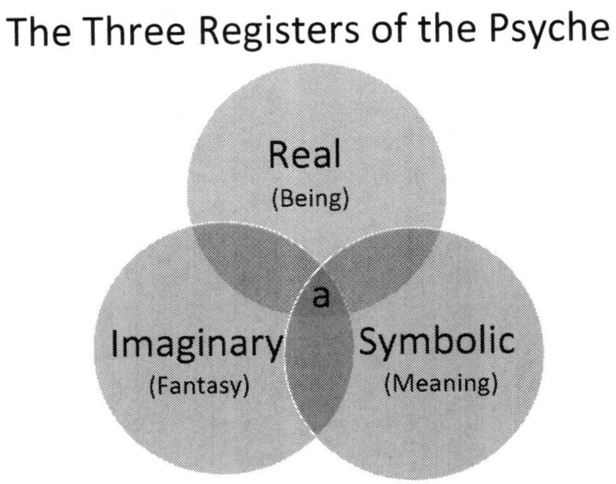

The Three Registers of the Psyche

Real
(Being)

a

Imaginary
(Fantasy)

Symbolic
(Meaning)

FIGURE 6.2 The three registers of the psyche

Suturing the Symbolic and Imaginary
Over the Real

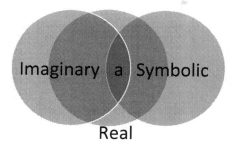

FIGURE 6.3 Suturing the Symbolic and Imaginary over the Real

early American civilization upon a brutal expression of base instincts that then root white identity in its signal notions of freedom and independence. As Toni Morrison notes, this fantastical and self-contradictory discourse is precisely what is articulated in the narratives white America would tell of itself in the literary works of its canonical gatekeepers. Morrison observes that "the major and championing characteristics of our national literature—individualism, masculinity, social engagement versus historical isolation; acute and ambiguous moral proble-matics; the thematic of innocence coupled with an obsession with figurations of death and hell—are [...] in fact responses to a dark, abiding, signing Africanist presence."[67] This presence, both internal to the self and externalized in the slave, functioned through a "black surrogacy" (p. 13) in which the "slave population was understood to have offered itself up for reflections on human freedom in terms other than the abstractions of human potential and the rights of man" extolled by the Enlightenment, for "nothing highlighted freedom—if it did not create it—like slavery."[68] Thus making freedom itself quantifiable in the literature and life of the nation and its people, the slave as surrogate functioned as the *object a* that both named and filled the lack of white America.

Constructing a soul and a racial self

The institution of slavery, we must therefore see, gave birth to our modern world, producing concomitantly new structures of subjectivity determined by an individual's relation to lack. What mediated this relation in early America was not only capitalism but also race, as itself an emergent, modern apparatus of *jouissance*, a fantasy *object a* forged within the crucible of slavery to define the core being of masters and slaves. Unlike the slave master, however, who positioned himself as free of lack, both the modernists of the 1920s and the slave of the Antebellum south were unable to easily manipulate this apparatus, and what defined these individuals as modern was a heightened sensitivity toward the alienation and fragmentation confronting the human psyche. Freud and artists like Eliot variously chart subjective fragmentation and alienation in a historical moment when the First World War had fractured dominant fantasies of the civilized white subject's univocality and racial superiority. However, these fantasies still clearly structure our contemporary world, and race remains a primary mediator of lack and subjectivity. This long conjunction of race and subjectivity demands, I suggest, a more expansive conception of the modern as extending from slavery through the postmodern into the contemporary, a conception that recognizes slavery as the natal source of a new racialized psyche that defines the expansively considered modern subject.[69] I will later show how this subject within today's American Symbolic remains reliant upon race in pursuit of alienated *jouissance*, and I will argue that this is especially true of today's African American subject. At what we may call the inception of our now modern America, however, African American slaves uniquely emerged as subjects of modernity by contending against race in its ability to mediate psychic states of fragmentation and alienation.

The racist discourse that reduced the slave to the position of *object a*, employing him or her as the instrument that sutures the constitutive gap of the white subject, sought traumatically to unsuture subjectivity for blacks.[70] Slavery assaulted the slave's Imaginary, fragmenting his or her psyche by employing the Symbolic to decimate personal fantasies of being. In the Lacanian understanding of the subject, such unsuturing can lead only to psychosis and the dissolution of subjective status. But the traumatic attacks upon being issued by slavery could never completely weed out the fantasies through which slaves, like all subjects, were able to establish—though at times only tenuously—a sustaining sense of being. Despite the fact that, as Patterson argues, slavery attempted to situate the slave as "a social nonperson" with "no socially recognized existence outside of his master," part of what slaves were able to do was construct a discourse of the self that shaped religious beliefs into folk narratives reflective of their personal and communal world views.[71] Through folk practices like storytelling, slaves attempted to create not only a counter-narrative to that facilitated by the master signifier of whiteness, but also, and more basically, a narrative of self that simply made life liveable, a narrative that recuperated for them a semblance of being, resuturing their fragmented selves and producing their own surplus *jouissance*.

Lacan notes that when there is an eruption of the Real, when something "is not going well" in our confrontation with the impossibility that lies at the frontier of our existence,[72] it is often religion that steps in to "soothe people's hearts"[73] and "give meaning to all the distressing things" one experiences.[74] In slavery, religion became a means of ordering an impossible existence through the salvation of a communal sense of being. By converting to Christianity, slaves accessed a "language and a flexible vocabulary" that allowed them to express their own conceptions of freedom, salvation and their natural rights.[75] Through a "syncretistic religion, sharing features of Protestant Christianity and traditional

African religions," they created the sense of a group identity based, not on the master's constructs of race, but on a shared experience and worldview.[76] Slaves situated themselves within the community through the aid of religious expressive structures like "the call and response pattern Negroes brought with them from Africa," which allowed a slave to "dialogue" with the community in a manner that "preserve[d] his voice as a distinct entity" while also "blend[ing] it with those of his fellow."[77] This group identity affirmed the being of the individual slave, countering the slave's "natal alienation" and "social death" by constructing the *object a* as an internal object found in African Americans as the core of their religious selves, the souls of the slaves.

In its connection to being, the Lacanian *object a* allows us to adumbrate a genealogy of this African American soul. Such a genealogy makes visible what I will later argue has been a striking repositioning of race as the fantasy *object a* structuring African American communal identity. Lacan argues that the Christian notion of the soul articulates a fantasy of the *object a* as a "semblance of being" that remains in man to link him to the Supreme Being.[78] Man tolerates "the intolerable in [his] world" through the notion of a soul that guarantees his return to that which embodies a plenitude of being, absolute being[79]; and this relation to being structures also communal and group identity. Bonded by being itself, individuals "recognize and choose each other" as "friends," as members of a re-envisioned kinship, through "their courage in bearing [an] intolerable relation" to being, through apprehension of the distinguishing commensurable manner in which they each compensate for the loss of being.[80] What unifies the group is the fantasy insertion of a soul within the other who, to the subject, suffers like me, a soul that mirrors mine, rooting me in what Lacan calls a process of "soulloving,"[81] whereby I love the other because s/he fantastically holds that foreign body ever lost to me that yet resonates with the lack that is "in me more than me."[82] This conflation of the other with the subject's absent being is the source of not only religious love but also racial identity; and it roots contemporary African Americans in what I will describe after Lacan as an ethical struggle over personal and group identity as a means of accessing *jouissance*—a struggle that, as one sees through the work of Freud, is germane to all subjects, but is especially visible in the lives of black Americans.

Within slavery, African Americans could not directly resignify and redeploy the concept of race to recuperate *jouissance* and a sense of being. Instead, what they fashioned in being's defense was this syncretic notion of the slave's eternal soul. In the folk narratives related by African American slaves, we find both the fantasy construction of such a soul as the foundation of being and the reshaping of *jouissance* by slave communities into the source of an African American cultural identity not yet explicitly reliant upon race. Zora Neale Hurston, in her anthropological study of African American folk culture, *The Sanctified Church*, relates a version of the folktales slaves told about High John de Conquer, a mystical figure who supplied a discursive means for slaves to tolerate their enslavement. High

John, Hurston's narrative recounts, was a "whisper, a will to hope,"[83] who had come from Africa by "walking the very winds that filled the sails of ships" in the middle passage[84] before becoming "a natural man."[85] Traversing the plantations unrecognized by slave masters, High John, the "hope-bringer," supplied slaves with the means to fight "a mighty battle without outside-showing force" and win their "war from within."[86] High John functioned as a paradigmatic model for the slave community's discourse; at times "touristing around the plantations as the laugh-provoking Brer Rabbit," he embodied the stories slaves told themselves.[87] He served his people in the same way as "King Arthur of England,"[88] granting them through storytelling a means of "making a way out of no-way."[89]

What the figure of High John provided slaves with was, as Hurston's tale specifies, "an inside thing to live by," a fantasy *object a* that could root their sense of possessing an individualized soul that links them in perseverance against suffering.[90] This soul was bound to a conviction that "something better was coming."[91] When "the lash fell on a slave in Alabama," High John could be "in Texas," but "before the blood was dry on the back he was there," causing someone "in the saddened quarters" to "feel like laughing," and say, "Now High John de Conquer, Old Massa couldn't get the best of *him*. That old John was a case."[92] Remaining "unbeatable," John defied "the impossible" by winning over slavery "with the soul of the black man whole and free."[93] Curating and shaping this soul, John showed the slaves that "he who wins from within is in the 'Be' class. *Be* here when the ruthless man comes and *be* here when he is gone."[94] Generating a notion of *conquest* that positions the slave's soul as eternal, whole and free both within and after slavery, High John helped provide slaves with a vivifying sense of the permanence of their being, an internal conviction that could counter the hierarchical structure of being through which slavery justified their subjugation. Thus opposing the eruptive *jouissance* that characterized the slave master's drive for immediate gratification, the figure of High John de Conquer helped temper the slave's desire through a knowledge received "a hundred years ahead of time that freedom was coming," an insight acquired "long before the white folks knew anything about it at all."[95]

This insight roots slaves in an "inside feeling and meaning" that generates the courage they manifest in bearing the intolerable relation to nonbeing that slavery bestows upon them.[96] Their conviction of the permanence of being enables them to not only sacrifice eruptive *jouissance* for the delayed gratification of desire, but also transform pain and suffering into pleasure. The slaves of Hurston's narrative recognize with amusement that their masters don't "know where us gets our pleasures from,"[97] but they themselves locate their source of pleasure in a "gift song" bequeathed to them by the "Old Maker" during their storied journeys with High John.[98] Leaving their "work-tired bodies" behind, they and John visit heaven and receive from the Maker a "tune that you could bend and shape in most any way you wanted to fit the words and feelings that you had."[99] The tune itself functions as a narrative of the soul, a gift from God that united a people in the expressive forms through which they recover lost *jouissance*. Where slave owners like Jefferson read the pleasure displayed in such forms as proof that pain is transient in the insensate slave, the narrative conveys that the "secret of black song and laughter" is its ability to fortify an eternal sense of being that seems ever quiescent in slavery.[100] Their journey toward acquisition of their "gift song" required that the slaves "reach inside [them]selves and get out all those fine raiments [they've] been toting around," and it supplied them access to musical instruments that "were right inside where they got their raiments from."[101] Through High John, slaves established an internal means to refashion themselves in the drapery of expressive religious and musical practices that cohere the community. By bending the Maker's tune to fit their words and feelings, they transformed the master's *jouissance* into the slave's pleasure.[102]

Giving later birth to such cultural forms as the blues, this process of bearing *jouissance* through its transformation into pleasure marks a central aesthetic in the culture developed by the slaves and their descendants. However, there is not only aesthetics involved in this relation to *jouissance*, but also ethics. Lacanian ethics privileges desire over *jouissance*, proposing that, "from an analytic point of view," what each subject must do is act "in conformity with the desire that is in" him or her.[103] This ethical stance, Lacan argues, is what the subject may achieve at the "termination of an analysis," a process that allows the "function of desire [to] remain in a fundamental relationship to death."[104] But without the resource of analysis, what slavery traumatically enabled through its very brutality was precisely such a relationship. Presenting the possibility for the slave to confront what Lacan calls "the reality of the human condition," slavery stripped away the fantasies by which subjects mask lack, reducing the slave to a signifier and confronting him with his social death.[105] This stripping away opened up the potential for what Lacan terms a traversal of the fundamental fantasy, the illusions of univocality that evade the fact of subjective fragmentation. Lacan argues that a subject who "has traversed the radical phantasy [may] experience the drive" as the agitation that fuels a new relation to desire.[106] Here the drive, as a "will to destruction," may be more productively embraced as a "will to create from zero, a will to begin again."[107] It is this process of starting from zero, from the decimation of one's being, that slavery imposed upon the slave, and the cultural productions that emerge from this process are perhaps among the nearest circumscribable examples of a Lacanian creation "ex nihilo."[108]

Here we may conceive of African American culture—with its people's unique understanding of "freedom," their play with discourse and language, and their aesthetic transformation of pain into "laugh" and "song"—through Lacan's description of the potter.[109] As the potter "creates the vase with his hand around" the "emptiness at [its] center," so too did African American culture involve a creation that is built around the gap of their lack.[110] Jazz music, as an "art which traditionally thrives on improvisation,"[111] and the blues, which is both "an autobiographical chronical of personal catastrophe expressed lyrically" and an effort to "finger [the] jagged grain" of catastrophic loss in order to aesthetically "transcend it," are both illustrative of this kind of creation.[112] However, such fashioning of a container for lack can only emerge within the discourse of the Symbolic, through the agency of the signifier; and while fundamental to the signifier is its essential function as "the cause of jouissance," signifiers of race, as we have already seen, aim precisely at the *jouissance* and wholeness of being.[113] In narratives such as High John's, African Americans constructed not only expressive religious and musical forms shaped around lack, but also the rudiments of a fantasy object to fill this lack, a soul as *object a* that gave substance to a notion of the group's essential difference. And this difference, which initially constituted through the soul a conception of being that rejected the master's fantasies of race, came in time to be conflated with race itself as the fantasy essence that defines African Americans.

Lacan shows that "we make reality out of pleasure."[114] Slavery and racism have produced race as an illusory but determinant mediator of subjective access to pleasure and being in our American society. We have seen how in the case of white Americans this mediation urges their unification into racial-communal structures that, as Freud recognizes, pits the community against the interests of the broader society or civilization. But the experiences of African Americans also show how communal identity, while mediating their political realities, can simultaneously impede personal desire. It is the political exigencies of racism combined with the greater pleasures promised by racial identity as *object a*—as an internal fantasy-essence that fills the lack that is merely framed and contained by cultural forms—that continually steer African Americans off what Lacan identifies as the path in which a subject may "recognize the topology of [his own] desire."[115] This less pleasurable path of lack, Lacanian ethics makes clear, individualizes subjective desire, granting the subject understanding of "the deepest level of himself"[116] and "support[ing] an unconscious theme" that roots each subject not in the fantasies of the Symbolic, but in "the tracks of something that is specifically [his] business."[117]

But one finds consistently a struggle over the pleasures of racial fantasy and the revelations of individualized desire playing out across the cultural and literary productions of African Americans, appearing quite noticeably in the work of Hurston herself and other "modernist" African American authors like W.E.B. Du Bois. Du Bois' famous articulation of the African American subject as traumatized and split by race into a doubled consciousness has become a defining portraiture of black American identity.[118] It is an image of identity that supplants what Du Bois calls "the religious feelings of the slave" with race as the center of the individual and communal self.[119] Maintaining that "for the Negro to-day" religion is a "complaint and a curse, a wail rather than a hope,"[120] Du Bois foregrounds race in an attempt to "conserve," revalue and politically redeploy this concept in efforts to produce social change.[121] But Hurston's own work, particularly her famous novel *Their Eyes Were Watching God*, emerges as a blanket rejection of race as the core of personal identity, demonstrating how without race the lacking self may be contained within the encapsulating exploration of an individualized unconscious theme.

The protagonist of Hurston's novel, Janie Crawford, is first confronted with the fact of her blackness when she is pointed out by others in a photograph of herself and her white playmates. Though Janie's youth and racial difference deprive her of any self-defined space in the Symbolic, allowing others to mock her liminality by renaming her "Alphabet," Janie is never unsettled by racial difference[122]; unconcerned with race before the picture, she reacts to its discovery only with the sedated words, "Aw, aw! Ah'm colored!"[123] In what is clearly Hurston's own response to Du Bois' notion of race as splitting the conscious self, Janie narrates insistently that her "conscious life had commenced" not with the earlier discovery of race, but at her "Nanny's gate," when a boy's "kiss over the gatepost" awakened her sexuality.[124]

Individualizing Janie's identity, Hurston's novel roots this sexuality in an experience under a blossoming pear tree that had "called [Janie] to come and gaze on a mystery" that personally "stirred her tremendously."[125] In isolation under the pear tree, Janie experiences her libido as an internally directed force in pursuit of external resonances. As she attentively observes everything from "leaf-buds to snowy virginity of bloom" and arduously listens to "singing she heard that had nothing to do with her ears," Janie finds a connection to "other vaguely felt matters that had struck her outside observation and buried themselves in her flesh."[126] Her experience under the pear tree starts to articulate an unconscious theme that will drive her actions throughout the book. Discarding race and progressively rejecting the illusions of the Symbolic that promise her satisfaction in an other, Janie moves through each new experience in her life with a determination that "her old thoughts were going to come in handy [...] but new words would have to be made and said to fit them."[127] Clinging to a thematic experience that to her "is the truth"[128] while simultaneously remaking the dream and manufacturing words within the Symbolic to name it, Janie exemplifies an ethics rooted in desire, a self-explorative, self-constructive ethics grounded in a metonymic search not for eruptive *jouissance* or the "illusions" one confronts "on the path of desire,"[129] but for something more fundamentally her own, something that resonates with the "constant force" of her own lost being.[130]

Hurston's vision of the racialized subject who reconstitutes herself through an individualized desire would be supplanted by the political focus already urged by figures like Du Bois. In the 1930s, the work of Richard Wright in particular would insist on an alignment of art and politics that lead to the rejection of Hurston's writings, causing Hurston herself to fall into obscurity until the 1970s.[131] By this point in African American history, race had already been cemented to politics and conflated with religion. Seminal figures of the Civil Rights movement like Martin Luther King Jr. had attempted to balance spiritual salvation of the soul with political liberation of the race; King had argued that "segregation distorts the soul and damages the personality" by creating false senses of racial "superiority" and "inferiority."[132] But the need to fight against racial inferiority, or what King described as the "denigrating sense of 'nobidiness'" that assaults not just the individual but the race as a whole, had urged insistently African Americans' endeavors to fight racism with race.[133] Today, frequently superseding both the individualized understanding of personality Hurston extolled and the function of the soul created in slavery, race in contemporary America has solidified as what I would call a Lacanian Até, an infinitely alluring object that binds us both to dreams of recuperating our lost being and to atrocities of the past that shattered being.

This Até, which appears in Lacan's work as a precursor to the *object a*, is defined as an atrocity that has been subjected to a process of divinization, becoming an ascension that situates itself at the entranceway onto the beyond. Lacan describes the Até through the image of the crucifixion, which protects us from subjective self-annihilation by barring our direct access to the overwhelming *jouissance* and absolute being we position in this beyond. But the Até only protects the subject by attracting "to itself all the threads of [his or her] desire."[134] It fundamentally stagnates desire, leaving the subject trapped in an unbearable fixation with the atrocity that has risen in the place of being. Race, I argue, is an alluring Até that agitates and attracts desire through an ascension in which it comes to stand as the gateway onto being.

In a racial Symbolic that has already collapsed subjective lack with the social experiences of African Americans, race, as Até, positions itself as both the root of atrocities confronted by black Americans and the seductive, political expedient that can protect blacks from further horrors. Alluringly conflating the social and the psychic, race presents itself as a means to regain that semblance of being struck from the subject by language and unveiled in its absence by slavery and racism. The danger, however, is that this Até positions not just being but also slavery as its beyond. Whereas the fantasy notion of the soul aligned being with the Supreme Being, the Até of race seeks after a being that, in the racism of the Symbolic, is produced as the correlative of an impossible whiteness most fully secured in the racist past. With this Até, slavery and racism come to function like the divine, ministering to subjects the proper contours of their actions, granting them a particular ontology of self, and constructing for them the fantasy paths through which to regain their lost being. Manifesting a historicized upsurge of *jouissance*, slavery has produced race as an object that both unveils and fills the gaping void opened up at the very frontier of the racialized subject's being; and in contemporary America, it does so equally for black and white subjects. As Até, race seduces the American subject with the promised pleasures of communal racial identity, stifling personal desires that may allow subjects to forego *jouissance* for exploration of an ethics that can remake both the self and the "civilized" nation.

Conclusion: masking and unveiling the real

Lacan has described psychoanalysis as a "symptom" of the Real that intrudes upon the Symbolic in a particular historical moment[135] to express "the discontents of civilization Freud spoke about."[136] His reading situates Freud and psychoanalysis at the place of the gap opened up by this intrusion, as mediating agents that make it possible to "perceive what the intrusion of the real is."[137] I have shown throughout, however, that slavery marks an earlier intrusion not acknowledged by Freud, an eruption in which the master's visible pursuit of the *jouissance* of the Real and the slave's ostensible transformation into a signifier of lack come to express a civilization's discontents with the limits placed upon enjoyment by psychic reality. In slavery, such limits were breached, revealing the atrocity at the heart of the human subject, who, when given social sanction to pursue *jouissance*, would seek, as Freud only recognized decades later, to "exploit [his or her neighbor's] capacity for work without compensation, to use him sexually without his consent, to seize his possessions, to humiliate him, to cause him pain, to torture and to kill him."[138]

Before Freud himself, it was ex-slaves who gave true meaning to this intrusion of the Real. Particularly through authoring narratives of their former enslavement, ex-slaves highlighted and critiqued this brutality's paradoxical coexistence with ideals of freedom that structure American national identity. Indeed, in the very first novel published by an African American, the escaped slave William Wells Brown paints a telling image of America as split between two fully integrated but divergent modes of accessing surplus *jouissance*. Brown, in 1853, fictionalizes the then popular and now validated claim of Thomas Jefferson's sexual exploits with his slave-mistress in a tale Brown titles *Clotel or, The President's Daughter*.[139] While rendering this daughter as a slave who escapes her pursuers by jumping to her death from the center of a bridge joining the "capitol of the Union," Washington D.C., to the slave state of Virginia, Brown contextualizes slavery within a revisionary origin-narrative that ties the birth of the nation to the trafficking of two ships.[140] Both arriving in 1620, one ship is the "May-flower anchored at Plymouth Rock," and the other is "the slave-ship in James River" carrying the "first cargo of slaves on their way to Jamestown."[141]

These ships, each serving as what Brown refers to as a "parent" of the society to come, mark the birth of the nation through a fracturing of ideas that defined the Enlightenment.[142] They embody, on the one hand, abstract idealisms that seek to equalize access to pleasure through notions of the rights of man and, on the other, rationalizations for immediate, quantifiable forms of *jouissance* rooted in eruptive transgressions against those rights.[143] But, contrary to what Freud's theory would anticipate, the free rein of unrepressed impulses that this fracturing allowed did not lead naturally to the crumbling of early American society. Instead, it stratified the nation into North and South, establishing, as Brown notes, two "parallel" and equally viable social structures.[144] What defined these structures was the divergent manner in which they pursued *jouissance*. Expressed in contending approaches to race and capital that are clearly exemplified for Brown in the contrast between "unpaid labour" in the "peculiar institution of the South" and the "labour-honouring, law sustaining" practices of institutions in the North, this contention culminated in the Civil War as a struggle over unreconciled modes of accessing *jouissance* that had already become internal to each region.[145] But the Civil War did not bring a resolution to America's contentions over *jouissance*; and, indeed, the stratifying impulses toward racial violence and humanistic idealism still exist in parallel with each other in an American Symbolic that has sutured to itself notions of race that yet today accrue to whiteness its unique capacity to mask the Real.

In recognition of the subject's reliance upon such masks, Lacan has predicted that "humanity will be cured of psychoanalysis" as a symptom through use of "religious meaning" to "repress" the unveiled Real psychoanalysis makes perceivable.[146] But what must be acknowledged is how race, perhaps exceeding religion, continues to function as a prevailing screen for the Real in our American society. By extending our analysis backward beyond the modernist moment of the 1920s that gave birth to Freud's racialized recognition of the brutal impulses driving discontent, we have shown that race mediates access to *jouissance*, generating notions of identity that not only sustain the historical allure of whiteness, but also attract even African Americans toward communal, racial identities. Both offering a means to fend against social oppression and conflating the self with the group and its pursuits, such identities incorporate and even supplant religious notions of the soul with race as the essential core of the subject. This new version of the soul, race as the core self that emerges out of slavery's ensuing legacy, noticeably implicates African Americans in psychic struggles with *jouissance* and being that play out for every subject, though often in less dramatic or readily perceivable ways. It was finally the extreme brutality of the First World War that traumatically unveiled the Real Freud himself was able to perceive in his analysis of the human psyche and its subjective instincts. In a similar fashion, the extremity of African Americans' struggles against social manifestations of psychic discontent offers yet untapped understandings of the relationship race and *jouissance* hold to each of us as subjects of a modernized American civilization.

Notes

1   We are grateful for the generous permissions granted by Springer to reprint this chapter, which previously appeared in *Psychoanalysis, Culture & Society* 23, no. 3 (2018), 267–289.

2   Sigmund Freud, *Civilization and its Discontents* (London: Hogarth Press, 1986), 95.

3   Sigmund Freud, *Thoughts for the Times on War and Death* (London: Hogarth Press, 1986), 282.

4   Sigmund Freud, *Civilization*, 119.

5   Ibid., 86.

6   Ibid., 87.

7   Ibid., 95.

8 Ibid., 112.
9 Sigmund Freud, *Thoughts,* 276. As Sander Gilman notes, though Freud identified himself as a Jew and struggled against contemporaneous stereotypes that associated Jews with mental illness, it is clear from this racial formulation presented above that "the Jews, seen as a people of culture, were," in Freud's estimation, "to be considered 'white' and, therefore, civilized" (1993, p. 98).
10 Jacques Lacan, *The Seminar of Jacques Lacan Book VII: The Ethics of Psychoanalysis,* translated by D. Porter (New York: Norton, 1997), 194.
11 Ibid., 194.
12 Ibid., 194.
13 Paul Gilroy, *The Black Atlantic: Modernity and Double Consciousness* (Cambridge, MA: Harvard University Press, 1993), 42.
14 Ibid., 63.
15 T.S. Eliot, *The Waste Land,* edited by M. North (New York: Norton, 2001), 5.
16 Sigmund Freud, *Thoughts,* 299.
17 Ibid., 286.
18 Ibid., 297.
19 Sigmund Freud, *Totem and Taboo* (London: Hogarth Press, 1913/1986), 154.
20 Ibid., 150.
21 Ibid., 143.
22 Eugene Genovese, *The Political Economy of Slavery* (London: MacGibbon and Kee, 1966), 33.
23 Sigmund Freud, *Civilization,* 95.
24 Lacan, *Ethics,* 322.
25 Jacques Lacan, *The Seminar of Jacques Lacan Book XI: The Four Fundamental Concepts of Psychoanalysis,* translated by A. Sheridan (New York: Norton, 1998), 167.
26 Ibid., 198.
27 Ibid., 197.
28 Ibid., 164.
29 Lacan, *Ethics, 209.*
30 Ibid., 210.
31 Lacan, *Four Fundamental,* 26.
32 Ibid., 243.
33 Jacques Lacan, *Ethics,* 212.
34 Ibid., 211.
35 Lacan, *Four Fundamental,* 212.
36 Ibid., 212.
37 Jacques Lacan, *The Seminar of Jacques Lacan Book XVII: The Other Side of Psychoanalysis* (New York: Norton, 2007), 177.
38 Ibid., 177.
39 Ibid., 126.
40 Ibid., 103.
41 Ibid..
42 Ibid..
43 Ibid..
44 Henry Louis Gates Jr, *Loose Canons: Notes on the Culture Wars* (New York: Oxford University Press, 1992), 54.
45 Ibid., 55.
46 Ibid., 64.
47 Gilman, S.L. "Black bodies, white bodies: Toward an iconography of female sexuality in late nineteenth-century art, medicine, and literature," (Chicago: University of Chicago Press, 1986), 235.

48   Thomas Jefferson, *Notes on the state of Virginia* (New York: Library of America, 1787/1984), 270.
49   Ibid., 265.
50   Lacan, *Other Side, 188.*
51   For more on whiteness as the master signifier, see Kalpana Seshadri-Crooks, Desiring Whiteness: A Lacanian Analysis of Race (New York: Routledge, 2000).
52   Lacan, *Other Side, 201.*
53   Lacan, *Four Fundamental, 157.*
54   Jacques Lacan, *Ècrits: The First Complete Edition in English*, translated by B. Fink (New York: Norton, 2006), 679.
55   Jacques Lacan, *The Triumph of Religion,* translated by B. Fink (Boston: Polity Press, 2013), 74.
56   Lacan, *Ècrits,* 686.
57   Orland Patterson, *Slavery and Social Death: A Comparative Study* (Massachusetts: Harvard University Press, 1982), 8.
58   Ibid., 10.
59   Ibid., 5.
60   Ibid..
61   Lacan, *Other Side, 107.*
62   Ibid., 70.
63   Ibid., 20.
64   Ibid., 189.
65   Here my deployment of the concept of "suture" is more in keeping with its original use in Lacan's theory than with its now more popularized use in film theory as a concept that "figures the lack at the core of intersubjectivity in narrative film" (George Butte, *Suture and Narrative: Deep Intersubjectivity in Fiction and Film* (Columbus, Ohio: Ohio State University Press, 2017), 3).
66   Lacan, *Four Fundamental, 118.*
67   Toni Morrison, *Playing in the Dark: Whiteness and the Literary Imagination* (New York: Vintage Books, 1992), 5.
68   Ibid., 38.
69   As far as alienation is concerned, it can be argued that what we find across time periods is differences in intensity, and less so differences in kind. Jean Baudrillard,for example, aligns the postmodern and the contemporary with an increased sense that we engage the world through "simulacra," or "models of a real without origin or reality" (p. 1).
70   For more on this trauma, see my book *Trauma and Race: A Lacanian Study of African American Identity.*
71   Patterson, *Social Death, 5.*
72   Lacan, *Triumph,* 72.
73   Ibid., 64.
74   Ibid., 65.
75   Mevlin Dixon, *Singing Swords: The Literary Legacy of Slavery* (New York: Oxford University Press, 1985), 300.
76   Ibid., 298.
77   Lawrence W. Levine, *Slave songs and slave consciousness*, edited by A. Weinstein, F. O. Gatell, and D. Sarasohn (New York: Oxford University Press, 1979), 152.
78   Lacan, *The Seminar of Jacques Lacan Book XX: Encore, On Feminine Sexuality*, 92.
79   Ibid., 84.
80   Ibid., 85.
81   Ibid..
82   Lacan, *Four Fundamental,* 263.
83   Zora Neale Hurston, *High John de Conquer* (New York: Marlowe & Company, 1981), 69.

84   Ibid., 70.
85   Ibid, 69.
86   Ibid., 70.
87   Ibid.
88   Ibid., 71.
89   Ibid., 70.
90   Ibid., 69.
91   Ibid., 69.
92   Ibid., 69.
93   Ibid., 70.
94   Ibid., 71.
95   Ibid., 72.
96   Ibid., 73.
97   Ibid., 78.
98   Ibid., 77.
99   Ibid.
100 Ibid., 78.
101 Ibid., 76.
102 For an overview of High John's cultural transformation after slavery, see Carolyn Morrow Long, *Spiritual Merchants: Religion, Magic, and Commerce* (Knoxville, Tennessee: University of Tennessee Press, 2001).
103 Lacan, *Ethics,* 314.
104 Ibid., 303.
105 Ibid.
106 Lacan, *Four Fundamental,* 273.
107 Lacan, *Ethics,* 212.
108 Ibid.
109 Hurston, *High John,* 78.
110 Lacan, *Ethics,* 78.
111 Ralph Ellison, *Living With Music* (New York: Random House, 2002), 35.
112 Ibid., 103.
113 Lacan, *Encore* 24.
114 Lacan, *Ethics, 225.*
115 Ibid., 315.
116 Ibid., 323.
117 Ibid., 319.
118 W.E.B. Dubois, Of our Spiritual Strivings, (New York: Norton, 1999), 11.
119 W.E.B. Du Bois, *The Religion of the American Negro* (Boston: Houghton Mifflin, 1900), 615.
120 Ibid., 622.
121 W.E.B. Du Bois, *The conservation of races* (Washington, D.C.: American Negro Academy, 1897), 15.
122 Zora Neale Hurston, *Their Eyes Were Watching God* (New York: Harper and Row, 1990), 9.
123 Ibid., 9.
124 Ibid., 10.
125 Ibid.
126 Ibid.
127 Ibid., 31.
128 Ibid., 1.
129 Lacan, *Ethics, 219.*
130 Lacan, *Four Fundamental,* 164.
131 See Wright's "Blueprint for Negro Writing," for example.

132 Martin Luther King, Jr., *Letter from Birmingham Jail*, edited by J. James (Maryland: Rowman and Littlefield, 2003), 38.
133 Ibid.
134 Lacan, *Ethics*, 262.
135 Lacan, *Triumph*, 65.
136 Ibid., 66.
137 Ibid., 67.
138 Freud, *Civilization*, 111.
139 For more on Jefferson and his slave, Sally Hemings, see Gordon-Reed.
140 Wells W. Brown, *Clotel or, The President's Daughter* (New York: Penguin 1853/ 2004), 184.
141 Ibid., 156.
142 Ibid.
143 Ibid.
144 Ibid., 155.
145 Ibid., 156.
146 Lacan, *Triumph*, 67.

References

Baudrillard, Jean. *Simulacra and Simulation*. Translated by Sheila Faria Glaser. Michigan: University of Michigan Press, 1994.

Brown, William Wells. *Clotel or, The President's Daughter*. New York: Penguin, 2004.

Butte, George. *Suture and Narrative: Deep Intersubjectivity in Fiction and Film*. Columbus, Ohio: Ohio State University Press, 2017.

Dixon, Melvin. "Singing Swords: The Literary Legacy of Slavery." In *The Slave's Narrative*, edited by C. T. Davis and H. L. Gates Jr., 298–318. New York: Oxford University Press, 1985.

Du Bois, W.E.B. "The conservation of races." Occasional Papers, No. 2., 5–15. Washington, D.C.: American Negro Academy, 1897.

Du Bois, W.E.B. "The Religion of the American Negro." In *The New World: A quarterly review of religion, ethics and theology*. Vol. 9, December, 614–625. Boston: Houghton, Mifflin, 1900.

Du Bois, W.E.B. "Of Our Spiritual Strivings." In *The Souls of Black Folk*, edited by H. L. Gates Jr. and T. H. Oliver, 9–16. New York: Norton, 1999.

Eliot, T.S. *The Waste Land*, edited by M. North. New York: Norton, 2001.

Ellison, Ralph. *Living With Music*. New York: Random House, 2002.

Freud, Sigmund. *Totem and Taboo*. Standard Edition 13, 1–162. London: Hogarth Press, 1986.

Freud, Sigmund. *Thoughts for the Times on War and Death*. Standard Edition 14, 273–302. London: Hogarth Press, 1986.

Freud, Sigmund. *Civilization and its Discontents*. Standard Edition 13, 57–145. London: Hogarth Press, 1986.

Gates Jr., Henry Louis, *Loose Canons: Notes on the Culture Wars*. New York: Oxford University Press, 1992.

George, Sheldon. *Trauma and Race: A Lacanian Study of African American Identity*. Waco Texas: Baylor University Press, 2016.

Genovese, Eugene. *The Political Economy of Slavery*. London: MacGibbon and Kee, 1966.

Gilman, Sander L. "Black bodies, white bodies: Toward an iconography of female sexuality in late nineteenth-century art, medicine, and literature." In *"Race," Writing and Difference*, edited by Henry Louis Gates, Jr. Chicago: University of Chicago Press, 1986.

Gilman, Sander L. *Freud, Race and Gender*. Princeton, NJ: Princeton University Press, 1993.

Gilroy, Paul. *The Black Atlantic: Modernity and Double Consciousness*. Cambridge, MA: Harvard University Press, 1993.

Gordon-Reed, Annette. *The Hemingses of Monticello: An American Family*. New York: Norton, 2008.

Hurston, Zora Neale. "High John de Conquer." In *The Sanctified Church*, 69–78. New York: Marlowe & Company, 1981.

Hurston, Zora Neale. *Their Eyes Were Watching God*. New York: Harper and Row, 1990.

Jefferson, Thomas. "Notes on the state of Virginia." In *Writings*, 123–325. New York: Library of America, 1984.

King Jr., Martin Luther, "Letter from Birmingham Jail." In: *Imprisoned Intellectuals: America's Political Prisoners Write on Life, Liberation, and Rebellion*, edited by J. James, 34–45. Maryland: Rowman and Littlefield, 2003.

Lacan, Jacques. *The Seminar of Jacques Lacan Book VII: The Ethics of Psychoanalysis*. Translated by Dennis Porter. New York: Norton, 1997.

Lacan, Jacques. *The Seminar of Jacques Lacan Book XX: Encore, On Feminine Sexuality*. Translated by Bruce Fink. New York: Norton, 1998.

Lacan, Jacques. *The Seminar of Jacques Lacan Book XI: The Four Fundamental Concepts of Psychoanalysis*. Translated by Alan Sheridan. New York: Norton, 1998.

Lacan, Jacques. "The subversion of the subject and the dialectic of desire in the Freudian unconscious." In *Écrits: The First Complete Edition in English*, 671–702. Translated by Bruce Fink. New York: Norton, 2006.

Lacan, Jacques. *The Seminar of Jacques Lacan Book XVII: The Other Side of Psychoanalysis*. Translated by Russel Grigg. New York: Norton, 2007.

Lacan, Jacques. *The Triumph of Religion*. Translated by Bruce Fink. Boston: Polity Press, 2013.

Levine, Lawrence W. "Slave songs and slave consciousness." In *American Negro Slavery: A Modern Reader, 3rd ed.*, edited by A. Weinstein, F. O. Gatell, and D. Sarasohn, 143–172. New York: Oxford University Press, 1979.

Long, Carolyn Morrow. *Spiritual Merchants: Religion, Magic, and Commerce*. Knoxville, Tennessee: University of Tennessee Press, 2001.

Morrison, Toni. *Playing in the Dark: Whiteness and the Literary Imagination*. New York: Vintage Books, 1992.

Patterson, Orlando. *Slavery and Social Death: A Comparative Study*. Massachusetts: Harvard University Press, 1982.

Seshadri-Crooks, Kalpana. *Desiring Whiteness: A Lacanian Analysis of Race*. New York: Routledge, 2000.

Wright, Richard. "Blueprint for Negro writing." In *The Portable Harlem Renaissance Reader*, edited by D. L. Lewis, 194–205. New York: Penguin, 1995.

7

THE NASTY WOMAN

Destruction and the Path to Mutual Recognition

Tracy Sidesinger

Not long ago and unbeknownst to my conscious mind, I began to follow the
Nasty Woman into the woods. She appeared to me as Durga, the Hindu goddess
of loving destruction. Like many other Nasty Women in mythology, her temples
are often located deep within dark forests. This immediately conjures fear and
avoidance, which are protective, dissociative processes that nevertheless keep valuable experience and knowledge at bay. The impetus for this chapter was the sociocultural emergence of the Nasty Woman in the 2016 U.S. presidential election
between Hillary Clinton and Donald Trump, and the reactive response to dissociate and control her. An important archetypal image has come into the spotlight
but with confusion over whether she should be further dissociated, appreciated, or
integrated. Through personal, clinical, and mythological work, I argue that the
Nasty Woman archetype needs attending to as a destructive force whose destruction is paradoxically loving and in the service of mutual recognition.

Herein the Nasty Woman is defined as one who operates from her own subjectivity and asserts this through many means including autonomous desire or
creativity. This is rooted in Simone de Beauvoir's 1949 articulation that the subjective experience of woman has been denied by an embedded worldview that
sees the masculine as the point from which to define all else. In her words,
"'feminine reality' has been constituted... woman has been defined as Other...
from men's point of view."[1] Although much has changed to shift our conscious
point of view, this patriarchal orientation still exists as a strong unconscious
underpinning in society. The Nasty Woman's assertion of herself is not necessarily aggressive, but is often received as such because it is so counter to embedded
conceptions of what is acceptable for Woman. In the current social climate, the
Nasty Woman receives a split response, simultaneously dissociated and re-claimed
as central to identity. Following on the work of Sullivan[2] and Bromberg,[3] there

are those who would disidentify with the Nasty Woman as "not-me," and others who would resonate and identify with her as "me!" The more complicated work is standing between these identities and knowing how the Nasty Woman can be present with others. If dissociation theory has anything to teach us, the Nasty Woman is not about furthering splits. Rather, she is at the center of patriarchy's last stand, what could become the final cultural struggle for any one form of otherness to remain dominant. Realizing a different solution than dominance to the struggle for relationship affords a fuller and more mutual engagement with otherness. However, in the present moment, the Nasty Woman has to bring down the ruling cultural view that is one of dominance, or else there is no chance for equality in a fuller acceptance of the self and others.

Through its patriarchal roots, American culture has dissociated from the Nasty Woman or "dark feminine" who is, in fact, a member of the feminine pantheon. In reaction to this dissociation and with the growing momentum of feminism and civil rights, the Nasty Woman is being reclaimed in equal force. At times this reclaiming can perpetuate dissociation through what Benjamin[4] calls "complementary dual unity," where parties alternate between dominant and submissive positions and hierarchy nevertheless remains. At other times, however, identification with the Nasty Woman can cut through the strictures of domination and open up a path to mutuality, especially if she is recognized as one among many members in the pantheon of the self. Conscious recognition of the destructive dark feminine actually opens up the way for more authentic inclusion of other feminine energies that had previously been accepted in isolation (i.e., nurturance, beauty, patience). The mythological story of Durga, as well as clinical examples that follow a similar trajectory, demonstrate the archetypal reality whereby inclusivity comes through destruction. As such, the Nasty Woman can offer our culture not ultimate destruction, but a new vision of a mature relatedness and mutual recognition.

An overview of dissociation, complementarity, Oedipal problems, and gender

Philip Bromberg[5] argued that the most revolutionary thesis of psychoanalysis is not about the self's subjectivity in isolation, but that there is *no* solitary autonomous self. The self is by nature decentered, multiple, and dissociable from its various points. Indeed, a brief review of psychoanalytic history reminds us that the concept of dissociation has been around since its inception through Janet, Breuer, and Freud and their originary work on hysteria.[6] However, the dissociability of the psyche was seen as a pathological process in most early clinicians, except for Jung who saw it as a universal phenomena in his theory of complexes.[7]

Since the 1980s, many theorists, most notably with relational orientations, have returned to the idea of dissociation as a normative process.[8] Ideas on dissociation have been broadened to conceptualize psychological development in terms of relatedness to multiple, non-linear, and de-centered parts of the self and others. Integral to this is a recognition of interpersonal enactments. Enactments are seen as inevitable manifestations of dissociated parts of the self that occur in interpersonal experiences, as a means of bringing that which is unformulated into a conscious sense of self.[9]

Dissociation and enactments are normal, inevitable aspects of psychological functioning that arise from some level of trauma but are also permeable to change. While living forward may involve repair, it always brings with it the possibility of further destruction. To avoid this, there is the problematic possibility that rigid walls will remain between multiple self-states; one state cannot tolerate or negotiate the conflict that exists between itself and another, and thus defenses against knowing otherness are reinforced. What constitutes psychoanalytic work, in contrast, is an ethic of openness to otherness. It cultivates an ability to stand in the spaces between self-states, from which one can have dialogue and relatedness.[10] This applies to both internal and external otherness. In both cases, dissociation implies an experiencing subject that sees all others as its objects, but as we break down the walls of dissociation we also break down false hierarchies into multiple subjectivities. In terms of the Nasty Woman, her subjectivity has been excluded from the dominant conscious viewpoint, and her consequent nastiness is the destruction of dissociation's walls.

It is therefore anticipated that untouched, rigid walls exist between multiple self-states, and defenses against knowing otherness are reinforced. Interpersonally, Benjamin[11] outlines this subject/object hierarchy as a complementary dual unity in which individuals immaturely complement each other by filling linked roles of dominant/submissive, doer/done-to. Complementarity serves to contain identity in an illusory sense. It is a trap of bondage for both the dominant subject who needs an other to define, and for the submissive object who looks to another for their definition.

Complementarity remains a problem, particularly within the psychoanalytic narratives of individuation and of mature Oedipal development. As it was originally formulated, mature Oedipal development and thus mature relational capacity requires turning away from the mother as the desired object.[12] Many female theorists have attempted to re-work Oedipal theory and thus preserve the value of such long-standing theory, while also adding more feminine perspective.[13] The psychoanalytic Oedipus narrative has helped to elaborate the triangulation between a child and their parents that needs to be reckoned with for mature relating under any definition. This narrative has also accurately recognized the presence of the phallus as a signifier of desire throughout history. It can be problematic to remain within this narrative, however, as when the phallus dominates our theorizing[14] and obscures other perspectives. By setting up a linear model of development—moving from enmeshed relatedness with the mother toward autonomy and eventual possession of another desired one—the Oedipal narrative is premised in patriarchal complementarity and prohibits a theory of sustainable mutual relatedness.[15] Thus, even with modifications, it can be problematic to remain within the Oedipal narrative as singularly foundational.[16] While the issue is implicitly addressed here, a full discussion of the limits of Oedipal theory, its revisions, and alternatives is beyond the scope of this chapter.

In discussing patriarchy, sociocultural views of women, and feminine and masculine concepts, it must be noted that there is an important and wide range of considerations about what constitutes gender. There are theories oriented around a Freudian frame that tend to be more essentialist and claim some aspect of the physical body as primary in understanding gender.[17] Similarly, archetypal theories reference myths that by and large fall along a gender binary, but are also considered as inner images that can apply to any individual. Alternately, there are theories working from a more postmodernist, constructivist stance, frequently of a relational orientation that focus on gender as context-based.[18] As Harris points out,[19] however, multiplicity of self also applies to gender development, whereby all the vicissitudes of physical bodies, historical, relational, and social contexts interact.

Likewise, reclaiming the subjectivity of those who have been objectified by a dominant culture applies to any minority. Gender problems share many overlaps with racism, including objectification and its overturning. It is my hope that these parallels will be read as a subtext throughout the chapter, even as I focus on women for the sake of specificity. For the purposes of this chapter, I refer to Woman with a capital "W" in reference to the archetypal feminine present in all individuals. But this is deeply tied to women's experiences, with appreciation for the literal physical body and an awareness that language is derived from material reality.[20] We cannot pretend to have a symbolic language of masculine phallus and feminine lack that is divorced from the physical bodies of those about whom we are speaking. To remain in Oedipal terminology, Irigaray suggests, means that women's development "can never be characterized with reference to the female sex itself."[21] Gender is constituted to a significant degree by the physical body, both in terms of the characteristics one embodies, and the social treatment of individuals based on their biology. This is evident in Trump's remark that he grabs women "by the pussy."

The Nasty Woman is thus one who has to reclaim her identity from a dominant other who has attempted to define it for her. Many times definition-by-another manifests in the treatment of women's bodies, as well as in gender stereotypes that don't recognize a wide range of gender possibilities. Certain characteristics like self-defense or assertion of desire are socially constructed as unwomanly, consistent with the early essentialist view of women that emphasized the vagina as naturally receiving. Consciously in some and unconsciously in many is the notion that Woman is passive, empty, and waiting to be defined by the masculine subject.

Active dis-association from patriarchy

The Nasty Woman presents herself because, in alchemical terms that here take their most literal form, "the king must die." "King... refer(s) to the ruling principle of the conscious ego and to the power instinct. At a certain point these must be mortified in order for a new center to emerge," says Edinger.[22] The ruling principle that has become over-inflated—the rule of the father, a.k.a. patriarchy—must die. Interpersonally, destruction is a necessary part of relating because only then can ideas that are safely held about another be challenged by the actual subjectivity of the other. Gilligan and Snider[23] describe interpersonal resistance and protest as efforts to be heard as a differentiated other in relationship, not to leave relationship.

What has been known within the limits of the ego and personal neuroses will sometimes need to be shed in order to grow into deeper knowledge. Destruction is a requirement of growth because oftentimes "the price of self-knowledge will be self loss," the loss of ideas which later experience shows to be one-sided and limited.[24] The Nasty Woman brings a disruption and destruction to existing social structure, akin to destruction of the ego, *for the sake of its enlargement.*

What has been passive and unconscious, a dissociation done to the Nasty Woman by excluding her subjectivity, can become active when she refuses to be complicit. In defense and creation of herself, the Nasty Woman ruptures the patriarchal orientation which includes 1) a dichotomy of dominance and submission, 2) a linear model of development from relatedness to separateness, 3) phallocentrism which defines woman-as-lack, and 4) a demand for empathy at the expense of Woman's own desire.

Firstly, the Nasty Woman cuts off from a dichotomy where Woman is either all-controlling or all-controlled. The feminine has become established as either one of possible extremes, both of which remain fantasied projections inaccessible to true alterity. de Beauvoir identified the image of Woman in history as both "the source of [man's] being and the kingdom he bends to his will."[25] The archetypal creatrix and source of all is re-imaged in every woman, but also controlled in insecure efforts to not be overwhelmed.[26] Dominance, or submission.

A highly successful, wealthy male patient with a narcissistic disposition enacted this complementarity with me and others. Through his career he was able to support his wife and daughters extravagantly, but did not see his wife as an intellectual equal, nor his daughters as interesting or easy to connect with. He harbored a love object who he found intellectually and erotically captivating, and in turn he offered her many lavish gifts. Together he and I had a productive and mutually enjoyable therapeutic relationship, until I realized I was accepting from him a weekly fee that was less than what he paid for his daily lunch. I realized my own complicity in denigrating my professional value, and that we had together enacted a power structure of male success through female helpmates. However, we were unable to work through it, as the patient asked for a further reduction in fee during this time and terminated when it was not granted. It became clear that the walls of dissociation were too firm to be penetrated. Although symptoms of marital distress encouraged him to seek a new relationship to the feminine, he could only sustain commitment to the relationships that reiterated what he already knew and allowed him to maintain a position of dominance.

In psychological theorizing, a linear model of development perpetuates this all-controlling or all-controlled dichotomy, and the Nasty Woman cuts off from such a model. Specifically, I am referring to the separation-individuation trajectory that sees separation from an initial, all-containing symbiosis as the necessary way to achieve maturity. It is outlined in Mahler's theory of child development,[27] and a common, central theme in both Oedipal theory and the Jungian ideal of individuation. For example, in the lineage of Freud and Lacan, Chasseguet-Smirgel[28] articulates father as essential to developing a sense of reality by cutting off from symbiotic tie to the mother: "The original meaning of the word nomos [law in Greek] is 'division,' 'separation.' A fatherless universe where fusion with the mother is possible is a world without law and without separation." In the lineage of Jung, Neumann saw "reality" as developing an ego autonomous from the mother. "When the ego begins to emerge from its identity with the uroboros, and the embryonic connection with the womb ceases, the ego takes up a new attitude to the world."[29] There is always some level of separation that needs to happen, but, as Benjamin[30] points out, separation-individuation theories problematically conceptualize maturity as a linear progression away from relatedness toward individualism.

The other pole which sees Woman to be all-controlled contains the idea that the essence of Woman is her lack, and is dependent upon a phallocentrism which sees the phallus as the only signifier of desire.[31] We are well aware that Freud psychologized the view that woman's identity is rooted in her empty readiness. For the girl according to Freud, "the two wishes—to possess a penis and a child—remain strongly cathected in the unconscious and help to prepare the female creature for her future sexual role."[32] According to Lacan,[33] these are the only ways women can become even temporarily whole. While this idea may not often be expressed so overtly, I see little evidence that psychoanalytic theorizing has deviated from this position. Its original connection to and biased definitions of biological reality cannot be overlooked. Many have criticized such a viewpoint on the basis that it does not allow Woman to know or exist in herself.

Objectification, or denial of Woman's subjectivity, may occur across a variety of roles. In some versions of mothering, the child is the subject whose experience defines her. Benjamin[34] acknowledged that "we have only just begun to think about the mother as a subject in her own right... No psychological theory has adequately articulated the mother's independent existence." For Freud, the pre-Oedipal "boy regards his mother as his own property." That she is property remains a given; what is at stake in the Oedipal conflict is whose property she is. As noted by Atlas-Koch and Kuchuck,[35] the Hebrew word for husband is synonymous with ownership of the wife, and many examples bear this out today.

A further extension from the ideas of woman-as-lack and the developmental demand of separation is the idea of mother as oppressive, refusing to let go of what she holds, a symbiotic, all-containing unity that doesn't allow for differentiation or individuality. This falsely sets up mother as the problem, mother as the engulfing one, lacking consciousness, and castrating the males around her who would otherwise seek independence and differentiation. Yet, if Woman lacks existence for herself, how could she be anything but uroboric, dependent on others to remain inside her to sustain her? If some perpetuate this myth by demanding separation, others do so by passively assuming their identity from who they are for others.

Empathy is the ability to understand and share in the feelings of another, a definition that stems from a one-person psychology of dominance and submission, one person leaving themselves to enter the experience of another. Empathy is the patriarchal mandate of the feminine that requires Woman's unilateral renunciation of her own desire. Novelist Claire Messud argues that the socially-constructed acceptable feminine is "not supposed to be appetitive."[36] Woman is disallowed her appetite in general—whether it be for things physical, emotional, or intellectual—and Messud observes that this construct is reiterated by a cultural expectation that beautiful women are those who are thin (lacking appetite) but curvaceous (available for the appetites of others). Within a patriarchal context, the drives for sex and aggression that are overt in Freud's theory are nevertheless unacceptable for women.

Danger of cutting off and staying separated

We work in a society and theories premised on a linear model of development away from the mother, of woman-as-lack and someone else's object, and see Woman as oppressive when she desires connection yet expect her to empathize with otherness. All of these suppositions need cutting off from. They all negate Woman's identity so implicitly and so thoroughly that they prime us for a violent, hysterical rupture that itself follows the model of separation to achieve individuation.

However, positioning women as the subjects who define men or anyone else as their objects would be no truer a form of alterity than patriarchy has been. Here I must quote Irigaray at length. After an unhealed rupture with Lacan, she argued for mutuality that requires a break from complementarity in *This Sex Which is Not One*: In a reversal within Oedipal theory,

> the question of the woman still cannot be articulated… For what is important is to disconcert the staging of representation according to exclusively masculine parameters, that is, according to a phallocratic order. It is not a matter of toppling that order so as to replace it—that amounts to the same thing in the end - but of disrupting and modifying it, starting from an "outside" that is exempt, in part, from phallocratic law.[37]

Whether subjective experience comes in the form of desire, outrage, or any other form, sometimes the distance of separation has been so hard won that any return to togetherness seems unthinkable, a betrayal of self. Yet, this would be to remain within the structure of doer and done to, a complementarity where only one voice can be heard at a time, perpetuating dissociation at the loss and expense of the other. Just as the one who was bullied becomes the bully, the Nasty Woman who has cut off from others' definitions of her can remain nasty too long, unable to see the other in her cut off state.

The Women's March on Washington and allied sister marches brought light not only to the Nasty Woman, but also to the tension that can come from any single group identifying as the subject. Some women from minority and lower socioeconomic classes vocalized that they continue to be sidelined even as white women gain privilege,[38] and so-called identity politics still operate on subject/object divisions but with a different subject as its center. The Women's March attempted to address these concerns by encouraging inclusiveness of multiple subjectivities, but there is a tension around the extent to which this is possible. This was already a difficulty for second wave feminists: "No sooner had they appropriated subjectivity than they switched roles, now in the position of subject obliged to recognize the identity of the racialized" and, one could add, Queer, "Other."[39] Recognition of multiple subjectivities continues to be a struggle, to the extent that domination and dissociation vie as primary psychological defenses.

Much of contemporary civilization has been built on the objectification of minority classes. This includes "the exchange of women," as Irigaray wrote in *Women on the Market.* "The circulation of women among men is what establishes the operations of society, at least of patriarchal society."[40] Women are not the only ones who have been objectified to sustain civilization according to another's terms. The displacement of Native Americans and widespread slave labor are well-known examples of this dialectical tendency to use some in the service of others. Yet, it is perpetuated today in unequal minority labor practices, over-criminalization of racial minorities, and gentrification (to name but a few examples). It is this dialectical tendency that the Nasty Woman addresses, more than any class in isolation.

With this in mind, we are careful not to simply reverse the hierarchy of domination. When the Nasty Woman defends against misconceptions of the feminine, she runs the risk of remaining dissociated, albeit from characteristics which were formerly accepted. The fluid birth-death-rebirth process involves first dissociation *and then association* between its known parts. It has been said that "death involves renewal through the integration on a higher level of what has been sacrificed. Without that integration, death is murder."[41] The Nasty Woman's gift is not primarily in cutting off, though this is unavoidable. Her ultimate gift is that she clears the way for a new kind of relatedness: mutual recognition that includes the subjectivity of all involved, in conversation with one another.

Examples from mythology and clinical practice

Examples from archetypal, personal, and clinical realms can each add dimension to understanding the Nasty Woman. Together they help us see themes that are eternally present, yet are reified through each new experience and individual choice. Here I explore the Hindu goddess Durga who is an archetypal Nasty Woman par excellence. Her stories help to articulate the relationship between destructiveness and mutual recognition.

Durga cohabitates with Kali, Ishtar, and other dark goddesses in destructive territories. She is typically imaged with eight arms, riding an all-powerful tiger and wielding implements of destruction, including a bow and arrow, trident, sword, mace, chakra, conch shell, and lotus flower. Contradictory to the patriarchal Western mindset, such a goddess is foremost a mother figure. Her maternal nature is one of protection, discernment, and fiercely fighting through evil to defend what is good. Durga is the middle of a triad of divine mother goddesses: she is nestled between Parvati who is nurturing and family-oriented, and Kali who is likened to the rat with unbridled destructiveness. Durga is both loving and destructive, holding the tension of these energies. One of her attributes is that she cuts through illusion to see what is real.

Personally, when I began to feel the unavoidable force of destruction in my life, I realized how appropriate Durga's image is to the story of mutual recognition. Durga—or if you prefer, the energy she personifies—destroyed my marriage and she destroyed me. I became a force of destruction when I could not remain in my marriage, and my own physical and psychic health demanded that I defy the conventional family structure I had. After tearing my husband and children away from the cohesive family they had known, it was easy to identify as the Nasty Woman and all the negativity that comes with such an identity.

In this spirit, I naively set out one evening to approach a temple dedicated to Durga, following the Nasty Woman into the woods. I was in remote mountains after dark, where I knew such a temple existed though I had not been to it before. The path was in complete darkness except for what light was cast by the night stars, and it descended downhill into a tunnel carved out of thick tree cover. In this cold, dark moment I realized that I—my ego, my choices—cannot be identified with destructiveness because of the extent to which I am also susceptible to it. I did not go further that evening but left with an awareness of how the inner and outer are synchronized: I was both destroyer and destroyed. I had also lost the shared safety and pleasure of family as I knew it. But on the other side of a family narrative in which we shared everything and expected to be all resolution for one another, each of us have a greater sense of who we are, and who we are not. Perhaps this is what Louise Bourgeois[42] meant when she said, "I have been to hell and back and let me tell you, it was wonderful." My own version would go something like, "I have been to hell and back, and it was terrible; but let me tell you, life is fuller and possible again because of it."

Stories of Durga are found in various Hindu texts and often revolve around her unique role in destroying demonic forces.[43] Specifically, she is said to defeat Mahisha, the demon king. Mahisha was given a boon by the gods to be invincible, except he had to choose one class of beings to which he was not immune.

He chose Woman, believing this was a loophole and women did not actually possess the ability to kill him. This seemed largely true, and without impediment he gained tremendous power over the earth and gods alike, raping and pillaging everything he could. The gods desperately approached Durga who was steadfast, austere, and repentant. As a faithful and strong woman, they believed she possessed the ability to overcome the demon. When Durga first appeared to the demon, her beauty captivated him, and he wished to possess her as he had many women before her. When she challenged him and asserted her own desire for Shiva instead, he fought back harder to control her, appearing as an immense buffalo who raged at the earth with his horns. Durga knew that the matter was severe, but first she tried to resolve it by offering wise instruction. She spoke openly to the demon to repent, to turn toward virtuousness and a kind of inclusiveness that allowed others to live in harmony. Only when the demon raged against this advice did Durga send forth all forms of female warriors and ultimately defeat him. And although she was encouraged by the gods to pursue this course, she immediately returned to repentance out of distress for having killed even the demon king.

Devotees of Durga do not use her story to justify violence, but they do recognize that certain forms of inclusiveness can obscure the goal of actual recognition. To accept the position of Mahisha with overt love would mean to accept a position of domination. This story shows that without destruction, recognition is impossible, because the narrative of the subject who sees themselves as the center continues to absorb, deflect, and re-define whatever else might be posited.

A clinical example further describes how feminine destructiveness is needed in both individuation and recognition. Steve has come to experience validation of himself through the eyes of another, often in the form of hooking up with women who take him into a more fulfilling experience of himself. However, this fulfillment seems all too fleeting, and he sought therapy in order to have a steadier relationship to himself and more lasting fulfilment with others. For Steve, women at times receive him passively and give him permission to release his libido. Alternately, he feels shame for sexual desire and dependence, and suffers thoughts that he is psychologically ill because of it. Early in psychotherapy with me, he had a dream that considered castration as a possible resolution: "We (the patient and therapist) are in a medical office considering different options for performing castration. A butter knife is selected. The therapist says that the reaction of others is not so much pain, maybe a flinch. We discuss the kind of person this operation is for, and the patient decides it's not for him."

The patient's work continued to demonstrate that the all-controlling castrator was not the Nasty Woman he needed to encounter. Indeed, the castrator would be a reversal of complementarity, and perpetuate unfulfillment.

In his 30s, Steve realized his need to "cut the cord," both in terms of familial dependence and the women he admitted he makes into gods. The following dream appeared: "I am at a pool, where my sister is breastfeeding my 7-year-old nephew. I immediately go over to them and say this has to stop. My 12-year-old niece defends her mom but she doesn't know what she's talking about; I tell her she can talk to me about this when she's [my current age]. I tell my sister and my family, 'our being coddled is 100% related to our still being financially dependent on our parents.' They all don't understand me, and our argument ends the dream." In his own childhood, sharing a family bed was more problematic than extended breastfeeding. Until he was an adolescent, he slept in his parents' bed, "winning" this opportunity by beating his father in rigged games that was then passively accepted by his mother. He lacked a mature other to tell him "no" so that he could experience validation of himself through autonomy, rather than dependence.

In a male patient, we may be especially inclined to identify heroic separation as the goal. In such a view, individuation is a function modeled and mandated by the father. Individuation resulting from separation from the parents is integrated as a developed Oedipus complex. The individual recognizes he cannot remain possessively connected to his own mother but must face the tragedy of separating from her when his father sets this prohibition and limit. In the case of Steve, we could accept such a theory as it stands.

This perspective certainly addresses some aspects of the problem and the cure. Yet, the male choice of a female analyst is also informative. Relationally, there was the experience of having to be the Nasty Woman myself, at times disallowing connection where the patient sought it. A significant theme of our work was destroying the illusion that love is all-inclusive, and that saying no at times is more loving than saying yes. As therapist, I was asked by Steve in different ways to participate in his life outside of the set boundaries (i.e., attending a milestone event in his life). This always appeared to be a conscious effort to find more peace and validation of himself. Admittedly, "no" did not immediately present itself, and I was a ready participant in complying with the patient's dependence and desire for more definition of himself through me, as if his requests were in his best interest and those were the benchmarks of right action. This formula is remarkably similar to the patriarchal one that holds Woman as object and man as experiencing, deciding subject. When I considered my personal reactions and schedule conflicts, "no" came more regularly into the room with Steve, in ways that also proved more useful for him. Concurrent with this transference phenomenon, Steve sought out a version of the feminine that included more limits, and he cultivated an inner image that stepped in to offer the maternal "no." To name this action as belonging to a "phallic mother"[44] also misses the point of female subjectivity by locating feminine experience within a male narrative. Steve sought a Nasty Woman to reiterate boundaries and destroy his tendency to permeate them.

Generally speaking, what constitutes psychoanalytic work is an ethic of openness to otherness, both internal and external. It cultivates an ability to stand in the spaces between self-states, from which one can have dialogue and relatedness. As we break down the walls of dissociation we also break down false hierarchies into multiple subjectivities. In terms of the Nasty Woman, her subjectivity has been excluded from the dominant conscious viewpoint, and her consequent nastiness is the destruction of dissociations walls.

Relational maturity: the nasty woman's child

Out of the assertion of her subjectivity, the Nasty Woman bears a child: relational maturity. Relational maturity requires the presence of all involved as active subjects. This includes the feminine presence that has often been denied under a patriarchal orientation. In the words of Irigaray, "If women are such good mimics, it is because they are not simply resorbed in this function. They also remain elsewhere: another case of the persistence of 'matter,' but also of 'sexual pleasure.'"[45] That is to say, to be truly available as Woman is to have a presence from which to be available. Irigaray identifies that this feminine presence is rooted in two things. The first is "matter," including the material body's desires and limits. The second means of feminine presence is "sexual pleasure." This remains the most forbidden place for women to articulate themselves, though it is also the most necessary, in order not to remain a receptacle for the projections and desires of others. Women's desire has too long been viewed as need for her void to be filled. In the words of contemporary female critical theorists, "desire isn't lack, it's an excess of energy,"[46] and furthermore, "Desire makes us a subject."[47] Integral to mutuality is the realization that while the phallus is a signifier of desire, Woman also is her own subject and experiences desire in all its forms from a place of presence, not absence.

This point has been reiterated specific to psychological theorizing: "self-psychology is misleading when it understands the mother's recognition of the child's feelings and accomplishments as maternal mirroring. The mother cannot (and should not) be a mirror; she must not merely reflect back what the child asserts; she must embody something of the not-me; she must be an independent other who responds in her different way."[48]

When we don't see woman as lack, we can acknowledge what is present. In a small conference with archetypal psychologist James Hillman (pers. comm.), I asked him a question which I no longer remember, but his answer to me was this: "There are more ways to be a woman than the Virgin Mary." I was coincidentally in the early months of pregnancy with my first child, not yet visible to others but already marking the ways body is essential in helping to map identity. Contrary to existing theory, pregnancy and the physical acts of mothering have allowed me to recognize the feminine as active. Indeed, even some of Freud's contemporaries criticized his theory for being phallocentric and worked toward a theory of "primary rather than compensatory femininity."[49] Horney is most notable among these. Her work on womb envy recognized that women, too, possess something which men lack and desire.[50] Yet, the active presence of woman's identity remains dissociated in much of contemporary theory and culture.

The Nasty Woman is in the archetypal territory of Durga, Ereshkigal, Isis, Demeter/Persephone, as well as Black Madonna figures that take us to an earthy dark feminine and to the underworld. The underworld is a place of destruction, but through destruction, renewal. As elaborated in the image of Durga, this feminine is strong, discerning, cutting even. The Nasty Woman first appears as cold and dark when we expect feminine presence to bend to our own will instead. She appears as unproductive because she is undesirable and destructive to our conscious will, but she shows herself to enhance the relational capacity of all affected by her.

This is a call to take seriously that the Nasty Woman is not just one kind of person in society from whom we would like to dissociate, but she is in every woman attempting to speak her subjectivity and difference. Such a shift takes us to a place where we can relate with maturity, equality, and mutuality. This describes the accomplishment of what Winnicott termed object usage,[51] the ability to see others as real, changeable, and free to connect or disagree at any moment. It also includes what Benjamin[52] describes as the intersubjective Third, where every self is also the other's Other, and acknowledgement of the other means responsiveness and change happen often. For this to take place, the total capacity of the Nasty Woman must lodge itself in the hearts of the feminine in all stages—mother, lover, daughter, professional, old woman. Likewise, the Nasty Woman and her refusal to comply with the desires of others as a matter of course must be internalized by those who do not identify as women for mature relationships to take place between them.

Conclusion

In conclusion, it is interesting to note that Freud's conception of the resolution of the Oedipus complex was not that it "passed," or "dissolved," as it came to be translated, but that it was "destroyed."[53] Loewald observed that the German word Freud used, Untergang, "literally means a going under, going down. It is used for the sun's going down in the evening (Sonnenuntergang) as well as for the destruction of the world (Weltuntergang)." Freud[54] allowed that the Oedipal complex could be overcome naturally, either by witnessing the precondition of the mother's so-called castration, or the implicit victory and prohibition by the father. In either case, destructiveness by the mother herself was not considered.

If instead we take cues from Freud's strong language emphasizing destruction when it comes to the development of mature relational capacities, and from mythic examples which typically involve a dark feminine as the harbinger of destruction and new birth, relational maturity is born not by separating from the totality of Woman but by the separateness that the Nasty Woman herself demands. In this sense, the mother destroys the Oedipal fantasy because she, like the father, asserts her subjectivity and difference as part of being in relationship.

On this foundation, both independence and relatedness look different than pervasive models of separation-individuation and complementarity suggest. Independence occurs within the context of relatedness, not above it.

The Nasty Woman thus offers a different kind of "no." Recall Chasseguet-Smirgel's observation that no comes from the Greek word *nomos* which means separation.[55] In French, Lacan was able to connect no to the symbolic order, law, and prohibition of the father in the word *nom* (Name) because it sounds identical to *non* (No), further establishing the link between language and separation.[56] But as Carol Gilligan observed, also by way of a spoken pun in English, saying *"no"* is made possible because of what one does *know.* [57]

The Nasty Woman shows us that separation is not only a masculine function, but that this feminine form of separation enhances recognition of each individual. Connection to others is not based in a passive sense of compliance, or a dominant definition of the other, but of you-and-I. This is consistent with theories that posit mutual recognition of multiple subjectivities as the goal, but we have not come to realize enough the place that destructiveness has in this effort. I am reminded of this fact when patients ask me to be "more harsh," destroying existing notions of the self and longing for recognition by asking to be told more of what I think or what I desire for them. In these moments no one is asking to be dominated, but for the presence of you to speak deeply to the presence of I in that place where we meet together.

As we have witnessed in the political and social climate where the Nasty Woman has been named, defamed, silenced, and risen up to unavoidable proportions, complementary objectification of others still exists fiercely. Yet, the age of dissociating woman as "not-me," or not a subject, is waning. The Nasty Woman rises up to claim her subjectivity, and thus signals a turn to recognition. However, this is not meant to be a recognition of herself as the solitary subject, or at the cost of the ultimate destruction of the other. We are desperately in need of listening to this voice, in all her destructiveness, to resolve the longstanding Oedipal model of domination. By asserting her difference, the Nasty Woman ushers us into a dialogue of mutual recognition and relational maturity.

Notes

1 Simone de Beauvoir, *The Second Sex,* tran. Constance Borde and Sheila Malovany-Chevallier (New York: Vintage Books, 2011), 17.
2 Harry Stack Sullivan, *The Interpersonal Theory of Psychiatry* (New York: W.W. Norton & Company, 1953).
3 Philip Bomberg, *Awakening the Dreamer: Clinical Journeys* (New York: Routledge, 2006).
4 Jessica Benjamin, *The Bonds of Love* (New York: Pantheon, 1988), 48.
5 Philip Bromberg, "Standing in the Spaces: The Multiplicity of Self and the Psychoanalytic Relationship," *Contemporary Psychoanalysis,* no. 32 (1996): 59–535.

6 Eugene Taylor, *Shadow Culture: Psychology and Spirituality in America* (Washington, D. C.: Counterpoint, 1999).

7 R. Noll, "Multiple Personality, Dissociation, and C.G. Jung's Complex Theory," *Journal of Analytical Psychology* 4, no. 34 (1989): 353–370; Carl Gustav Jung, "A Review of the Complex Theory," in *The Structure and Dynamics of the Psyche*, trans. Gerhard Adler and R.F.C. Hull (Princeton: Princeton University Press, 1970), 92–104.

8 Philip Bromberg, "Standing in the Spaces: The Multiplicity of Self and the Psycho-analytic Relationship," *Contemporary Psychoanalysis*, no. 32 (1996): 59–535; Irwin Hirsch, "The Widening of the Concept of Dissociation," *Journal of American Academy of Psychoanalysis* 4, no. 25 (1997): 603–615; Donnel Stern, *Unformulated Experience: From Dissociation to Imagination in Psychoanalysis* (Hillsdale: The Analytic Press, 1997); Jodi Messler Davies, "Love in the Afternoon: A Relational Reconsideration of Desire and Dread in the Countertransference," *Psychoanalytic Dialogues*, no. 4 (1994): 153–170; Adrienne Harris, "Gender in Linear and Non-Linear History," *Journal of the American Psychoanalytic Association* 4, no. 53 (2005): 1079–1095.

9 Donnel Stern, *Unformulated Experience: From Dissociation to Imagination in Psychoanalysis* (Hillsdale: The Analytic Press, 1997); "The Fusion of Horizons: Dissociation, Enactment, and Understanding," *Psychoanalytic Dialogues*, no. 13 (2003): 843–873.

10 Philip Bromberg, "Standing in the Spaces: The Multiplicity of Self and the Psycho-analytic Relationship," *Contemporary Psychoanalysis*, no. 32 (1996): 59–535.

11 Jessica Benjamin, *The Bonds of Love* (New York: Pantheon, 1988).

12 Sigmund Freud, "The Dissolution of the Oedipus Complex," in *The Standard Edition of the Complete Psychological Works of Sigmund Freud, Vol. XIX (1923–1925): The Ego and the Id and Other Works* (London: Hogarth Press, 1961), 171–180.

13 Janine Chasseguet-Smirgel, "From the Archaic Matrix of the Oedipus Complex to the Fully Developed Oedipus Complex - Theoretical Perspective in Relation to Clinical Experience and Technique," *Psychoanalytic Quarterly*, no. 57 (1988): 505–527; Rosemary Balsam, "Where Has Oedipus Gone? A Turn of the Century Contempla-tion," *Psychoanalytic Inquiry* 6, no. 30 (2010): 511–516.

14 Jane Gallop, "Of Phallic Proportions: Lacanian Conceit," *Psychoanalysis and Con-temporary Thought* 2, no. 4 (1981): 251–273.

15 Jessica Benjamin, *The Bonds of Love* (New York: Pantheon, 1988).

16 Carol Gilligan and Naomi Snider, "The Loss of Pleasure, or Why We Are Still Talk-ing About Oedipus," *Contemporary Psychoanalysis* 2, no. 53 (2017): 173–195.

17 Jacques Lacan, *The Seminar of Jacques Lacan: Feminine Sexuality, The Limits of Love and Knowledge, 1972–1973*, trans. Bruce Fink and ed. Jacques-Alain Miller (New York: W. W. Norton & Co., 1999); Luce Irigaray, *This Sex Which is Not One* (Ithaca: Cornell University Press, 1985); Juliet Mitchell, "Commentary on 'Deconstructing Difference: Gender, Splitting, and Transitional Space,'" *Psychoanalytic Dialogues* 3, no 1 (1991): 353–357; Doris Bernstein, "The Female Superego: A Different Perspective," *Interna-tional Journal of Psycho-Analysis*, no. 64 (1983): 187–201; Janine Chasseguet-Smirgel, "From the Archaic Matrix of the Oedipus Complex to the Fully Developed Oedipus Complex - Theoretical Perspective in Relation to Clinical Experience and Techni-que," *Psychoanalytic Quarterly*, no. 57 (1988): 505–527; Rosemary Balsam, "Where Has Oedipus Gone? A Turn of the Century Contemplation," *Psychoanalytic Inquiry* 6, no. 30 (2010): 511–516.

18 Muriel Dimen, "Deconstructing Difference: Gender, Splitting, and Transitional Space," *Psychoanalytic Dialogues* 3, no. 1 (1991): 335–352; Jessica Benjamin, "Sameness and Difference: Toward an 'Overinclusive' Model of Gender Development," *Psycho-analytic Inquiry* 1, no. 15 (1995): 125–142; Jessica Benjamin, "In Defense of Gender Ambiguity," *Gender and Psychoanalysis* 1, no. 1 (1996): 27–43; Adrienne Harris, "Gender in Linear and Non-Linear History," *Journal of the American Psychoanalytic Association* 4, no. 53 (2005): 1079–1095; Nancy Chodorow, *The Reproduction of*

Mothering: Psychoanalysis and the Sociology of Gender (Oakland: University of California Press, 1979).

19 Adrienne Harris, "Gender in Linear and Non-Linear History," *Journal of the American Psychoanalytic Association* 4, no. 53 (2005): 1079–1095.

20 David Abram, *The Spell of the Sensuous: Perception and Language in a More-Than-Human World* (New York: Random House, 1996), 100.

21 Luce Irigaray, *This Sex Which is Not One* (Ithaca: Cornell University Press, 1985), 69.

22 Edward Edinger, *Anatomy of the Psyche: Alchemical Symbolism in Psychotherapy* (Chicago: Open Court, 1985), 151.

23 Carol Gilligan and Naomi Snider, "The Loss of Pleasure, or Why We Are Still Talking About Oedipus," *Contemporary Psychoanalysis* 2, no. 53 (2017): 173–195.

24 Judith Butler, "Longing for Recognition: Commentary on the Work of Jessica Benjamin," *Studies in Gender and Sexuality* 3, no. 1 (2000): 286.

25 Simone de Beauvoir, *The Second Sex,* trans. Constance Borde and Sheila Malovany-Chevallier (New York: Vintage Books, 2011), 163.

26 Jan Abram, *The Language of Winnicott: A Dictionary of Winnicott's Use of Words* (London: Karnac Books, 2007).

27 Margaret Mahler, "Symbiosis and Individuation: The Psychological Birth of the Human Infant," *Psychoanalytic Study of the Child,* no. 29 (1974): 89–106.

28 Janine Chasseguet-Smirgel, "From the Archaic Matrix of the Oedipus Complex to the Fully Developed Oedipus Complex - Theoretical Perspective in Relation to Clinical Experience and Technique," *Psychoanalytic Quarterly,* no. 57 (1988): 513.

29 Erich Neumann, *The Origins and History of Consciousness* (Princeton: Princeton University Press, 1954), 39.

30 Jessica Benjamin, *The Bonds of Love* (New York: Pantheon, 1988).

31 Jane Gallop, "Of Phallic Proportions: Lacanian Conceit," *Psychoanalysis and Contemporary Thought* 2, no. 4 (1981): 251–273.

32 Sigmund Freud, "The Dissolution of the Oedipus Complex," in *The Standard Edition of the Complete Psychological Works of Sigmund Freud, Vol. XIX (1923–1925): The Ego and the Id and Other Works,* 171–180. (London: Hogarth Press, 1961), 179.

33 Jacques Lacan, *The Seminar of Jacques Lacan: Feminine Sexuality, The Limits of Love and Knowledge, 1972–1973,* trans. Bruce Fink and ed. Jacques-Alain Miller (New York: W. W. Norton & Co., 1999).

34 Jessica Benjamin, *The Bonds of Love* (New York: Pantheon, 1988), 23.

35 Galit Atlas-Koch and Steven Kuchuck, "To Have and To Hold: Psychoanalytic Dialogues on the Desire to Own," *Psychoanalytic Dialogues* 1, no. 22 (2012): 93–105.

36 Ruth Franklin, "The Hunger Artist," *The New York Times Magazine,* August 13, 2017: 29.

37 Luce Irigaray, *This Sex Which is Not One* (Ithaca: Cornell University Press, 1985), 68.

38 Karen Grigsby Bates, "Race and Feminism: Women's March Recalls the Touchy History," *NPR,* January 21, 2017, http://www.npr.org/sections/codeswitch/2017/01/21/510859909/race-and-feminism-womens-march-recalls-the-touchy-history.

39 Jessica Benjamin, *Beyond Doer and Done To: Recognition Theory, Intersubjectivity and the Third* (New York: Routledge, 2018), 19.

40 Luce Irigaray, *This Sex Which is Not One* (Ithaca: Cornell University Press, 1985), 184.

41 Marion Woodman, *Leaving My Father's House: A Journey to Conscious Femininity* (Boston: Shambhala, 1992), 113.

42 Louise Bourgeois, *I Have Been to Hell and Back,* ed. Iris Muller-Westermann (Ostfildern: Hatje Cantz Verlag, 2015).

43 Krishna Dharma, *Beauty, Power, and Grace: The Book of Hindu Goddesses* (New York: Simon & Schuster, 2014); *Devi Mahtatmyam,* trans. Thirugnanam (Internet Archive, 2012), https://archive.org/stream/DeviMahatmyamEnglishTransiteration/Devi%20Mahatmyam%20English%20Transliteration_djvu.txt.

44 Melanie Klein, "The Oedipus Complex in the Light of Early Anxieties," *International Journal of Psycho-Analysis*, no. 26 (1945): 32.

45 Luce Irigaray, *This Sex Which is Not One* (Ithaca: Cornell University Press, 1985), 76.

46 Chris Kraus, *I Love Dick* (Los Angeles: Semiotext(e), 2006), 3024.

47 Jessica Benjamin, *Beyond Doer and Done To: Recognition Theory, Intersubjectivity and the Third* (New York: Routledge, 2018), 10.

48 Jessica Benjamin, *The Bonds of Love* (New York: Pantheon, 1988), 24.

49 Martha Feldman Herman, "Depression and Women: Theories and Research," *Journal of American Academy of Psychoanalysis* 4, no. 11 (1983): 495.

50 Karen Horney, "The Flight from Womanhood: The Masculinity-Complex in Women, as Viewed by Men and by Women," *International Journal of Psycho-Analysis*, no. 7 (1926): 330.

51 Donald W. Winnicott, "The Use of an Object," *International Journal of Psycho-Analysis*, no. 50 (1969): 711–716.

52 Jessica Benjamin, *Beyond Doer and Done To: Recognition Theory, Intersubjectivity and the Third* (New York: Routledge, 2018).

53 Hans Loewald, "The Waning of the Oedipus Complex," *Journal of the American Psychoanalytic Association*, no. 27 (1979): 752.

54 Sigmund Freud, "The Dissolution of the Oedipus Complex," in *The Standard Edition of the Complete Psychological Works of Sigmund Freud, Vol. XIX (1923–1925): The Ego and the Id and Other Works*, 171–180 (London: Hogarth Press, 1961).

55 Janine Chasseguet-Smirgel, "From the Archaic Matrix of the Oedipus Complex to the Fully Developed Oedipus Complex - Theoretical Perspective in Relation to Clinical Experience and Technique," *Psychoanalytic Quarterly*, no. 57 (1988): 513.

56 Emily Zakin, *The Stanford Encyclopedia of Philosophy*, Summer 2011 Edition, s.v. "Psychoanalytic Feminism," https://plato.stanford.edu/archives/sum2011/entries/feminism-psychoanalysis/.

57 Carol Gilligan, *The Birth of Pleasure: A New Map of Love* (New York: Vintage Books, 2003), 25.

References

Abram, David. *The Spell of the Sensuous: Perception and Language in a More-Than-Human World*. New York: Random House, 1996.

Abram, Jan. *The Language of Winnicott: A Dictionary of Winnicott's Use of Words*. London: Karnac Books, 2007.

Atlas-Koch, Galit and Kuchuck, Steven. "To Have and To Hold: Psychoanalytic Dialogues on the Desire to Own." *Psychoanalytic Dialogues* 1, no. 22(2012): 93–105.

Balsam, Rosemary. "Where Has Oedipus Gone? A Turn of the Century Contemplation." *Psychoanalytic Inquiry* 6, no. 30(2010): 511–516.

Bates, Karen Grigsby. "Race and Feminism: Women's March Recalls the Touchy History." *NPR*, January 21, 2017. http://www.npr.org/sections/codeswitch/2017/01/21/510859909/race-and-feminism-womens-march-recalls-the-touchy-history,

Benjamin, Jessica. *The Bonds of Love*. New York: Pantheon, 1988.

Benjamin, Jessica. "Sameness and Difference: Toward an 'Overinclusive' Model of Gender Development." *Psychoanalytic Inquiry* 1, no. 15(1995): 125–142.

Benjamin, Jessica. "In Defense of Gender Ambiguity." *Gender and Psychoanalysis* 1, no. 1 (1996): 27–43.

Benjamin, Jessica. *Beyond Doer and Done To: Recognition Theory, Intersubjectivity and the Third*. New York: Routledge, 2018.

Bernstein, Doris. "The Female Superego: A Different Perspective." *International Journal of Psycho-Analysis*, no. 64(1983): 187–201.

Bourgeois, Louise. *I Have Been to Hell and Back*. Edited by Iris Muller-Westermann. Ostfildern: Hatje Cantz Verlag, 2015.

Bromberg, Philip. "Standing in the Spaces: The Multiplicity of Self and the Psychoanalytic Relationship." *Contemporary Psychoanalysis* no. 32(1996): 59–535.

Bromberg, Philip. *Awakening the Dreamer: Clinical Journeys*. New York: Routledge, 2006.

Butler, Judith. "Longing for Recognition: Commentary on the Work of Jessica Benjamin." *Studies in Gender and Sexuality* 3, no. 1(2000): 271–290.

Chasseguet-Smirgel, Janine. "From the Archaic Matrix of the Oedipus Complex to the Fully Developed Oedipus Complex—Theoretical Perspective in Relation to Clinical Experience and Technique." *Psychoanalytic Quarterly*, no. 57(1988): 505–527.

Chodorow, Nancy. *The Reproduction of Mothering: Psychoanalysis and the Sociology of Gender*. Oakland: University of California Press, 1979.

Davies, Jodi Messler. "Love in the Afternoon: A Relational Reconsideration of Desire and Dread in the Countertransference." *Psychoanalytic Dialogues*, no. 4(1994): 153–170.

De Beauvoir, Simone. *The Second Sex*. Translated by Constance Borde and Sheila Malovany-Chevallier. New York: Vintage Books, 2011 (Originally published 1949).

Devi, Mahtatmyam. Transliteration by Thirugnanam. Internet Archive, 2012. https://a rchive.org/stream/DeviMahatmyamEnglishTransiteration/Devi%20Mahatmyam%20Eng lish%20Transliteration_djvu.txt

Dharma, Krishna. *Beauty, Power, and Grace: The Book of Hindu Goddesses*. New York: Simon & Schuster, 2014.

Dimen, Muriel. "Deconstructing Difference: Gender, Splitting, and Transitional Space." *Psychoanalytic Dialogues* 3, no. 1(1991): 335–352.

Edinger, Edward. *Anatomy of the Psyche: Alchemical Symbolism in Psychotherapy*. Chicago: Open Court, 1985.

Franklin, Ruth. "The Hunger Artist." *The New York Times Magazine*, August 13, 2017.

Freud, Sigmund. "The Dissolution of the Oedipus Complex." In *The Standard Edition of the Complete Psychological Works of Sigmund Freud, Vol. XIX (1923–1925): The Ego and the Id and Other Works*, 171–180. London: Hogarth Press, 1961.

Gallop, Jane. "Of Phallic Proportions: Lacanian Conceit." *Psychoanalysis and Contemporary Thought* 2, no. 4(1981): 251–273.

Gilligan, Carol. *The Birth of Pleasure: A New Map of Love*. New York: Vintage Books, 2003.

Gilligan, Carol and Naomi Snider. "The Loss of Pleasure, or Why We Are Still Talking About Oedipus." *Contemporary Psychoanalysis* 2, no. 53(2017): 173–195.

Harris, Adrienne. "Gender in Linear and Non-Linear History." *Journal of the American Psychoanalytic Association* 4, no. 53(2005): 1079–1095.

Herman, Martha Feldman. "Depression and Women: Theories and Research." *Journal of American Academy of Psychoanalysis* 4, no. 11(1983): 493–512.

Hirsch, Irwin. "The Widening of the Concept of Dissociation." *Journal of American Academy of Psychoanalysis* 4, no. 25(1997): 603–615.

Horney, Karen. "The Flight from Womanhood: The Masculinity-Complex in Women, as Viewed by Men and by Women." *International Journal of Psycho-Analysis*, no. 7(1926): 324–339.

Irigaray, Luce. *This Sex Which is Not One*. Ithaca: Cornell University Press, 1985.

Jung, Carl Gustav. "A Review of the Complex Theory." In *The Structure and Dynamics of the Psyche*, translated by Gerhard Adler and R.F.C. Hull, 92–104. Princeton: Princeton University Press, 1970 (Originally published in 1948).

Klein, Melanie. "The Oedipus Complex in the Light of Early Anxieties." *International Journal of Psycho-Analysis*, no. 26(1945): 11–33.

Kraus, Chris. *I Love Dick*. Los Angeles: Semiotext(e), 2006.

Lacan, Jacques. *The Seminar of Jacques Lacan: Feminine Sexuality, The Limits of Love and Knowledge, 1972–1973*. Translated by Bruce Fink and edited by Jacques-Alain Miller. New York: W.W. Norton & Co., 1999.

Loewald, Hans. "The Waning of the Oedipus Complex." *Journal of the American Psychoanalytic Association*, no. 27(1979): 751–775.

Mahler, Margaret. "Symbiosis and Individuation: The Psychological Birth of the Human Infant." *Psychoanalytic Study of the Child*, no. 29(1974): 89–106.

Mitchell, Juliet. "Commentary on 'Deconstructing Difference: Gender, Splitting, and Transitional Space'." *Psychoanalytic Dialogues* 3, no 1(1991): 353–357.

Neumann, Erich. *The Origins and History of Consciousness*. Princeton: Princeton University Press, 1954.

Noll, R. "Multiple Personality, Dissociation, and C.G. Jung's Complex Theory." *Journal of Analytical Psychology* 4, no. 34(1989): 353–370.

Stern, Donnel. *Unformulated Experience: From Dissociation to Imagination in Psychoanalysis*. Hillsdale: The Analytic Press, 1997.

Stern, Donnel. "The Fusion of Horizons: Dissociation, Enactment, and Understanding." *Psychoanalytic Dialogues*, no. 13(2003): 843–873.

Sullivan, Harry Stack. *The Interpersonal Theory of Psychiatry*. New York: W.W. Norton & Company, 1953.

Taylor, Eugene. *Shadow Culture: Psychology and Spirituality in America*. Washington, D.C.: Counterpoint, 1999.

Winnicott, Donald W. "The Use of an Object." *International Journal of Psycho-Analysis*, no. 50(1969): 711–716.

Woodman, Marion. *Leaving My Father's House: A Journey to Conscious Femininity*. Boston: Shambhala, 1992.

Zakin, Emily. *The Stanford Encyclopedia of Philosophy*, Summer2011 Edition, s.v. "Psychoanalytic Feminism." https://plato.stanford.edu/archives/sum2011/entries/feminism-psychoanalysis/.

8

ANOTHER VOICE FROM RADICAL ETHICS

Denmark's Knud Løgstrup

Donna M. Orange

What may I do? What must I do? What must I never do? And why or why not? Ethics—usually taught as a calculus of justice or risk and reward, in the rationalistic, individualistic, and thoroughly Western voices of Kant and the utilitarians—claims an indispensable place in ordinary human life, whatever that may be. Promises, contracts, even medical triage. In a distinctly secondary place, we have descriptive ethics, from Aristotle to Paul Woodruff,[2] teaching us to ask what makes a human character good, and what in human life is worth pursuing. Intuition ethics, with a long British history and now resurrected in social psychologist Jonathan Haidt's *The Righteous Mind*,[3] explains why people hold moral positions for which they can give no grounds except that they feel so convinced. Some behaviors evoke disgust and extreme disapproval, even when we cannot explain why. Arguably, however, we once again live in times where all these normal ethics fail us. Radical ethics—our topic here—attempts to meet the challenges of what Hannah Arendt described as the "dark times;" those times, no, rather, *these times* when everything is at stake. Times when, for example, human life has no value whatever to our systems of prejudice, powerful economic forces, or ecological destructiveness. Radical ethics, as the ancient prophets knew, orients everyday life but becomes crucial in emergencies.

And yet, the voices of radical ethics sound strange. Can one be both a philosopher and a prophet? Most philosophers would immediately say no, and I think most prophets would say no, perhaps more slowly. Many of us still wonder about such questions. Though we may have learned the relational ethic of Martin Buber long ago, many of us know a truly radical ethical voice primarily or only in the work of phenomenologist and Talmudist Emmanuel Levinas. Thanks to his fellow survivor of totalitarianism and liquid modernity theorist Zygmunt Bauman (lost in 2017 after a prolific and challenging old age), as well as to my

Levinas teacher Simon Critchley,[4] I have now been discovering a second border-crosser who often upset rigorous disciplinarians in theology and philosophy both: the Danish Lutheran philosopher of ethics Knud Ejler Løgstrup.

Bauman tells[5] of his mid-1980s sabbatical in Newfoundland before he wrote *Postmodern Ethics*:[6] "Ethical philosophy of the modern era," he believed, "could not but reflect the legislative and order-building ambition, the defining trait of modernity."[7] Searching the library shelves, having previously found only Emmanuel Levinas to challenge traditional rationalistic ethics, he had nearly given up when he came upon a probably unread copy of Løgstrup's *The Ethical Demand* in English translation, where, he recounts, he found his lost time compensated many times over. Now he could counter the calculus of philosophers like Stephen Toulmin's so-called moral person. For both Bauman and Løgstrup, this righteous fellow was a "dreadful person" who would return John's book just because everyone must return what is borrowed. This "moral person," a good Kantian universalizer, "cares not two pins about John but is merely concerned with his own fidelity to his promises so that the social order may be preserved."[8]

Perhaps the most important Danish philosopher since Kierkegaard and born in 1905, Løgstrup lived through the Nazi occupation of Denmark, taught philosophy and theology at the University of Aarhus, and died in 1981. His magnum opus, translated into English as *The Ethical Demand*, [9] claims that the impossible command to love one's neighbor, as heard in Christianity, need not be linked to institutional religion or dogma but instead must be understood humanly as *silent, radical, one-sided*, and *impossible*. He believed that the basic phenomenological fact of human trust in each other, absent abuse of this trust, means that our lives come to us as a gift and that we have a fundamental duty to take care of each other.

> The other person must to such a degree be dependent upon me that what I do and say in the relationship between us—I alone and nobody else, here and now and not at some other time or in some other manner—is of decisive importance. If my relation to the other person is the place where my relation to God is determined, then it must at the same time be the place where that person's existence is so totally at stake that to fail him is to fail him irreparably.[10]

Immediately we hear an unusual voice: clear, straightforward, uncompromising, without philosophical or theological jargon. And yet, this clarity carries an implicated[11] message. Let us look more closely.

He called the ethical demand silent because it comes to us without words in two senses. Unspoken but implicit in all conversation, the other's dependence on me means I must not mistreat or abandon this raw vulnerability. "Regardless of how varied the communication between persons may be," he wrote, "it always involves the risk of one person daring to lay himself or herself open to the other in the hope of a response."[12] "There is self-surrender in all forms of communication."[13] Our vulnerability to the other generates pre-emptive shame, keeping the ethical demand silent: "It must at all costs never become apparent to the other person, and preferably not even to ourselves, that it is a matter of disappointed expectation, because though we have been exposed we are at pains not to admit it. We would much rather admit blemishes and weaknesses, mistakes and stupidities than admit to our having laid ourselves open."[14] The silent demand, though it commands response, does not specify its content and leaves each of us to work that out. Like the humanitarians to whom nurse-educator Jean Watson[15] recommends both Løgstrup and Levinas, the recipient of the demand must find its content in the context. An ethical response, one that takes care of the vulnerability of the other, differs depending on the age of the child, the illness and capacities of the patient, the resources of the surrounding world, and the precarity Judith Butler's recent work[16] foregrounds. The demand remains silent on its content, but does not permit or exonerate bystanding. Racial vulnerabilities, for example, concretize the precarity to which Butler refers, to which prophetic figures like Martin Luther King, Jr. have spoken out the summons. Bystanders like King's "white moderate" in *The Letter from the Birmingham Jail* reject the ethical demand, as do the perpetrators of actual violence.[17]

Though the ethical demand remains silent and pervasively implicit, Løgstrup insists on its radicality, not in words and actions but in the demand itself. This ethics requires that what I do and say in relation to the other be done unselfishly, for the sake of the other:

> The demand, precisely because it is unspoken, is radical. This is true even though the thing to be done in any particular situation may be very insignificant. Why is this? Because the person confronted by the unspoken demand must him or herself determine how he or she is to take care of the other person's life. If what he or she does is to result in something of real value to the other person, he or she must think and act unselfishly...[18]

The radicality of the demand consists, further, in that it asks me to take care of the other person's life not only when to do so strengthens me but also when it is very unpleasant, because it intrudes disturbingly into my own existence. And this is not all. Even in distrust the other person is still delivered over into my hands. Even my enemy is to a large degree dependent upon me and upon the manner in which I respond to him or her.[19]

Finally, he concludes, as if he had studied Levinas on the ethical constitution of subjectivity: "...the demand has the effect of making the person to whom the demand is directed a singular person. Ethically speaking the demand isolates him or her."[20] I respond, therefore I am. Løgstrup leaves his inversion of the Cartesian and Kantian versions of subjectivity to speak for itself. Nor has he subscribed to Husserlian intentionality, where the knower points to the known. The ethical demand's directionality comes from the other to me, putting me on the spot. But neither does he become a Kierkegaardian, seeking his own ethical purity. Instead, each of us is vulnerably exposed by the demand that the other's need creates. We cannot hide.

He notes that we are not required to "turn ourselves inside out...to abandon all spiritual reticence."[21] Rather, we must protect the life of the other who has been delivered over into our hands. Løgstrup cautions that our responsibility for the other does not mean taking over the responsibility for the other's own responsibilities. He further cautions that mistaking radical responsibility for limitlessness can easily lead us to encroach on the other in the name of taking care. The radicality of the demand may require us to do less-than-radical actions.

The demand is, thirdly, one-sided, because it can claim nothing in return. If, as Løgstrup took as axiomatic, my life is a gift, I have nothing to which I am entitled. I possess nothing that I have not received and cannot, as he said, make counter demands.

> A person is a debtor not because he or she has committed some wrong but simply because he or she exists and has received his or her life as a gift. The demand that he or she take care of the other person's life is rooted in the very fact of his or her indebtedness for all the different potentialities he or she has him or herself received: intelligence, speech, love, and many others.[22]

Some will object, Løgstrup knew, to characterizing life as a gift, especially in the face of suffering and death, loss and despair. But, he concludes, "the thing that makes us dispute that life is a gift is not death or suffering, it is our own will to be worshiped and feel our own power."[23] He notes that suffering becomes bearable only if others support life as gift. I am reminded of Levinas's description in *Totality and Infinity* [24] of the non-demanding caress.

One-sidedness, the demand's third trait, shows up most clearly when the other feels less like a gift and more like a nuisance:

> It is when we regard him or her as something entirely other than a gift because he or she is a bother and an inconvenience to us. The demand that we nevertheless take care of his or her life is therefore directed to us on the presupposition that our own life has been given to us as a gift...Through the demand we are...asked whether we intend to make ourselves masters of our own life to the point of deciding for ourselves who shall and who shall not be a part of it, or whether we will accept our life as a gift in order to use it for taking care of the other person's life.[25]

So the question of reciprocity, what does the other owe to me, receives the same answer from Løgstrup as from Levinas: that is his affair.[26] My only concern is that the other comes first. The common or divergent sources of their convictions on this one-sidedness or asymmetry would make a larger study than I can undertake here. Both equally opposed any social contract ethics based on reciprocity or mutual recognition.

And last, the demand is impossible or unfulfillable, because it so seems to contradict our acquired selfishness. The demand is further impossible because we can never know whether we have truly acted unselfishly. The demand does not tell us *how* we are to take care of the other—sometimes the other would seem to prefer to be left in the rubble—but that we must take care. Nor can we know if we have done enough. Løgstrup acknowledges that the demand sometimes involves us in knotty problems of thinking we know better, like a parent, what is good for the other, but insists that these problems cannot allow us to become bystanders.

The Good Samaritan is Løgtrup's model. The Samaritan has no time to consider what his duty may be in this case—then Løgstrup would name him a "Kantian Samaritan," or whether the stranger left for dead is Jewish or Samaritan like him. Thus Løgstrup's reading of this story offers no specific guidance for us who face devastated refugees or inherit racial injustice from which we profit and walk by, like those in the story who did not respond. The ethical demand does not prescribe what exactly we who observe and live with injustice should do; it requires that we respond and leaves us all the problems of practical wisdom.[27] The needs are infinite and we are not. We thus live divided between the demand and our possibilities.

Though his emphasis on trust could seem to place Løgstrup among the promise-keeping Kantians, his ethics utterly transcends a calculus of what we owe to each other based on any kind of social contract. He described instead a radical vulnerability into which we are born, and in which we live. Trust, he wrote, "is essential to every conversation. In conversation as such we deliver ourselves over into the hand of another."[28] He continues:

> What happens is that simply in addressing the other, irrespective of the importance of the content of what we say, a certain note is struck through which we, as it were, step out of ourselves in order to exist in the speech relationship. For this reason the point of the demand—though unarticulated—is that the speaker is accepted as the note struck by the speaker's address is accepted. For a person inadvertently or even intentionally not to hear the note in what we say, therefore, means that it is we ourselves who are being ignored, provided it is we ourselves who dared to make the overture. That all speech takes place in such fundamental trust is evident in the fact that the most casual comment takes on a false note if one believes that it is not accepted in the sense that it is intended.[29]

Parenthetically, we might note that misunderstandings and ruptures, therapeutic and in intimate relationships, occur when the other feels some important nuance unheard, and trust breached. The silent demand is to protect trust, the pre-condition for everything.

Løgstrup's ethical philosophy, like that of Emmanuel Levinas with whom he begs to be compared, mostly emerged from his reflections on the behavior of bystanders and of courageous people during the Nazi period. He wrote of the differences in ethical decision required in Norway and Denmark during WWII. In Denmark, he thought, the presence of a government that persisted between the people and the Nazis meant time for deliberation. In Norway, with nothing but Nazi government, people constantly faced radical choices where protecting the vulnerable meant immediate risk of death or concentration camp for themselves or their families. Løgstrup thought that their previous patterns of response to the ethical demand would probably predominate in their choice to collaborate, resist, or protect the lives of vulnerable others. "There is a psychic maturity," he wrote, "which can make the direction of many an instant decision a foregone conclusion. Even where much is at stake, a person need not therefore necessarily be in doubt about what he or she will do."[30] Although we may, in our present moment, still have time to deliberate, to "sleep on it," I find it useful to realize that every choice I make may be preparing a direction for fiercer challenges. Løgstrup himself, by the way, involved himself in much more active and dangerous resistance to the Nazi occupiers than many of his Danish colleagues were willing to do. So although his writings do not address racism directly, his own history makes it clear that the extreme racist program of National Socialism created the context for the radicality of Løgstrup's ethics, just as it did for Levinas. Both knew that the radical precarity of the hated racial other constituted a summons or demand on a subjectivity able to feel this demand.

Two further aspects of Løgstrup's thinking help to make his radicality clear. First he raged—as much as his reserved philosophical voice would let him—against Kierkegaard, dearly beloved ancestor of so many of us who grew up in the 1960s and 1970s with existentialism. In his view, Kierkegaard, putting away Regine Olsen and his love for her, focused much too much on his own purity of heart. In Løgstrup's view, ethics has little to do with how holy and pure the individual can become. Not that Kierkegaard's search for purity brought him any satisfaction—see *Fear and Trembling* [31]—but Løgstrup thought Kierkegaard dissatisfied because he was pursuing the wrong goal. In addition, my own satisfaction is beside the point; the other's need commands me.

Further, in the years after his most famous book, Løgstrup wrote of what he called the "sovereign expressions of life." This odd-sounding phrase refers to qualities of relatedness (he might have said character traits) like sincerity, trust, and mercy; characterizing response to the ethical demand, but contrasting with obsessive and self-enclosed phenomena, including betrayal, jealousy and envy.[32] Much of Løgstrup's later work involved describing these contrasts, so neglected, he thought, by Kierkegaard, and by conventional moral philosophy.

Løgstrup and Levinas.

Emmanuel Levinas, born in Lithuania in 1906, student and early admirer of Heidegger, came to mount an ethical and phenomenological critique of what he called "totalizing," every form of reducing people to things or categories, a tendency he found both violent and endemic to the western tradition.[33] From the time Hitler came to power, with Heidegger enthusiastically endorsing him, Levinas contrasted this murderous totalizing with response and responsibility to infinity and transcendence, to the face of the other, commanding me, accusing me. Presentiment and memory of the Nazi horror, he wrote, haunted all his work.[34] In his second great book,[35] substitution—the other's life before mine, the other's death of more concern than mine—takes center stage. Ethical saying— *hineni* (me here, yes)—replaces the objectifying, categorizing "said," now treating the naked and vulnerable other as of ultimate value. The face of the other now bears the trace of the infinite, and only in the other can the infinite be found.

So how do these two thinkers of radical ethics compare and contrast? Rooted in religion, Lutheran[36] and Jewish (respectively), both intended to work as phenomenologists but picked up different strains. Influenced by Bergson, Husserl, and Heidegger, both lived at the same times in Strasbourg—where Levinas was teaching when Løgstrup arrived as a student—and Freiburg (both Husserl and Heidegger were there in the early 1930s), though they seem never to have met. Where Levinas developed his phenomenology by inverting Husserlian intentionality—the other faces and accuses me—Løgstrup studied with Hans Lipps in Göttingen, absorbing the Heideggerian being-in-the-world conviction but following this being into ethical relatedness. Our very situatedness with others creates the ethical demand. Heideggerian thrownness became for Løgstrup basic trust, only destroyed by betrayal and trauma. Løgstrup, though neither novelist nor poet, often illustrated his ethical concepts with relational stories, creating a type of narrative phenomenology:

At four o'clock in the morning there is an insistent ring at the door. When the woman descends the secret police are outside, demanding that she open up. Once inside, they ask for her husband. They are informed that, as it happens, he is not at home but away on business. One of the two men, the subordinate, heavily armed, ugly as sin, and looking capable of every kind of brutality, starts searching the house. The other, possessed of an engaging manner, all amiability and courtesy, is talking to the woman meanwhile and assuring her that the visit is of no consequence, merely a routine procedure. The woman acts obligingly, appearing surprised—a composed and polished performance. She is perfectly aware that his charming insistence on the insignificance of their visit is aimed solely at getting her to talk, and is not taken in by anything that he says. She knows that from the least unconsidered remark ammunition will be forged for use against her husband and herself. In spite of that—and this is probably the oddest part of the whole business—she needs constantly to rein in an inclination to talk to the man as to another human being, as though he might be drawn from his destructive enterprise to properly human perceptions and good sense. Unremittingly, she must keep a cool head. Why? What manifests itself in that inclination? Nothing other than the elemental and definitive peculiarity attaching to all speech qua spontaneous expression of life: its openness. To speak is to speak openly.[37]

Here we have a good sample of phenomenological description in Løgstrup's hands. The basic trust exerts an almost instinctual hold. He justified his view of the ethical demand and of the sovereign expressions of life on grounds of experiences with which the reader or hearer could easily identify.

Levinas, directly Heidegger's student, but even earlier a translator and student of Husserl, found another phenomenological voice:

> The self is a sub-jectum: it is under the weight of the universe [...] the unity of the universe is not what my gaze embraces in its unity of apperception, but what is incumbent on me from all sides, regards me in the two senses of the term, accuses me, is my affair.[38]

Here we find a prophetic voice challenging the whole philosophical tradition. The first-person perspective so beloved by phenomenologists finds itself no longer agentic, no longer the constructor of experience; but subject as subjected, under the weight of incumbency, obligated from all sides, "more passive than all passivity."[39] Because Levinas (1906–1995) outlived Løgstrup (1905–1981) into the digital age, we have additional access to Levinas' distinctive voice in the form of interviews from his later years easily accessible to us. We can hear him repeat the importance of returning to texts, and like a mantra: "la sortie du soi, la sortie du soi" (the exit from self). Each thinker describes a radical ethical demand of responsibility to care for the vulnerable other in his own idiom. Both phenomenologists challenge what Critchley names the "autonomy orthodoxy" of Western moral theory; both describe ethical experience, rather than justifying ethical choices.

Both, in addition, share a Judeo-Christian sensibility. (The expression "Judeo-Christian" can, of course, seriously mislead.) Phenomenology gives both thinkers a secular language, one might say, for communicating their radical ethics in human terms. Raised in an intellectual strain of Judaism in Kovno, Lithuania, and ever allergic to more mystical forms, then profoundly educated in Russian literature in exile in Ukraine in his Gymnasium years, and in phenomenology in Europe with Husserl and Heidegger, Levinas emerged from five years in captivity during the war to study Talmud with the famous Chouchani, also the teacher of Elie Wiesel. Headmaster of a Jewish school (ENIO) in Paris, he gave weekly

Rashi commentaries, and produced Talmudic commentaries, published with a different publisher from his philosophical work. These, as well as his explicitly philosophical works, show a fascinating interdisciplinary voice, and resistance to theologizing.

Løgstrup, for his part, began his best-known work, *The Ethical Demand*, by framing its purpose as making the basic message of Jesus—love thy neighbor—accessible in human terms. Simon Critchley[40]—rightly in my view—hears Løgstrup throughout glossing Matthew 5:43–7, from the Sermon on the Mount:

> You have heard that it was said, "You shall love your neighbor and hate your enemy."
>
> But I say to you, Love your enemies and pray for those who persecute you,
>
> so that you may be sons of your Father who is in heaven; for he makes his sun rise on the evil and on the good, and sends rain on the just and on the unjust.
>
> For if you love those who love you, what reward have you? Do not even the tax collectors do the same?
>
> And if you salute only your brethren, what more are you doing than others? Do not even the Gentiles do the same?

How many times should I forgive my brother? Seventy times seven. A radical, one-sided, and unfulfillable demand—like the Levinasian ethic, this inordinate, excessive demand seems to echo "be perfect, as your heavenly Father is perfect" (Matthew 5:48).

But Løgstrup did not quote these words. Educated in theology and philosophy, he, like Levinas, avoided theologizing, preferring description and narrative of ethical experience. As Hans Fink and Alisdair MacIntyre write in their introduction to *The Ethical Demand*:

> Løgstrup did indeed take the ethical demand to be that which was commanded by Jesus when he repeated the injunction of Leviticus to love our neighbour as ourselves. But for Løgstrup ... the ethical demand is not laid upon Christians rather than non-Christians. There is not Christian morality *and* secular morality. There is only human morality.[41]

He saw people living out their acceptance of the ethical demand in the present, and struggling with it. Levinas would speak of a split in subjectivity, with the demand originating in the immemorial past, a demand to which I am always inadequate, thus torn apart by. In Judith Butler's straightforward words, "Let's face it. We're undone by each other. And if we're not, we're missing something."[42]

For both thinkers, Western religious sensibility grounded and shaped what they came to understand as the human ethical relation. How much either would be able to engage in interfaith dialogues beyond their partially shared traditions remains, for me, an open question. Both profoundly challenged the individualism underlying Western ontologies, colonialism, and other forms of reductive and murderous violence. Løgstrup substituted trust, Levinas solidarity. Both seem close to Buddhist compassion and to African *Ubuntu*, though to my knowledge neither mentioned these ideas.

A striking similarity between these two thinkers, absent from other major moral philosophers, is one-sidedness (Løgstrup) or asymmetry (Levinas). The ethical demand is on me. Not you. This stupefying, excessive, exorbitant quality defies the logic of justification. Only stories demonstrate its possibility, and even reasonableness. But I must mention that in his last years Levinas tended to call these examples of the ethical response holiness. Løgstrup, more reserved, thought they simply demonstrated true humanity.[43] But both would have taken interest in the story of Arnaud Beltrame, the French policeman who offered himself as substitute hostage, without hesitation. Løgstrup might have commented that Beltrame saw that the life of the woman hostage was delivered into his hands, or entrusted to him. Levinas would have explained that snatching the bread from one's own mouth to save the other is holy, if anything is.

Despite the striking parallels, we find in Løgstrup an emphasis on human inter-dependence underpinning his constant talk of basic trust, for him a phenomenological fundamental that finds no exact equivalent in Levinas, for whom an anarchic responsibility refuses all appeal to something foundational. But do they differ so much? Both stress one-sidedness and asymmetry, but the vulnerability of Løgstrup's speaker, and the nakedness of the face of Levinas' widow, orphan, and stranger share a common fragility and impose a common demand in these emergency times—you shall not turn away, you shall not remain indifferent, you shall not murder me with your categories, you shall not leave me to die alone.

Notes

1 Knud Løgstrup, *The Ethical Demand* (Notre Dame: University of Notre Dame Press, 1997).
2 Paul Woodruff, *Reverence: Renewing a Forgotten Virtue* (New York: Oxford University Press, 2014).
3 Jonathan Haidt, *The Righteous Mind: Why Good People are Divided by Politics and Religion* (New York: Pantheon Books, 2012).
4 Simon Critchley, *Infinitely Demanding: Ethics of Commitment, Politics of Resistance* (London; New York: Verso, 2007).
5 Zygmunt Bauman, *Liquid Times: Living in an Age of Uncertainty* (Cambridge: Polity Press, 2007).
6 Zygmunt Bauman, *Postmodern Ethics* (Cambridge: Blackwell, 1993).
7 Zygmunt Bauman, *Liquid Times: Living in an Age of Uncertainty* (Cambridge: Polity Press, 2007), 114.
8 Knud Ejler Løgstrup, *Beyond the Ethical Demand* (Notre Dame: University of Notre Dame Press, 2007), 104.

9 Knud Ejler Løgstrup, *The Ethical Demand* (Notre Dame: University of Notre Dame Press, 1997).

10 Ibid, 5.

11 I write "implicated" rather than "implied" here because Løgstrup seems to imply, as does Levinas, that the other's vulnerability accuses me, implicates me.

12 Knud Ejler Løgstrup, *The Ethical Demand* (Notre Dame: University of Notre Dame Press, 1997), 17.

13 Ibid, 8.

14 Ibid, 11.

15 Jean Watson, *Caring Science as Sacred Science* (Philadelphia: F. A. Davis Co., 2005).

16 Judith Butler, *Precarious Life: The Powers of Mourning and Violence* (London; New York: Verso, 2004).

17 Martin Luther King, Jr., *A Testament of Hope* (San Francisco: Harper & Row, 1986).

18 Knud Ejler Løgstrup, *The Ethical Demand* (Notre Dame: University of Notre Dame Press, 1997), 44.

19 Ibid, 45.

20 Ibid.

21 Ibid, 16.

22 Ibid, 116.

23 Ibid, 122.

24 Emmanuel Levinas, *Totality and Infinity: An Essay on Exteriority* (The Hague; Boston, Hingham: M. Nijhoff Publishers; Kluwer Boston, 1979).

25 Ibid,127–128.

26 Emmanuel Levinas and Philippe Nemo, *Ethics and Infinity* (Pittsburgh: Duquesne University Press, 1985), 98.

27 Hans Fink and Robert Stern, *What is Ethically Demanded?: K. E. Løgstrup's Philosophy of Moral Life* (Notre Dame: University of Notre Dame Press, 2017).

28 Hans Fink and Robert Stern, *What is Ethically Demanded?: K. E. Løgstrup's Philosophy of Moral Life* (Notre Dame: University of Notre Dame Press, 2017), 14.

29 Ibid, 15.

30 Ibid, 150.

31 Søren Kierkegaard, *Fear and Trembling* (Harmondsworth, Middlesex; New York: Penguin Books, Viking Penguin, 1985).

32 Knud Ejler Løgstrup, *Beyond the Ethical Demand* (Notre Dame: University of Notre Dame Press, 2007).

33 Emmanuel Levinas, *Totality and Infinity: An Essay on Exteriority* (The Hague; Boston, Hingham: M. Nijhoff Publishers; Kluwer Boston, 1979).

34 The young Levinas spoke of Heidegger's *Being and Time* (Oxford: Blackwell, 1967) as comparable to the work of Plato and Hegel, but, shocked and horrified, he abandoned his book on Heidegger when that philosopher joined the Nazis and, as rector, tried to impose their program on Freiburg University in 1933–34. In 1931 Levinas became a French citizen and in 1939 enrolled in the officer corps where he worked as an interpreter of Russian and German. In 1940 he was imprisoned in a labor camp near Hannover for five years until the war's end, while his wife and daughter were hidden by nuns. His status as a French officer kept him from transfer to the death camps, but as a Jew, he was made to work harder than the others. His entire Lithuanian family was murdered. His life was, he later said, "dominated by the presentiment and the memory of the Nazi horror." Emmanuel Levinas, *Difficult Freedom: Essays on Judaism* (Baltimore: Johns Hopkins University Press, 1990).

35 Emmanuel Levinas, *Otherwise Than Being: Or, Beyond Essence* (The Hague; Boston, Hingham: M Nijhoff Publishers; Kluwer Boston, 1981).

36 Robert H. Stern, "Freedom from the Self: Luther and Løgstrup on Sin as 'Incurvatus in Se,'" *Open Theology* 4, no. 1 (2018): 268–280, accessed July 18, 2018, http://doi.org/10.1515/opth-2018-0020.

37 Knud Ejler Løgstrup, *Beyond the Ethical Demand* (Notre Dame: University of Notre Dame Press, 2007), 83–84.
38 Emmanuel Levinas, *Otherwise Than Being: Or, Beyond Essence* (Pittsburgh: Duquesne University Press, 1981), 116.
39 Ibid, 146.
40 Simon Critchley, *Infinitely Demanding: Ethics of Commitment, Politics of Resistance* (London; New York: Verso, 2007).
41 Knud Ejler Løgstrup, *The Ethical Demand* (Notre Dame: University of Notre Dame Press, 1997).
42 Judith Butler, *Precarious Life: The Powers of Mourning and Violence* (London; New York: Verso, 2004), 23.
43 To my ears, these messages from a Lutheran and Jewish phenomenologist sound equally demanding; others, lacking such voices, must turn to practical philosophers like Dorothy Day, whom both Løgstrup and Levinas would have very well understood.

References

Bauman, Z. 2007. *Liquid Times: Living in an Age of Uncertainty*. Cambridge: Polity Press.

Bauman, Z. 1993. *Postmodern Ethics*. Cambridge: Blackwell Publishers.

Butler, J. 2010. *Frames of War: When is Life Grievable?*London; New York: Verso.

Butler, J. 2004. *Precarious Life: The Powers of Mourning and Violence*. London; New York: Verso.

Critchley, S. 2007. *Infinitely Demanding: Ethics of Commitment, Politics of Resistance*. London; New York: Verso.

Fink, H. and Stern, R. 2017. *What is Ethically Demanded?: K. E. Løgstrup's Philosophy of Moral Life*. Notre Dame: University of Notre Dame Press.

Haidt, J. 2012. *The Righteous Mind: Why Good People are Divided by Politics and Religion* (1st ed.). New York: Pantheon Books.

Heidegger, M. 1967. *Being and Time*. Oxford: Blackwell.

Kierkegaard, S. 1985. *Fear and Trembling*. Harmondsworth, Middlesex, England; New York: Penguin Books; Viking Penguin.

King, M. L. 1986. *A Testament of Hope*. San Francisco: Harper & Row.

Levinas, E. 1998. *Otherwise Than Being: Or, Beyond Essence*. Pittsburgh: Duquesne University Press.

Levinas, E. 1990. *Difficult Freedom: Essays on Judaism*. Baltimore: Johns Hopkins University Press.

Levinas, E. 1981. *Otherwise Than Being: Or, Beyond Essence*. The Hague; Boston, Hingham: M. Nijfoff; Kluwer Boston.

Levinas, E. 1979. *Totality and Infinity: An Essay on Exteriority*. The Hague; Boston, Hingham: M. Nijhoff Publishers; Kluwer Boston.

Levinas, E. & Nemo, P. 1985. *Ethics and Infinity* (1st ed.). Pittsburgh: Duquesne University Press.

Løgstrup, K. E. 2007. *Beyond the Ethical Demand* (English Language ed.). Notre Dame: University of Notre Dame Press.

Løgstrup, K. E. 1997. *The Ethical Demand*. Notre Dame: University of Notre Dame Press.

Stern, R. H. 2018. "Freedom from the Self: Luther and Løgstrup on Sin as 'Incurvatus in Se'." *Open Theology*, July 18: 268–280. doi:10.1515/opth-2018-0020.

Watson, J. 2005. *Caring Science as Sacred Science* (1st ed.). Philadelphia: F. A. Davis Co.

Woodruff, P. 2014. *Reverence: Renewing a Forgotten Virtue* (2nd ed.). New York: Oxford University Press.

9

IDENTITY-AS-DISCLOSIVE-SPACE

Dasein, Discourse and Distortion

Robin R. Chalfin

Introduction

Language presents as both a central problem and simultaneous possibility of Being. It is in language that Being is defined, in language Being is distorted, and through language Being is *disclosed*. Across the lifespan, human beings are in a process of becoming through, against, and with language. I quite vividly remember when my second grade teacher introduced the subject of gender bias in our language. Even he was unprepared for my enthusiasm for this issue. Every time he read a book or introduced a subject using "mankind" as representative of all people, I would jump up with my hand raised, simultaneously yelling out, "And women too!" Or "You mean humankind? Right? Right!" He had to talk with me about my timing, but this proved to be the early expression of my abiding interest in the power of language, and how it forecloses and discloses our existence.

Decades later this feels all the more urgent. While society rushes into post-identity discourses, it feels imperative that one proceeds with caution regarding this seductive iteration of universalizing: the ever psychologically complex and politically fraught experience of embodied difference must be languaged. A powerful force in human existence, the words used to identify oneself and others can hold violent and liberatory functions; words fuel what have come to be known as the "identity wars." At the heart of every social movement is a process of reclaiming marginalized identities, utilizing language to rename, and thus authentically live in the world. These very efforts, however, can lead to yet further reductionistic and dehumanizing language wherein personal and group cohesion function at the cost of reifying not only the "other" but the "self." Yet forsaking the language of identity in lieu of universalizing, colorblind, or post-identity discourses erases something of humanity itself—here lies the problem and the possibility. Here lies the paradox of Dasein where one's potentiality for being is predicated on being-in rather than escaping these very limitations of language.

This chapter considers the language of identity and difference through a Heideggerian lens. Typically, identity is altogether rejected, deconstructed or rendered a category, whereby it functions as explanations, defenses, or determinations of who someone may be or become in the world. Yet when Being is understood in the Heideggerian sense as a process of becoming, then identity too (whether related to ethnicity, race, sexual orientation, gender expression, disability, or any cultural affiliation) can and must be understood as a process or a becoming rather than a designation.[1] As such, identity is a core existential and is embodied as something that persons *live* rather than *possess*, like a cultural artifact or a finite category. One does not *have* a gender identity; rather, one *lives* gender identity. One does not *possess* a sexual orientation; one *lives* it. One does not *have* a disability; one *lives* disability or different ability.

As a feminist therapist and teacher trained in current postmodern approaches, examining identity from an existential, and in particular Heideggerian, lens is a fruitful, yet problematic endeavor. Considering identity involves embracing disparate parts of the self and contending with the tension among feminist, multicultural, and queer philosophical orientations. One could say that studying Heidegger has been an "opposites attract" endeavor: passionate, but conflicted, and with the initial romance quieting into a more complex evolution. Thus, while my Jewish family looked askance and my feminist colleagues looked perplexed, I persisted in my study of Heidegger; I was surprised to find the ethos of his work resonate with me so deeply, and found myself indebted to his life-long project of overturning dualistic and abstract thinking.[2]

Being-in-language

Heidegger poses a simple yet powerful question: Who is the Being that asks the question of Being? More importantly, he probes: how does one ask this question of Being without objectifying Being?[3] This central tension is at the heart of Heidegger's radical anti-reification stance and his emphasis on the relationship between Being and language.

Heidegger's uncommon use of visual, spatial, and often hyphenated and italicized language functions to evoke the *experience* of Being stripped bare of common abstractions. For Heidegger, language *is* Being.[4] This idea is ancient, of course, but Heidegger awakens it in a particularly useful way. For Heidegger, language is not a thing, but an *experience*. Dasein, meaning *"Being-there,"* reconceptualizes the person as a process, or as a relating. Dasein is always *"Being-in,"* or *with*, and in this regard Dasein is always already present in language. But this is not simply a peaceful relating—it is a necessary struggle. Dasein is "thrown"[5] into language, and in interpreting and grappling with its limits, Dasein discloses something beyond language. In this way, Dasein is *in* discourse and simultaneously *disclosive*: Heidegger concludes "Dasein is its disclosedness."[6] As such Dasein can be understood not only as a movement or a process but a space for Being. I would like to propose that we take Heidegger's disclosedness further and say Dasein is *Being-as-disclosive-space* (Robert Fox, personal communication, 2015–2018). One can then consider how identity is disclosed and received in this space. For Heidegger, discourse and existence are inextricably linked. So it follows that language always already constricts and constructs what it means to *be* human. If Dasein is always already in language, what happens when language is pervasively structured to render some persons inferior and others superior? In such oppressive conditions, can Being be a disclosive space?

It is useful to consider Heidegger's disclosiveness in this light. Discourse itself is never neutral, and so as Foucault has so eloquently articulated, one cannot speak of existence and one cannot speak of Being without also looking at structures of power.[7] Heidegger does not consider the existential tenets of difference, privilege, or power. Yet even for Heidegger, the notion that one can engage in ontology alone is humanly impossible and dangerous. Language and the production of knowledge are always situated.[8]

In feminist theory and praxis, dominant discourse is challenged when one asks questions about voice and context. Who is telling the story? Who does the author address? Who and what are omitted from the story, and finally, at what cost? Heidegger is telling *his* story. He begins where one must: where he is already entangled and untangling the defining conditions of his being-in-the-world. In reflecting on what is known about Heidegger's early existence, some pertinent details are salient. He was born of humble means to devout Catholic parents wholly involved with and financially dependent on the church.[9] The family lived in a rural, conservative town where Heidegger was raised as an altar boy amongst the priests and not surprisingly proceeded to join the Jesuit order as a young man.

As Heidegger progressed in his philosophical education however, he severed ties with the church and Christian theology.[10] In doing so, he abandoned his literal and figurative home in the world. He lost connection with his parents (who were devastated) and he relinquished the church's financial and educational support. He went further, not only breaking from the church, but defying his newfound academic world as he challenged all of Western tradition, collapsing the long-standing Cartesian split, and ventured toward unknown horizons.

Heidegger took over his thrownness, reinterpreting his potential for being-in-the world. He was bold, creative, and determined as he continually resisted the seduction of conformity. Out of this resistance, his most lucid writing is born. He writes about authenticity and inauthenticity, "the call," the "resolute stance" and his crucial understanding of the tranquilizing seduction of "the-they," or, in contemporary terms, the dominant discourse.[11] He understands guilt and all the ways persons neurotically defend against the anxieties surrounding their freedom and responsibilities to be their ownmost or authentic selves. It becomes clear that

Heidegger is writing to those (not unlike himself) who can belong, who wrestle with the seductions of security and sociocultural normativity, yet who have the responsibility to listen to the disruptive call of conscience.

What Heidegger neglects to address in himself and to address in his writings is the equally primordial need for and fear of the other. He neglects dependency, interdependency, grief, terror, and the more primitive or desperate and violent defenses that arise in protecting oneself against existential vulnerability. Robert Stolorow's psychobiographical monograph[12] offers particularly germane observations regarding Heidegger's own disavowed vulnerability. According to Stolorow, Heidegger does not so valiantly leave the priesthood. Rather, he escapes the pain, guilt, and probable fear surrounding this decision through somatization. He is released from the priesthood for medical reasons after a two-year period complaining of "heart pain," yet no heart symptoms are detected for the remainder of his life. Stolorow formulates that at this crucial time, somatization functions to protect Heidegger from his overwhelming feelings of attachment and loss, his guilt in abandoning his literal and spiritual family, and from his vulnerability in moving into the unknown. Perhaps, Stolorow suggests, the episodes Heidegger called heart pain were actual panic episodes.[13]

One also sees longstanding and disavowed vulnerability underlying Heidegger's alliance with the Nazi Party. In the context of the devastation and shame many Germans experienced following WWI, Heidegger nurtures pride in his rural, Bavarian cultural roots and in his sense of belonging to the common folk, or *his* German people. Heidegger's people embody a way of living that is both threatened and idealized. For him, the middle class and the urban Jews, who were considered privileged, were all seduced by technology and disconnected from his "pure" way of life; they threatened his hope of a better world and, as the dangerous and denigrated other, served to consolidate Heidegger's position of cultural arrogance.

These seeds of Heidegger's Nazism were long-standing, and are a cautionary tale on the dangers of polarization and idealization as a defense against sociopolitical vulnerability. Stolorow notes, however, even more personal precipitating factors that influenced Heidegger's affinity for Nazism. Just prior to his conversion to Nazism, Heidegger suffers several traumatic losses. His mother dies without reconciling with him. Hannah Arendt, who is Heidegger's muse, mistress, lover, and intellectual companion, breaks off their relationship and marries another man. In addition, *Being and Time* is published after years of laborious work, leaving him in a sort of postpartum loss exacerbated by very mixed initial responses to what is supposed to be his masterpiece. Heidegger is alone and vulnerable; his future uncertainty is acutely felt. He does not, however, show any evidence of processing these losses and fears.[14]

Soon thereafter, Heidegger joins the Nazi Party, resorting to personal grandeur and political extremism. In this instance, the imperative to ensure one's significance in the world overrides all else. Heidegger betrays himself and humanity.

He succumbs to the certainty of an answer, of power over, rather than living his vulnerability honestly and resolutely facing his own finitude. Thus, Heidegger not only omits the crucial question of social ethics in his writing, but he neglects parts of *himself*: his unintegrated needs, desires, fears, and most importantly, his grief. His somaticized struggle surrounding leaving the priesthood, his later flight from an unbearable broken heart, and his professional uncertainty are all resolved in Nazi idealizations.[15] The organizing effect Nazism seems to have on his sense of purpose in life suggests very primitive unintegrated needs. Heidegger does not grasp vulnerability. He does not grasp the power of distortion, but instead falls into its forces.

The contradictory brilliance of Heidegger's work on inauthenticity and the seductions of passivity, coupled with his failure to link this to the more primitive solutions of literal destructiveness towards the other, are devastating and yet not entirely surprising. While he elucidates the ontological destructiveness of conformity, he overlooks the ontic destructiveness of more sinister defences; the question of an ontology of belonging—a core existential of being-in-relation to the "other" rather than in resistance to "the-they" persists. How one contends with difference or otherness is crucial; this arena is where one exhibits the innermost primitive longings and defenses. When belonging and personal significance are threatened by the other, one typically resorts to dehumanization as a distorted attempt at self-preservation. Heidegger is a case in point where archaic defenses override and betray his very capacity for authentically living towards his own vulnerability.

Naturally wired to band together through evolutionary history, human beings create tribal affiliations in order to survive. To this purpose, categorizing unfamiliar others as inferior pre-emptively protects and controls against threats to interpersonal and intrapsychic cohesion, which for human beings in the contemporary world is so charged it can be understood as a matter of psychological life and death. While Heidegger is caught in these destructive identifications in his own life, he is unable to articulate it in his writing. He discusses the seduction of conformity, but not the related and highly urgent discussion of the force and function of otherization. The question remains: What if one cannot join "the-they", or only can do so as "the other," as "the object"? Here the discussion must turn from authenticity and freedom to oppression.

Being-in-distortion

Existential feminist Simone de Beauvoir's body of work, begun in 1946, is timeless, and continues to provide a critical foundation for considering how objectification, alterity, and abstraction work to protect certain groups of people and position others in exploitable and/or dispensable social roles. De Beauvoir identifies three primary forms of oppression: asymmetrical recognition, indifference, and aversion.[16]

With the symbiotic relationship of asymmetrical oppression, a loss of agency for the oppressed occurs, but also the comfort of belonging and the illusion of protection. This disparate yet complementary pattern is seen predominantly in the oppression of women and in some contexts of racial oppression. Oppression in the form of indifference renders one inferior and justifies scenarios of economic exploitation and cultural appropriation. This indifference often rationalizes and reinforces segregation and overt antagonism towards groups defined by race and religion. Ultimately, this indifference can become the basis for the most severe forms of dehumanization, and rationalization of acts of genocide and other atrocities. Finally, aversion manifests in a wide range of oppressions. These oppressions may include outright denial of existence, or the distortion of groups who threaten bodily norms and restrictions. Where silencing and erasing fail to sufficiently suppress a threatening expression of the human condition, other distortions—namely trivializing, criminalizing, or fetishizing—become primary modes. As a result, policing and pathologizing of embodiment functions against human variance in service of illusions of control; aging is prevented, different ability is rehabilitated, intersexuality is surgically corrected, and sexual and gender diversity is outlawed, cured, or rendered inconsequential. When asymmetry, indifference, and aversion are at work, the oppressed are asked to be useful in their assigned role and denigrate, hide, or change their existence as needed in order to uphold sociocultural normativity and protect against existential anxieties.[17]

Heidegger asserts that human beings are always free. This claim is indeed liberating albeit terrifying at times. What is less obvious is how this universal premise of freedom is shaming. This presumption of sovereignty implies that those who find themselves unable to act at will must be limited by personal deficiencies or, worse, act in bad faith. It follows that powerlessness is the problem of the individual: a matter of personal inferiority rather than a matter of unequal opportunity. Yet, subjected to massive mystification, those who are rendered "less than" are often unaware of what they are capable of, unaware even of the few opportunities for agency they do have.[18] While mystification may not always function to erase this consciousness, in its place remains an acute awareness of the costs of transgressing one's designated social role. Thus, even consciousness of oppression may not translate into actual freedom. It is clear that for the oppressed, in such constrained situations, change is nearly impossible and autonomy is distorted; whatever they may individually choose to do will only tend to further amplify their oppression. This dynamic is what feminist philosopher Marilyn Frye termed the "double bind" of oppression.[19] When persons are complicit, they further their own enslavement; if they subvert, they are further marginalized and condemned. Thus, while persons may have critical consciousness of their situation, they may even so remain complicit given the need for basic survival. From a feminist perspective, oppression not only constitutes an external impediment to action, but permeating subjectivity may also suppress the potential for ontological freedom itself.[20] In any case, social and ontological structures are rendered invisible, and all one sees is the individual that somehow does not thrive or manage to fly free. This invisible bind reconfirms the discourse of inferiority.[21]

While Heidegger addresses how conformity mutes one's full potentiality, complicity can be seen as more aggressive as it actively destroys one's capacities for Being and living in the world. The difference between the complacency and tranquillity of normative existence and complicity in one's own objectification, otherization, vilification, invisibility, and/or silence is crucial. Jean Baker Miller,[22] in her seminal work on the psychological costs of internalized sexism, argues that oppression requires persons be enlisted in their own enslavement through psychological forms or strategies, which results in what is generally categorized as neuroses or psychological troubles. She writes in *Toward a New Psychology of Women*, "…psychological problems are not so much caused by the unconscious (as Freud suggested) as by the deprivations of full consciousness…"[23] Additionally, in the trauma literature, dimming consciousness or dissociation is understood as a primary defense as it protects the psyche from threatening affects and experiences. Therefore, when one falls into complicity, while this may be a necessary survival strategy, one participates in personal diminishment and disembodiment, reinforcing one's marginal and ineffectual position in society.

Similar to Heidegger, I can see that during vulnerable times in my life, through complicity, I found refuge in superficial certainties. I remember the power I felt as a child to impact the world around me as well as the excitement regarding all the possibilities in my life. I remember a very different power that quickly took hold when I entered adolescence. I grasped at easy attention and social status via my conventional femininity. While I felt special being accepted into older crowds and experienced the thrill of playing along, one knows I was not actually *power-full*. Instead, I played out a narrative of asymmetrical recognition. I was no longer for myself but for the other. I lost interest in my creative and academic pursuits and even contemplated dropping out of school. It was in my first college level women's studies course that I began to make sense of this time in my development and with newfound analytic tools began to clear a space for my own becoming.

Feminists have sufficiently established that mutual recognition is essential for healthy development and self-assertion. Analyst and philosopher Jessica Benjamin[24] likens this recognition to sunlight. Just as photosynthesis needs the sun, human beings need the crucial element of recognition from primary others and their social world. Interestingly, with each different mode of oppression, the distortion of recognition and/or complete absence of recognition is at play. The restoration of recognition (involving not only connection but languaging) then becomes central to the project of developing what in psychological terms is called a positive identity.[25]

Being-in-identity

There is now substantial theorizing on the process of identity development for oppressed groups. In contexts of otherization, identity development involves a passage through stages, moving from dimmed consciousness and complicity, through crisis, towards cultural resistance and immersion in one's identity group.[26] One emerges with critical consciousness, self-assertion, and agency in the world. These developmental models are useful, but also problematic in that they tend to be linear and suggest there is a fixed or narrow endpoint of positive identity, which further marginalizes those who experience their intersecting identities in more varied or fluid ways. It suffices to say that recognition can easily devolve into reification.

My own grappling with identity gives me a sense of how crucial it is that the tension between recognition and reification in the process of identity formation is understood. My identity story can be told as a love story. When I came back from my lostness in high school, I fell in love with a wonderful, awkward, and earnest boy my own age. This was a time of great cohesion and certainty. It wasn't only that I naïvely thought I had found the one I would spend my life with, but that I felt clear about who I was in the world. Love *is* recognition of our significance or, as Benjamin asserts, the very sunlight necessary for life. And in this relational light, we become, we grapple with and grow into, who we already are.

Then as I came of age, I fell in love with a woman. While I somehow felt more of myself, I also felt, in the absence of familiar language and social recognition, more vulnerable. It became urgent to explain or to give an account of myself. There was enough resistance and doubt from family and peers that I felt an added necessity to be certain. I found language. I came out as a lesbian woman: my identity was clear, it was strong, and it was a new sense of belonging and solidarity. Still life continued to unfold. I fell in love with a man, and my certainty and belonging was disrupted again. Yet this time I had a much greater capacity to tolerate ambiguity, and my need to manage others had subsided. I recognized that I have an enduring ability to love a person irrespective of gender and irrespective of my initial identification as straight or lesbian and eventually bisexual.

Like transgender and mixed-race identities, bisexuality is treated with the third form of oppression: aversion (fetishizing, trivializing, pathologizing are examples), as it subverts the either/or categorization of sexual orientation. Bisexuality threatens both heteronormativity and homonormativity in lesbian and gay communities seeking cohesion in their identities and their efforts to politically organize. So I inhabit this identification not because it is always comfortable or even complete, but because it is a discursive space for Being: for disclosing my lived experience. This grappling with the language of who I am gives me an appreciation of reification as refuge as well as constraint, and the threatening reality of how diverse our identities actually are. I do not suggest that everyone is bisexual, or that all identity is or should be fluid, but rather that it is always dynamic.

How does one recognize oneself or the other without reifying? Critical race theorist and feminist philosopher Linda Martin Alcoff uses the metaphor of horizon, or a "horizon of agency."[27] Rather than discrete or stable sets of interests or a linear line of development, identity is a place from which one must engage in the process of interpretation and be engaged and open to the world. She writes, "The hermeneutic insight is that the self operates in a situated plane, always culturally located with great specificity even as it is open onto an indeterminate future and a reinterpretable past, not of its own creation."[28] Thus, once identity is understood as horizon, an opening *out*, a place from which to *see*, philosophically there is no conflict between Being-as-disclosive-space and what in a Heideggerian sense could be called "Being-as-identified" or "Being-towards-identity."

While philosophically there may then be no conflict, psychologically there most certainly is. This conflict persists when one rigidly holds onto identity for defensive or aggressive purposes. Alternately, this conflict persists when identity is disavowed in an attempt at minimizing the threat of difference at the cost of self-diminishment, constriction or even erasure. There is no peaceful escape from this struggle. Differences and identity must be contended with; race, gender, and sexuality (the ways in which Being is embodied and languaged) are inseparable from Being-in and with one's world, and therefore central to existence. Inevitably, so much of identity is formed in complicity with and reaction to oppression that it requires a critical consciousness to live identity in ways that are dynamic and liberatory. Modes of identifying, recognizing, resisting, interpreting, expressing, and living one's particular identities thus become a necessity. Language that discloses existence rather than constricts it must be generated and this disclosiveness requires the substantial task of speaking the multiplicitousness of Being.

Organizing, affiliating, and theorizing around singular and narrow identities necessitates that people split and/or constrict who they are in order to sustain much needed belonging. While this may be expedient when possible, oppression is further reinforced in the form of complementarity. Decentering white versions of feminism, radical women of color (from different ethnicities including Black, Chicana and Latina, Asian and Native American) changed academic discourse and the politics of identity as they contested the essentializing notion of the singular.[29] Patricia Hill Collins, in her seminal work *Black Feminist Thought*, articulates this foundational shift from "either-or" binary thinking to what she calls the "both-and" consciousness one must hold when living multiple loyalties.[30] One is not simply a woman: she is both woman *and* black, she is working class *and* lesbian, she is immigrant *and* academic, etc.

This shift from the predominate "either-or" discourse, which has long required the marginalized to sever and silence themselves, ushered in a new era of articulating and embracing rather than erasing difference. Not only did women of color bring attention to the particular violence of interlocking oppressions and the irreducibility of intersecting identities, but also to the complex consciousness that arises out of living at these fraught social and psychic junctures. Drawing on her experience as a Chicana and a bisexual woman, feminist philosopher Gloria Anzaldúa[31] speaks to the isolation and homelessness of those who are caught between identifications with different and often opposing cultural worlds. She likened the place one inhabits to a borderland where one is never completely at home in either country. Out of this fractious existence, a critical awareness she calls "mestiza" consciousness (meaning a state of being beyond binary "either-or" conception) arises out of necessity.[32] Others have called this state of "mestiza" consciousness a "world-traveling self," a "multi-voiced self," the "multiplicitous self," the one whose life is "on the hyphen." Heidegger would like this last one.[33]

Queer theorists have furthered the discussion, now moving from "both-and" to what could be called "neither." Sexuality and gender embodied outside the rigid and hierarchical binaries of gay/straight or male/female can be understood amidst the vast breadth of human variation and expression.[34] While psychic unease surrounds such multi-faceted and yet undefined dimensions of identity, a greater capacity for comprehending human Being emerges.

Critical consciousness materializes from the margins and (when one listens) implicates the very ground or ontology of *Being-in-the-world* thus changing the larger horizon of the dominant discourse. There is a complicated and ever important task at hand: while asserting one's own knowing, one must simultaneously be open to the unknown, to a future of oneself one cannot know. This idea is certainly the premise of queer theory and Judith Butler's[35] seminal work *Gender Trouble*, but also evokes the notion of Being-as-disclosive space. Heidegger emphasizes that Dasein is not *pre*determined, nor simply *de*termined or self-made. Rather, he holds that Being is always in an indeterminate process of becoming within its world. The conditions of the discursive world are indeed limiting, and yet, when one stands firmly in one's existence, *being-there,* looking outward, the horizons are already changing.

Being-disclosive-space

It is indeed psychologically challenging to dwell within these limitations, uncertainties, and responsibilities while being-towards one's ownmost potentiality. And yet one must not only be a space for one's own becoming but one must be towards the other's potentiality as well. Heidegger offers a beautiful ideal of Being as disclosedness. His use of reticence is crucial in relation to the other: with a measure of self-restraint one clears or holds open a space for the other's becoming.[36] However, the notion that this is practiced inclusively is naïve. Heidegger does not consider disclosedness within the socially stratified multicultural context. He does not account for implicit otherization already censuring and constricting disclosedness. How one is identified and how that allows and restricts the other's becoming leaps into that space whether one intends to be reticent or not.

Dasein is not only a space for being, but also a projection that takes over that space. While human beings are an opening, they are also a concealing, seeking a sense of security through abstraction, otherizing and objectifying of the self and other. Heidegger's resoluteness becomes all the more important in this instance, but requires some elaboration. Central to disclosing Being is the task of resolutely clearing a host of discourses that constrain Being. The use of the word "clear" in this context not only draws on Heidegger's notion of the clearing, but also specifically evokes the process of critically examining one's presuppositions and inherent defenses.[37] This practice requires a resolute stance towards difference and an existential integration of a contemporary understanding of cultural competency.

Most commonly, cultural competency efforts focus on cultural literacy, or learning as much as possible about specific cultures and identity groups.[38] These efforts are useful as they provide critical knowledge about the subjects' world from which they must make meaning, and give a sketch of their horizon. However, a stance of cultural literacy can become problematic when used to view culture as a homogenous system and when one assumes that everyone internalizes culture in the same way. Alternatively, an experiential-phenomenological approach anticipates that culture is always moving and changing, anticipates that each person internalizes and makes meaning of their culture in unique ways, and assumes a stance of "cultural naivety and curiosity."[39] In this process, the core paradox of cultural competency emerges. One must work hard to know as much as possible about the other *and* one must work equally hard at not knowing and simply Being an opening for Being.[40]

This existential, phenomenological approach to cultural competency is congruent with the original spirit of psychoanalysis, grounded in a similar paradox where the analyst works to know a great deal about human development while rigorously protecting a space for the patient's own becoming.[41] There is powerful convergence among talk therapy, language, logos, discourse, and disclosedness. To undergo an experience of language, as Heidegger states, is to experience the truth of Being.[42] Ironically, this experience is much more about language beyond words: the encounter with the impossibility of defining (of languaging) human Being. This is the revelatory experience of therapy and existential intimacy: the encounter and capacity to hold the powerful mystery and vulnerability of being oneself.

For Heidegger, the essential purpose of language is to reveal, or to show something authentic of oneself and existence.[43] Similarly, the purpose of psychoanalysis is to reveal oneself to an important other. Grounded in the feminist emphasis on mutual recognition and identity as horizon, this space can be authentically opened. The analyst need not leap in to interpret, fix, or define. Rather, one can allow through language that which is conflicted and disavowed to come forth and thus support the person's integration of vulnerability and capacity to be-in-the-world. Yet even this is not enough. The analyst, or the other, must also be willing to undergo the experience of language allowing oneself to be shaken and undone. The analyst must be open to the call of the unconscious, and to the other. This process opens the transcendent third space of intersubjectivity, mutual recognition, whereby relating to one another is reciprocally impactful and meaningful. Judith Butler speaks to this quite eloquently. In *Giving an Account of Oneself*, Butler writes:

[W]e must recognize that ethics requires us to risk ourselves precisely at moments of unknowingness, when what forms us diverges from what lies before us, when our willingness to become undone in relation to others constitutes our chance of becoming human. To be undone by another is a primary necessity, an anguish, to be sure, but also a chance—to be addressed, claimed, bound to what is not me, but also to be moved, to be prompted to act, to address myself elsewhere, and so to vacate the self-sufficient "I" as a kind of possession. If we speak and try to give an account from this place, we will not be irresponsible, or, if we are, we will surely be forgiven.[44]

Being-in-the-world is indeed a continual doing and undoing—a disclosing and foreclosing of existence. This is the relational experience of *undergoing* language, which requires one to grapple with the vulnerability, power, and the mystery that each person's life entails.[45] One must contend with existence on its ever uncertain yet finite terms, and finally, however risky, experience the genuine reward of relational authenticity and one's ownmost aliveness.

Authenticity requires the recognition of both possibility *and* vulnerability in oneself *and* in the other. Earlier I shared how I faltered in adolescence and now I turn to an experience of recognition during this same vulnerable time. When I moved midway through high school and first met with my new guidance counselor, he told me that, despite some failing grades, I could do better if I worked hard. He enrolled me in several advanced placement classes and gave me a second chance. I was encouraged by this opening. I *did* work hard and again flourished in school. I soon noticed, however, that *all* the black students and a handful of other kids with pink hair and piercings were in the remedial classes. I did not yet know this was called tracking, but I recognized that I was in advanced classes because my guidance counselor could *see* me and imagine me doing well (despite evidence to the contrary) because I was white, middle class, and conventionally feminine.

No one had *seen* the black students or the kids who appeared to be queer or deviant in some way. Their capacity to excel in school was quite literally overlooked, and their designation as inferior was systematically reinforced. On the other hand, I was recognized as a Being who was becoming and could afford to falter and make mistakes. I began to understand my privilege and the seductive myth of an inclusive meritocracy. This was my first encounter with relinquishing what I most wanted to hold onto: my cherished sense of personal accomplishment and significance. It is unsettling for many to realize that, while they have worked very hard to get where they are, the opportunities that have been given are a privilege afforded those who fit within the discourses of sociocultural normativity and dominance. In this light, I understood that I was involved not only in my own becoming but responsible for the undoing of others.

Humanity is implicated in a great mutual entanglement of systems of power, possibility and vulnerability. A letting go of protected positions, an undoing in order to let others in, and even more fundamentally a dismantling of "in and out" is called for here. However vulnerable, this loss of personal significance and security clears the way for mutual recognition, mutual empowerment, and mutual existence. Bearing this loss is central to individuation and the capacity for difference, conflict, and critical consciousness. It clears the way for new interpersonal and intrapsychic structures that need not rely on distortion, idealization, and otherization.

Heidegger longed to recover meaning in his rural folk roots and to restore national pride to his country, so broken from the First World War. Yet this recovery is quickly tarnished by the most sinister idealizing and otherizing and, in this case, anti-Semitism. It is seductive and dangerous indeed to believe that cultural groups are the carriers of some superior and enlightened way of Being. I know the feeling, however. I feel this way about queer culture. I think the world would be a better place if everyone could get in touch with a little more queerness in themselves. Queer culture is famously creative, daring, fiercely loyal, ridiculously playful, and doggedly intentional in forming families in all creative manners against severe odds. One could take this rich horizon further and into idealization. Queer culture bears the purest forms of human love, kinship, and sexuality—set free from heteronormativity, it embodies the full spectrum of human expression and existence. But even though essentializing in this way is comforting, it is problematic. How do individuals and groups have identity and these deep affiliative connections without superior tribalism, distortion and annihilation of the other? Herein lies the work. It is only in a conscious relationship with one's vulnerability that one can relinquish primitive defenses and allow oneself to be undone by a genuine encounter with the yet unknown other.

Conclusion

Being in the constraints of language is indeed definitive of existence. These limits, paradoxically, are not deterministic but rather the source of an interpretive and discursive process of becoming embodied in and beyond language. Holding a Heideggerian conceptualization of Being *as* its disclosedness situates identity in a hermenuetic space; one is neither entirely reduced to language nor is one free of language. Identity is a dynamic problem, a necessary tension, a linguistic and embodied process of becoming; one could say identity *is* Being. When one *lives* identity as a core existential it can thus be understood as a site, a horizon, a space for becoming—a disclosive space. This is neither passive nor peaceful. This living is possible when one resolutely embodies a particular throwness, languages this existence, and discloses its significance all the while being towards vulnerability— within oneself and in the other. This occurs in the context of mutually impactful recognition whereby Being is a disclosive space of becoming *and* becoming undone. I will end with the question one then must live: What possibilities for Being exist when one is not constructed in opposition to, power over, defended against oneself or the other, and when we are mutually-disclosive-space-being-towards-identity?

Notes

1 Chung-Hsiung Lai, "Re-writing the Subject: The Throwness of Being in the Multicultural Condition," *Canadian Review of Comparative Literature* 30, no. 3–4 (2003): 495–503. http://ejournals.library.ualberta.ca/index.php/crcl/article/view/10775/8332; Mariana Ortega, ""New Mestizas," "'World' Travelers," and "Dasein": Phenomenology and the Multi-Voiced, Multi-Cultural Self," *Hypatia: A Journal of Feminist Philosophy* 16, no. 3 (August 2001): 1–29, htpps://doi.org/10.1111/j.1527–2001.2001.tb00922.x; Craig Vasey, "Being and Race" (presentation, 20th World Congress of Philosophy, Boston, MA, August 1998).

2 John McCumber, *Metaphysics and Oppression: Heidegger's Challenge to Western Philosophy* (Bloomington: Indiana University Press, 1999).

3 Richard Sembera, *Rephrasing Heidegger: A Companion to Being and Time* (Ottawa: University of Ottawa Press, 2007).

4 Martin Heidegger, *Being and Time*, trans. John Macquarrie and Edward Robinson (New York: SUNY Press, 1962); *On the Way to Language*, trans. Peter D. Hertz (New York: Harper & Row, 1971); *Poetry, Language, Thought*, trans. Albert Hofstadter (New York: HarperCollins, 2001).

5 Chung-Hsiung Lai, "Re-writing the Subject: The Throwness of Being in the Multicultural Condition," *Canadian Review of Comparative Literature* 30, no. 3–4 (2003): 502. http://ejournals.library.ualberta.ca/index.php/crcl/article/view/10775/8332.

6 Martin Heidegger, *Being and Time*, trans. John Macquarrie and Edward Robinson (New York: SUNY Press, 1962), 171.

7 Michel Foucault, *Discipline and Punish: The Birth of the Prison*, trans. Alan Sheridan (London: Penguin, 1991); *The History of Sexuality: The Will to Knowledge*, trans. Robert Hurley (London: Penguin, 1998).

8 Sharon Rae Jenkins and Veronica Navarrete-Vivero, "Existential Hazards of the Multicultural Individual: Defining and Understanding 'Cultural Homelessness,'" *Cultural Diversity & Ethnic Minority Psychology* 5, no. 1 (1999), https://doi.org/10.1037/1099-9809.5.1.6.

9 Rudiger Safranski, *Martin Heidegger: Between Good and Evil*, trans. Ewald Osers (Cambridge: Harvard University Press, 1999).

10 Ibid, 7–9.

11 Martin Heidegger, *Being and Time*, trans. John Macquarrie and Edward Robinson (New York: SUNY Press, 1962).

12 Robert D. Stolorow, *World, Affectivity, Trauma: Heidegger and Post-Cartesian Psychoanalysis* (New York: Routledge, 2011).

13 Ibid, 88.

14 Ibid, 93–96.

15 Ibid, 97–98.

16 Simone de Beauvoir, *The Second Sex*, trans. Constance Borde and Sheila Malovany-Chevallier (New York: Alfred Knopf, 2010); Sonia Kruks, "Theorizing Oppression," in *Simone de Beauvoir and the Politics of Ambiguity* (New York: Oxford University Press, 2012).

17 Sonia Kruks, "Theorizing Oppression," in *Simone de Beauvoir and the Politics of Ambiguity* (New York: Oxford University Press, 2012).

18 Nancy J. Holland and Patricia J. Huntington, eds., *Feminist Interpretations of Martin Heidegger* (University Park: Pennsylvania State University Press, 2001).

19 Marilyn Frye, *Politics of Reality: Essays in Feminist Theory* (Trumansburg, NY: Crossing Press, 1983), 2–3.

20 Sonia Kruks, "Theorizing Oppression," in *Simone de Beauvoir and the Politics of Ambiguity* (New York: Oxford University Press, 2012).

21 Marilyn Frye, *Politics of Reality: Essays in Feminist Theory* (Trumansburg, NY: Crossing Press, 1983); Sonia Kruks, "Theorizing Oppression," in *Simone de Beauvoir and the Politics of Ambiguity* (New York: Oxford University Press, 2012).

22 Jean Baker Miller, *Toward a New Psychology of Women* (Boston: Beacon Press, 1987).

23 Ibid, 94.

24 Jessica Benjamin, *The Bonds of Love: Psychoanalysis, Feminism, & the Problem of Domination* (New York: Random House, 1988).

25 Charmaine L. Wijeyesinghe and Bailey W. Jackson III, eds., *New Perspectives on Racial Identity Development: Integrating Emerging Frameworks* (New York: New York University Press, 2012).

26 Ibid.

27 Linda Martin Alcoff, "The Political Critique," in *Visible Identities: Race, Gender and the Self* (New York: Oxford University Press, 2006), 42.

28 Ibid, 43.

29 Cherríe Moraga and Gloria Anzaldúa, *This Bridge Called My Back: Writings by Radical Women of Color* (New York: Kitchen Table Women of Color Press, 1983).

30 Patricia Hill Collins, *Black Feminist Thought: Knowledge, Consciousness and the Politics of Empowerment* (New York: Routledge, 2000).

31 Gloria Anzaldúa, "How to Tame a Wild Tongue," in *Borderlands/LaFrontera: The New Mestiza* (San Francisco: Aunt Lute Books, 1999).

32 Ibid.

33 Mariana Ortega, "'New Mestizas,' 'World' Travelers,' and 'Dasein': Phenomenology and the Multi-Voiced, Multi-Cultural Self," *Hypatia: A Journal of Feminist Philosophy* 16, no. 3 (August 2001): 1–29, https://doi.org/10.1111/j.1527–2001.2001.tb00922.x.

34 Sara Ahmed, *Queer Phenomenology: Orientations, Objects, Others* (Durham: Duke University Press, 2006).

35 Judith Butler, *Gender Trouble: Feminism and the Subversion of Identity* (New York: Routledge, 1990).

36 Martin Heidegger, *Being and Time*, trans. John Macquarrie and Edward Robinson (New York: SUNY Press, 1962).

37 Ibid.

38 Clemmont E. Vontress, "An Existential Approach to Cross-Cultural Counseling," *Journal of Multicultural Counseling and Development* 16, no. 2 (April 1988): 73–83, https://doi.org/10.1002/j.2161-1912.1988.tb00643.x.

39 Ibid.

40 Larry Dyche and Luis H. Zayas, "The Value of Curiosity and Naivete for the Cross-Cultural Psychotherapist," *Family Process* 34, no. 4 (1995): 389–399, https://doi.org/10.1111/j.1545.5300.1995.00389.x.

41 Kirk J. Schneider, *The Paradoxical Self: Toward an Understanding of Our Contradictory Nature* (Buffalo: Humanity Books, 1999).

42 Guy M. Thompson, "Logos and Psychoanalysis: The Role of Truth and Creativity in Heidegger's Conception of Language," *Psychologist Psychoanalyst* 20, no. 4 (2000), http://www.academia.edu/3613958/Logos_and_Psychoanalysis_The_Role_of_Truth_and_Creativity_in_Heideggers_Conception_of_Language; "Postmodernism and Psychoanalysis: A Heideggerian Critique of Postmodernist Malaise and the Question of Authenticity," in *Way beyond Freud: Postmodern Psychoanalysis Observed*, ed. Joseph R, Martin S., and Jane T. (London: Open Gates Press, 2004).

43 Ibid.

44 Judith Butler, *Giving an Account of Oneself* (Bronx: Fordham University Press, 2005) 136.

45 Martin Heidegger, *On the Way to Language*, trans. Peter D. Hertz (New York: Harper & Row, 1971); *Poetry, Language, Thought*, trans. Albert Hofstadter (New York: HarperCollins, 2001).

References

Ahmed, Sara. *Queer Phenomenology: Orientations, Objects, Others.* Durham: Duke University Press, 2006.
Anzaldúa, Gloria. "How to Tame a Wild Tongue." In *Borderlands/LaFrontera: The New Mestiza.* 75–86, 99–113. San Francisco: Aunt Lute Books, 1999.
Benjamin, Jessica. *The Bonds of Love: Psychoanalysis, Feminism, & the Problem of Domination.* New York: Random House, 1988.
Baker Miller, Jean. *Toward a New Psychology of Women.* Boston: Beacon Press, 1987.
Butler, Judith. *Gender Trouble: Feminism and the Subversion of Identity.* New York: Routledge, 1990.
Butler, Judith. *Giving an Account of Oneself.* Bronx: Fordham University Press, 2005.
Collins, Patricia Hill. *Black Feminist Thought: Knowledge, Consciousness and the Politics of Empowerment.* New York: Routledge, 2000.
De Beauvoir, Simone. *The Second Sex.* Translated by Constance Borde and Sheila Malovany-Chevallier. New York: Alfred Knopf, 2010 (Original work published 1949).
Dyche, Larry and Luis H. Zayas. "The Value of Curiosity and Naivete for the Cross-Cultural Psychotherapist." *Family Process* 34, no. 4(1995): 389–399. https://doi.org/10.1111/j.1545.5300.1995.00389.x.
Foucault, Michel. *Discipline and Punish: The Birth of the Prison.* Translated by Alan Sheridan. London: Penguin, 1991.
Foucault, Michel. *The History of Sexuality: The Will to Knowledge.* Translated by Robert Hurley. London: Penguin, 1998.
Frye, Marilyn. *Politics of Reality: Essays in Feminist Theory.* Trumansburg, NY: Crossing Press, 1983.
Heidegger, Martin. *Being and Time.* Translated by John Macquarrie, and Edward Robinson. New York: SUNY Press, 1962 (Original work published 1927).
Heidegger, Martin. *On The Way to Language.* Translated by Peter D. Hertz. New York: Harper & Row, 1971 (Original work published 1959).
Heidegger, Martin. *Poetry, Language, Thought.* Translated by Albert Hofstadter. New York: HarperCollins, 2001 (Original work published 1971).
Holland, Nancy J. and Patricia J. Huntington, eds. *Feminist Interpretations of Martin Heidegger.* University Park: Pennsylvania State University Press, 2001.
Jenkins, Sharon Rae and Veronica Navarrete-Vivero. "Existential Hazards of the Multicultural Individual: Defining and Understanding 'Cultural Homelessness.'" *Cultural Diversity & Ethnic Minority Psychology* 5, no. 1(1999): 6–26. https://doi.org/10.1037/1099-9809.5.1.6.
Kruks, Sonia. *Retrieving Experience: Subjectivity and Recognition in Feminist Politics.* Ithaca: Cornell University Press, 2001.
Kruks, Sonia. "Theorizing Oppression." In *Simone de Beauvoir and the Politics of Ambiguity.* New York: Oxford University Press, 2012.
Lai, Chung-Hsiung. "Re-writing the Subject: The Thrownness of Being in the Multicultural Condition." *Canadian Review of Comparative Literature* 30, no. 3–4(2003): 495–503. http://ejournals.library.ualberta.ca/index.php/crcl/article/view/10775/8332.
Martín Alcoff, Linda. "The Political Critique." In *Visible Identities: Race, Gender and the Self.* New York: Oxford University Press, 2006.
McCumber, John. *Metaphysics and Oppression: Heidegger's Challenge to Western Philosophy.* Bloomington: Indiana University Press, 1999.

Moraga, Cherríe and Gloria Anzaldúa. *This Bridge Called My Back: Writings by Radical Women of Color.* New York: Kitchen Table Women of Color Press, 1983.

Ortega, Mariana. "'New Mestizas,' 'World' Travelers,' and 'Dasein': Phenomenology and the Multi-Voiced, Multi-Cultural Self." *Hypatia: A Journal of Feminist Philosophy* 16, no. 3(August 2001): 1–29. https://doi.org/10.1111/j.1527-2001.2001.tb00922.x.

Safranski, Rudiger. *Martin Heidegger: Between Good and Evil.* Translated by Ewald Osers. Cambridge: Harvard University Press, 1999.

Schneider, Kirk J. *The Paradoxical Self: Toward an Understanding of Our Contradictory Nature.* Buffalo: Humanity Books, 1999.

Sembera, Richard. *Rephrasing Heidegger: A Companion to Being and Time.* Ottawa: University of Ottawa Press, 2007.

Stolorow, Robert D. *World, Affectivity, Trauma: Heidegger and Post-Cartesian Psychoanalysis.* New York: Routledge, 2011.

Thompson, M. Guy. "Logos and Psychoanalysis: The Role of Truth and Creativity in Heidegger's Conception of Language." *Psychologist Psychoanalyst* 20, no. 4(2000). http://www.academia.edu/3613958/Logos_and_Psychoanalysis_The_Role_of_Truth_and_Creativity_in_Heideggers_Conception_of_Language.

Thompson, M. Guy. "Postmodernism and Psychoanalysis: A Heideggerian Critique of Postmodernist Malaise and the Question of Authenticity." In *Way beyond Freud: Postmodern Psychoanalysis Observed.* Edited by Joseph Reppen, Martin A. Schulman, and Jane Tucker. London: Open Gate Press, 2004.

Vasey, Craig. 1998. "Being and Race." Paper presented at the 20th World Congress of Philosophy, Boston, MA, August 1998. http://www.bu.edu/wcp/Papers/Soci/SociVase.htm.

Vontress, Clemmont E. "An Existential Approach to Cross-Cultural Counseling." *Journal of Multicultural Counseling and Development* 16, no. 2(April 1988): 73–83. https://doi.org/10.1002/j.2161-1912.1988.tb00643.x.

Wijeyesinghe, Charmaine L. and Bailey W. Jackson III, eds. *New Perspectives on Racial Identity Development: Integrating Emerging Frameworks.* New York: New York University Press, 2012.

10

FINDING THE OTHER IN THE SELF

Nancy McWilliams

In[1] this chapter I explore how our psychological constructions of others, notably those from whom we differ in significant ways, affect how we go through life as members of the remarkably diverse human community. In particular, I wrestle with the ubiquitous human tendency to objectify and demean the other.

These thoughts owe a great deal to the memory of my father-in-law, Carey McWilliams—an attorney, writer, activist, and for twenty years the editor of *The Nation* magazine—who devoted his entire career to exposing toxic "othering" and its destructive social consequences. Most of my readers have probably not heard of him; he died in 1980, and although in his day he was quite well known, especially in left-wing circles, he was not unduly interested in promoting his own reputation or achieving personal fame. Long before there was a robust national conversation about such things, Carey McWilliams deconstructed numerous prejudices that were at the time unquestioned by the American majority. He was tireless in exposing the suffering of people excluded from what his contemporary, C. Wright Mills,[2] memorably called the "power elite." Among many ahead-of-his-time contributions, he wrote the first mainstream American book about anti-Semitism,[3] the first book objecting to the internment of the Japanese during World War II,[4] and an early volume about prejudice against Spanish-speaking immigrants.[5] His *Factories in the Field* exposed the suffering of migrant laborers and documented the evils of what later came to be called "factory farming."[6] His arguments about race influenced the 1954 U.S. Supreme Court ruling in *Brown vs. the Board of Education.* [7] His investigative journalism on the diversion of water rights to corporate interests in California (1946) inspired the movie *Chinatown* decades after its publication.

The psychological dynamics behind my searching out his work when I was in high school and eventually (via what psychoanalysts might call overdetermination) marrying his son, the late Wilson Carey McWilliams, an equally indefatigable advocate of understanding across differences, are dynamics central to my identity.[8] Writing about these topics is thus a kind of homecoming for me to the questions and passions that dominated my formative years.

A basic assumption of this chapter is that no amount of training to understand people from whom we differ—in privilege, power, wealth, ability, sexuality, gender, race, age, ethnicity, culture, health, belief, geography, and other potentially estranging phenomena—relieves us of the responsibility of trying to get to know the parts of ourselves that otherwise become dissociated and projected onto others. This is a simple idea, but a profound and elusive one. It represents, I believe, an inherently unattainable though worthy goal. I try to expand on this premise in useful ways, during which I suggest more questions than answers.

As a psychoanalyst, I feel both advantaged and disadvantaged in exploring issues of othering. Analysts have a mixed track record on inclusiveness. On one hand, Sigmund Freud insisted that the core psychological dynamics of "civilized" nineteenth- and twentieth-century readers were no different from those of people most Europeans referred to as "savages"—a radical idea in a time of colonial entitlement, unquestioned patriarchy, and enthusiasm for eugenics.[9] As a Jew in an anti-Semitic culture that limited his opportunities, he was sensitive to marginalization;[10] and, despite his own prejudices (for example, against Americans, whose commercialism he mocked by reportedly referring to the United States as "Dollarland"), he worked to extend analytic treatment to underserved groups and famously hoped that "the conscience of society will awaken and remind it that the poor man should have just as much right to assistance for his mind as he now has for the life-saving help offered by surgery ... Such treatment will be free."[11]

On the other hand, there may have been no community more self-satisfied and blind to the dynamics of privilege than some American psychoanalytic organizations in the mid-twentieth century, when becoming an analyst was a ticket to prestige. Many members of the dominant training institutes—overwhelmingly Caucasian, male, heterosexual, privileged physicians—were, unlike their venerated Professor Freud, remarkably uncurious about whether they could improve on their ideas about women, gay people, minority cultures, and others at some remove from their own experience.[12] Psychoanalysts have a lot to answer for. But I think that despite our problematic institutional history, the psychoanalytic project of exposing and taking seriously the unconscious parts of the mind, as far as it is possible to do so, remains critical to our efforts to understand and reduce poisonous attitudes and behaviors toward others. In defense of psychoanalysts, I want to note that psychologists as a community have even more to answer for. Our track record is replete with malignant othering, from our early enchantment with the eugenics movement, through our enthusiasm for IQ testing with no sensitivity to cultural context, to our more recent collusion with torture.

Melanie Klein is the first psychoanalyst I know of to have framed human psychology in terms of our *need* for the other to be our "bad object."[13] Klein had a vivid way of describing how we require and recruit others to be the negative background against which we can contrast our own sense of innocent virtue. She observed that, from our earliest understanding that there *are* others, we try to keep goodness in ourselves and relegate badness to the outsider. The Garden of Eden was perfect *until the snake interfered*—it was the "outside agitator" who tempted the originally blameless Eve into sin. The readiness to ascribe all badness to an evil outsider is denotative of what Klein called the paranoid-schizoid position, in contrast to the depressive position, a psychological orientation that emerges in children more slowly, in which we begin to be capable of seeing self and other in complex ways that integrate good and bad.

Subsequent psychoanalysts have made contributions compatible with Klein's work. For example, Peter Fonagy's scholarship has evolved into a therapeutic stance that helps clients move from an unreflective psychology ("psychic equivalence"), in which one cannot take distance on one's own thoughts and feelings and cannot fully appreciate the separate subjectivities of others, to a capacity to "mentalize."[14] Mentalization involves getting our minds around the fact that another person has motives that come from that person's internal experience, which is not equivalent to our own psychology. This capacity is a version of what behavioral scientists have called "theory of mind"[15] and correlates with the Kleinian idea of moving from paranoid-schizoid *"projection of intent"* toward knowledge that others act out of their personal motives, separate from one's own internal interpretation of a situation.[16]

I view projection of intent as an underappreciated concept. What it means is that when someone has an impact on us, we conclude (because we are seeing the transaction through only our own individual psychological lenses) that the *consequence* of the person's behavior equates with *motive*. For example, a boss who likes an employee reluctantly lays her off because the company is not doing well. She is naturally devastated to lose her job. But instead of simply grieving and figuring out what to do next, she concludes that her sense of devastation was her employer's *goal*, that the boss has hated her and sadistically intended to devastate her. She may then become preoccupied with revenge fantasies. She feels hurt, and so she assumes the boss intended to hurt her. Another example of projection of intent: I once interviewed a man who said of his nine-month-old son, "That baby really knows how to push my buttons." This man for some reason could not mentalize a baby. To him, his son's *effect* on him was the infant's *motive*.

This capacity to mentalize, or transcend projection of intent, or have a theory of the other's mind, is similar to what Jessica Benjamin has explicated as the process of getting out from under "doer" versus "done-to" polarities by finding a third way to conceptualize a dilemma when the situation seems to define one person or action as all-good and the other person or action as all-bad.[17] Her concept of "recognition" is similar to Fonagy's notion of the capacity to mentalize. There are other psychoanalytic ways of describing the achievement of a capacity to see the other as a subject as well as an object, including the original Freudian idea that the oedipal phase is central to psychological growth—when the child can grasp that its caregivers have a relationship *with each other* that is not about oneself, this amounts to a developmental leap forward from normal childhood egocentrism into the capacity to imagine other people's separate psychologies.

It is critical to note that Klein carefully, and with good reason, framed the paranoid-schizoid and depressive orientations as "positions" rather than "phases" or "stages" of maturation that can be fully outgrown.[18] Even though it is more archaic then the depressive stance, the paranoid-schizoid disposition remains active throughout life. In states of intense feeling, even the most psychologically mature and emotionally nuanced among us can fall into a paranoid-schizoid state in which we look not for an understanding of what happened but for who is to blame. When a lover has betrayed one's trust, the injured person rarely concludes, "I can understand, given my lover's history, the origins of that behavior and appreciate how pained my beloved must have been to act in a way that made me suffer." Reactions to such experiences tend to be more like "That snake!"

This chapter emerged from a conference that was centrally concerned with understandings of, and remedies for, what I take to be the incontrovertible fact that we all have powerful and enduring psychological motives to attribute our own iniquities, errors, and limitations to others—especially when we are thrown off balance. When we are attacked, suddenly the world contains several "Evil Empires." (Are we surprised that after being equated with evil, North Korea intensified an identity as America's arch-enemy?) The paranoid-schizoid response is both basic to our identity and a defense against intolerable shame. Shame is one of the most unbearable affects we can experience. I say more about it shortly. But first, some thoughts about the relationship between destructive othering and normal needs for identity and self-esteem.

Distinguishing self from other

Let me reflect on my pride in my father-in-law's lifelong activism to segue into a central psychological paradox. If we take seriously the observations of centuries of thoughtful commentators on the human condition, and many decades of psychoanalytic reflection, we have to admit that no one can escape the wish to feel different from, and superior to, others. Like other mammals, members of the species *homo sapiens* seem naturally to think hierarchically and prefer to be on a higher rather than a lower rung of the implicit ladder by which our fellows rank our status. Neuroscientists have found we are hard-wired for dominance and submission.[19] Some sense of being "better than" seems central to our self-esteem. Christian ascetics who distain competitive strivings may nonetheless find themselves competing to be the *humblest* in their reference group.

Thus, even in earnest meetings about diversity and intersectionality, one sometimes senses an underlying smugness that *we* are the people who are really on top of these matters, unlike the prejudiced hordes. And if we are aware of that conceit, and able to be self-critical about it, we may then take narcissistic satisfaction in the depth of our honest self-scrutiny. Whatever the nobler aspects of my wish to honor my father-in-law's memory, I am implicitly asserting a kind of pedigree of enlightenment, or relationship to a claim of moral authority, that I suspect is of a piece with the dynamics that characterize versions of narcissistic entitlement and othering that are more patently ugly to most people reading this article.

That position of framing myself as among the enlightened, by the way, is not only problematic in its unattractive narcissistic relationship to an imagined other who is not so morally sensitive, but also sets me up to be hurt and humiliated whenever I am caught out in some prejudice or microaggression, at which point I tend to resort to paranoid-schizoid defenses against such feelings. This hazard may be the flip side of *any* assumption that one has achieved enough moral gravitas to be given a pass on small deviations from one's obvious good-enough-ness. This phenomenon may be of a piece with empirical findings that privileged people tend to feel more entitled to break rules than less advantaged individuals.[20] Like generations of Calvinists who eschewed the sin of pride and then worried there was pride in their assiduous modesty, we face certain embarrassments and enigmas when we grapple with this topic.

Part of the dilemma of how to improve attitudes vis-à-vis other selves involves the vicissitudes of normal cognitive and emotional maturation toward a feeling of having a self at all. We develop a sense of our separate existence and worth as individuals as much by establishing who we are *not* as by discovering who we are. The ancient Hebrew God notably tells the Israelites, "Do not, *as the Philistines do…*" Attachment to one's own reference groups, as differentiated from others, is central to identity and self-esteem. Developmental psychologists have found that children originally understand who they are through binaries involving big and little, male and female, and bad and good. Then other polarized concepts follow, helping to consolidate a relatively stable sense of "me." And yet, that sense of identity and belonging is what can make us oblivious to the competing moral claims of others.

Philosophers, poets, writers, theologians, and social scientists have addressed such contradictions for centuries, and political theorists from Plato on have wondered how citizens can feel part of, and responsible to, any community larger than a small city-state—a pressing issue in our current global context. What psychoanalysis may bring to the conversation is a paradoxically consoling pessimism, a sense of the impossibility of eradicating the darkest sides of our nature, and yet some ideas about psychological conditions under which we can embrace rather than project them. In this vein, Mark Twain famously stated: "I have no color prejudices nor caste prejudices nor creed prejudices. All I care to know is that a man is a human being, and that is enough for me; he can't be any worse."[21]

One core question to deal with here is how we can have a sense of our realistic differences from others without importing notions of better and worse into our perceptions. Psychologists and other clinicians once tried to handle this problem with efforts to be "value free" and "nonjudgmental." But most of us have acknowledged over the years that it is psychologically impossible, and even dangerously dishonest, to claim neutrality or strive to be free of what were once, judgmentally, called "value judgments." Therapists embody certain values. The ways we talk about other subjectivities and sensibilities are replete with assumptions of better and worse. I have been party to several agonized listserv discussions about how to respond when a patient mentions casually a prejudice that the therapeutic community finds offensive. When we thought it was too moralistic in tone to ask clients if they thought their behavior was right or correct or proper, we appropriated the word "inappropriate" to signal our disapproval. Within this pale contextualism, we continue to comment on right and wrong.

Therapists have never been impartial or indifferent about the directions in which we hope our patients will go. We want to be of use to people who suffer mentally and emotionally. To do so, we need some notion of what mental and emotional wellbeing is, and how a person's psychology may fall short of an ideal of wellness. For example, we may come to believe a client needs to have more tolerance of strong emotions, or more realistic and reliable self-esteem, or more resilience when stressed, or more capacity to love and work and play. It would be disingenuous to take on a role that invites people to come to us for help and at the same time to deny that we have any enlightened perspective on what would help them toward an ideal of wellness. But it is also hard to avoid slipping into objectifying those who struggle psychologically in ways that bother us—as illustrated, for example, by the judgmental responses typically evoked by the term "borderline."

I have struggled throughout my career with how to talk about individual differences without objectifying and othering. We need language that allows us to think about what is "wrong" or "not working" with a client that does not imply that the person is an inferior human being. To do this, we tend to develop nomenclature that we hope is simply descriptive and then revise it as it starts to take on overtones of disparagement. For example, we replaced the once-professional terms "idiot" and "moron" with "retarded," and then with "developmentally delayed," and then with "developmentally challenged." I am pretty sure, because the whole idea of mental limitations frightens us, that we will in the future continue revising our terms for cognitive difficulty. Any category that disturbs us gets this treatment, in an apparently doomed attempt to sanitize language so that overtones of better and worse are avoided. It has happened with "moral insanity," which became "psychopathy," which became "antisocial personality disorder." It happened with sexual "perversion"—originally an effort at nonjudgmental terminology, via the implication from the Latin that a person had simply *turned a different direction* in the road—which became "deviation," which is now officially "paraphilia." We will probably soon do this with "borderline." These cures by rewording may succeed for a while, but they eventually run into the problem that it is the phenomenon itself that evokes defensive othering, not the label.

Whatever the preoccupation of the person or group struggling to capture difference without implications of better and worse, a tendency to revert to contempt for the other seems to run deep in our psychological marrow. Each generation of intellectuals, for example, in the effort to contribute something new under the sun, tends to oversimplify, misrepresent, and devalue the ideas of those who preceded them. Falling into the most objectifying and alienating kinds of othering involves the processes of disavowal and projection, the two core defensive operations in the paranoid states in which painful or shameful feeling is relegated outside the self. And you don't have to be paranoid to use paranoid defenses regularly. I want to look here at four affect states—not the only ones, but perhaps the most common—that tend to incite the need to objectify, reify, or demean; namely, *fear, rage, envy,* and *shame.*

Othering and fear

This dynamic is perhaps the easiest to observe. In recent years, we have witnessed how fears of terrorist attack have unleashed the demons of hatred and rejection toward immigrants, Muslims, non-Europeans, and the liberal elites who defend them. I assume that alarm about these developments are part of what motivated the organizers of the conference at which my ideas were first presented. But let me share a less dramatic but still socially and politically consequential example of how fear can turn into objectification and domination, namely, the currently conventional treatment of those who have gone mad.

In recent years, I have been attending conferences of the International Society for Psychological and Social Approaches to Psychosis, which, in addition to mental health professionals, welcomes to its meetings and its governing bodies people who have been diagnosed with schizophrenia and other psychotic disorders ("experts by experience"), as well as family members of those individuals. I have now become acquainted with a number of men and women who have had significant psychotic breaks, usually accompanied by a diagnosis of schizophrenia and sometimes many years of involvement in in-patient facilities, yet whose lives have become satisfying and meaningful after psychotherapy. Many of them still hear voices. The fascinating autobiography of Elyn Saks,[22] attorney and psychoanalyst, suggests she may fit this description. I had known for some time that people who suffer trauma-based dissociative states but are not diagnosable as psychotic will often admit to hearing voices once they trust a therapist not to send them immediately to a psychiatric hospital, but until recently I had not had many opportunities to get to know individuals diagnosed as psychotic, especially those voice-hearers who are completely comfortable with the perceptual habits of their mind.

Interestingly, although professionals who have not had psychotic experiences themselves tend to see any non-substance-related hallucinations as pathognomonic of serious mental illness, and to reach unreflectively for heavy neuroleptic medication without considering psychotherapy, many people who hear voices regard them as incidental features of the terror, confusion, and self-dissolution that is *in their own experience* the central catastrophe of their psychosis. They may develop a positive relationship with their voices, viewing them as relics of the histories and vulnerabilities that caused them to fall into psychotic states, and not see them as problematic in themselves—much as a person whose leg was crushed and treated surgically might be accepting of a limp after the fractured limb has healed as well as nature and science allow. They may or may not appreciate help from ongoing antipsychotic medication.

So why do we rush to give profoundly sedating doses of chemicals to anyone who mentions hearing voices? Some of that knee-jerk response reflects reasonable worries about both safety and professional criticism, or client or family litigation, if the patient turns out to be violent to self or others. But I think the main psychological explanation is that the experience of these terrified, hard-to-comprehend people frightens us, and so we resort to othering and dominance. Specifically, we do not want to believe that with enough bad luck, we ourselves could descend into madness, and so we find it appealing to construe those who do as having a brain disorder without psychological meaning that requires only medication and "management." In this way, we have denied a needed therapeutic relationship to thousands of our most anguished fellows.

Othering and rage

Most of us have seen a toddler trip over a plaything and then hit or yell at the toy. The child's anger immediately attaches to the proximate object. When teased, dogs will bite even the hand that feeds them. Frustration does indeed provoke aggression. Jaak Panksepp's work in affective neuroscience has established that all mammals so far studied are prone to a rage reaction when systematically aggravated.[23] Our world continually irritates us. And when we are angry, it is hard to acknowledge that we are just pissed off for no higher reason than that we have been inconvenienced. We need a bad object, and we tell ourselves a story that supports our taking our anger out on that person or class of people.

In addition to anger deriving from the irritations of daily life, we know that people with trauma histories can be thrown into states of blind rage when something in their environment triggers a dissociated fury. Jonathan Shay, among many others, has explored this in his writing about the posttraumatic states suffered by combat veterans.[24] Again, the human tendency is to look for an object on which one's rage can be discharged. To make ourselves feel more in control and less crazily reactive, we tend to create narratives that make the attack on others seem rational. We convince ourselves, often in a nanosecond, that a particular person or group deserves to be the target of our rage, whose sources in our prior traumatic experiences may be completely out of consciousness. On the continuum from quotidian aggravations to wild posttraumatic fury, there is a lot of room for disowning angry feelings and convincing ourselves that someone else deserves to be their target. (At the same time, our deep understanding that hated others are also human beings may eventually surface in the form of guilt and a sense of moral injury.)

The art of politics includes, among other things, accepting this reality. Effective political leaders develop a story about who is responsible for one's anger and designate a platform and a nominee to do battle with that enemy. What candidates offer psychologically to their constituencies is relief of their inchoate rage and reduction of the emotional and intellectual exhaustion caused by the battering we take from dizzying change and complexity: the immigrants took your job. The corporate elites are brainwashing you. The government wastes your money. The evangelicals hate you. In my youth, our helpless anger and fear of the draft led us to shout "Off the pigs!"—not exactly a mentalized understanding of individuals wearing police uniforms. Drew Westen found, rather to his disappointment, that the brain processes activated by listening to political accounts of who is to blame are no different in right-wingers than in people on the left.[25]

Othering and envy

It is not hard to see the envy that lies behind our glee in lampooning the rich and powerful; Lorne Michaels and Jon Stewart made themselves culturally iconic by comforting us this way. And it is not hard to see envy in the schadenfreude we feel whenever a privileged adversary is laid low. But envy is also a factor, though a less intuitively obvious one, in our attitudes toward those at a *disadvantage* vis-à-vis a majority population. I have noticed this in myself many times—though I'm sure I have experienced it less consciously many more times. When I was a young child, even though there was anti-Semitism in my town, I was jealous of Jewish friends for being God's "chosen people." Later, I envied them for some of the values central to the Jewish tradition, but also for their creativity and wit. Jewish jokes are certainly the humor of the chronically oppressed, but that makes them even funnier.

I remember in college being acutely envious of people of color. I felt I had no ethnicity or cultural distinctiveness. This is often how majorities feel, though it is never true. But more vitally, I felt that darker people had a moral high ground that I would have loved to claim. Numerous heterosexual women have told me they envy lesbians—not just for not needing men, but for the joyous, provocative, edgy quality of some gay sub-cultures. Agnostic and atheistic people frequently comment on their envy toward individuals in religious minorities whose faith supplies them with clear-cut answers to the great, troubling human questions. When people attack "welfare queens," there is surely envy in the picture they have constructed of lazy, greedy women sitting back and being spoon-fed by Uncle Sam. Their own sloth or greed is thus disowned and projected into an enviable image of unearned gratification of dependency needs.

Unconscious envy seems intimately related to the ugliest kinds of othering. Envy that is conscious does not need to be dissociated and projected. But envy is usually, like fear and anger, a pretty intolerable state of mind. Some common kinds of envy, such as that of the old toward the young, are familiar enough to cause us to expect certain dissociations and projections. In this context, I remember a startling comment made by an elderly, rather conservative relative of mine in the early 1970s. He had been a teacher and eventually school super-intendent, and he kept abreast of trends among the young. About the "sexual revolution" of the era, he remarked to me and my husband, "These young people today! If I'd had those freedoms when *I* was young" (he shook his head ruefully, and we braced ourselves for the sermon) …"All the sex I could have had!" I bet he was a fine teacher and administrator—he embraced his envy and did not have to make young people into bad objects.

Othering and shame

Accompanying fear, anger, and envy can be unconscious shame about having those reactions in the first place. Shame about one's internal life seems to me the common denominator of most toxic othering. Because the feeling of exposure is so excruciating, the whole shame spectrum, from chagrin to humiliation to mortifi-cation, presses us to disavow and project. Bullying is a sure way to cause shame, and bullying has been empirically connected to later paranoid projection.[26]

One of the most valuable outcomes of my personal psychoanalysis was its access to disowned parts of myself of which I was profoundly ashamed. Mortify-ingly, the worst things that emerged in the transference were not my sexuality and aggression, but all kinds of othering utterly alien to my conscious self-image. For example, after three dreams in which a greedy Jewish thug stole my money, I had to accept my analyst's gentle suggestion that these images might have some-thing to do with his being Jewish. Admitting this was almost unbearable to my pro-Semitic conscious self. Disturbing racist images arose as well (they may have come up faster if my analyst had been black), even though I was close to several people of color and had participated in the Civil Rights movements of my era. My internalized sexism ran deep, as well. Whenever I dreamed I was doing something powerful, the dream portrayed me as male; unconsciously, I fully subscribed to the gender binary that power is inherently masculine and weakness inherently feminine. My emergence from that polarity, as from other areas of othering, has been long, arduous, and incomplete. All these journeys through what one of my colleagues calls "winces" were accompanied by a degree of shame that could only have been reduced by its exposure to a trusted other who loved me in all my depravity.

Many people feel automatic shame whenever they feel afraid; they construe even realistic fear as somehow a childish reaction that a grown-up should never indulge. It was striking on September 11, 2001, to hear one after another of our leaders characterizing the actions of the plane hijackers as "cowardly." The behavior of the jihadists may have been many things, but it was hardly symptomatic of a craven timidity. These men were willing to die for what they believed. The only way to understand the attribution of cowardice, I think, is to view it as a projection of the fears that we Americans were feeling, combined with an effort to shame people who, we assumed (again via projection), would be humiliated by our refusal to acknowledge that however evil it was, what they did was brave.

Myths of psychological and moral progress

Because we are chronically prone to affects that are hard to bear, I see the problem of othering as an unending one, requiring constant self-monitoring. The project of owning our own darkness, tolerating the shame it causes, and trying not to project it never ends. A sober look at the history of our species suggests it is dangerous to assume we will soon get, or have gotten, ahead of the process of disowning and projecting our badness. We have to keep working on improving things *as if* we are headed toward increasingly just solutions—and we do make progress in some areas—but we cannot expect our gains to be permanent, and we cannot safely divert our gaze from the ongoing moral responsibility of thinking about what kinds of people we may be othering even when we improve our treatment of some groups.

There is, especially among people in Western industrialized regions, a shared illusion, often referred to by social scientists as the "myth of progress," to the effect that not only do we move forward scientifically and technologically (and even that assumption can be challenged, as we know that valuable knowledge has been lost for centuries throughout the part of human history about which we know anything), but that we also progress psychologically and morally. What is the evidence for that? The best I have seen was marshalled in Steven Pinker's *The Better Angels of Our Nature.* [27] But while reading it, just when I was starting to feel persuaded of our species' progress toward greater overall humanity, we started hearing about the beheadings of journalists, the kidnapping and sexual slavery of young girls, and in the previously more putatively scrupulous United States, an increasing enthusiasm for torture.

Even as we ravage our planet, the belief that life is somehow going onward and upward persists. People who would not necessarily subscribe to assumptions that goodness will ultimately prevail can be heard making comments such as, "Who would have imagined that this could happen in the twenty-first century?!" As if a process of continuing moral improvement has some kind of historical inexorability. When Donald Trump won the 2016 election, part of the devastation and incredulity that followed among those who had opposed him seems to have been the destruction of a not-entirely-conscious fantasy that we were moving consistently forward toward progressive ideals: we had elected our first African-American President, we were about to elect our first female President, the Supreme Court had endorsed gay marriage, and we saw our political life as embracing closer and closer approximations of social justice. Our confidence that we were marching up the high road may have had a lot to do with our defeat in that election.

Sometimes one hears laments about people from a subordinated minority whose alleged failings are difficult to fathom because they, having suffered, should "know better." Individuals who survive mistreatment and who move into leadership roles among groups that once excluded them often inspire fond hopes for the ongoing improvement of the species. When the Abu Graib atrocities were reported, a feminist friend confided, "I could have believed that *male* soldiers were capable of such cruelty, but not *females!*" Whenever Barack Obama disappointed his admirers, it was not uncommon for them to lament that, as a black man, he should have had more perspective and worked harder for the oppressed. This is an unfair burden to lay on any human being who has already borne more criticism and rejection than his non-minority followers can imagine, and another symptom of our human tendency to project our own disavowed qualities. To blame trailblazers for not being superhuman is a defection from our own responsibility to keep working on social justice issues.

Some implications

Having reflected on how deep the process of othering goes, and having suggested at least by implication how unlikely it is that we can eliminate it simply via exhortation, example, and faith in the long-term effectiveness of cultural competency and diversity training initiatives (all of which are valuable but limited in their effects when up against the power of unconscious defensive processes), what am I recommending? Alas, I have no answers that have not been offered by many greater thinkers. But as a psychoanalyst, I find myself starting with the issue of shame. If I am right that shame about the contents of one's mind underlies most or all forms of othering, then we need to set a cultural tone of acceptance of the thoughts, feelings, fantasies, and impulses that are most often denied and projected, along with clear boundaries about what cannot be acted out. This was a vital part of the original Freudian project, and a part that I think is in danger of being thrown out with the bathwater of Freud's limitations and mistakes, as well as the rigidities and conceits of some mid-twentieth-century analysts.

A climate of acceptance of the uglier parts of our natures does make it easier not to be crushed by shame and thereby tempted toward denigration of others. The natural converse of shame is contempt—for self or other. The more ashamed we are of our insides, the more we loathe them, externalize them, and treat their projected targets with scorn. Some of the earliest analysts set a tone of remarkable honesty about exposing to one another their own shadow sides; their letters suggest an almost manic delight in confessing their aggression, their petty jealousies, their lust, their crippling "complexes." Their acceptance of those aspects of themselves did help the rest of us own some darker places and soften our defenses against them, even if, later, this identification with their moral courage morphed into a perverse pride that expressed itself in overt and covert messages to the effect that "I've been analyzed, so I'm better than you"—arguably the most historically destructive (and self-destructive) psychoanalytic version of othering.

Professionally, the early analysts were *not* so disclosing about their personal struggles. Their case presentations tended to sound like tales of the benign fairy godmother who rescues the benighted victim. In my view, one of the greatest achievements of the relational movement is its having changed the tone of clinical presentations such that the analyst's subjectivity is acknowledged in all its unattractiveness and complexity. Writers like Irwin Hirsch, for instance, have urged us to look more honestly at *all* our countertransference reactions, even our painful, greedy envy toward wealthy patients.[28] But we need to be careful lest, as with some of our analytic predecessors, contempt for those outside our community sneak into our discourse.

Respect

The natural antidote to the shame-contempt axis is *respect*. Ever since my former student, Oren Blass, wrote a doctoral thesis on the topic of the therapist's respect for the patient, I have been intrigued with the concept of respect.[29] In our field, we have countless articles about empathy, but in a literature review, Dr. Blass found only five articles about respect in the clinical situation. So he interviewed a number of seasoned therapists, asking them whether they found themselves giving thought to the issue of respect for their patients. It turns out they did. Interestingly, most said something like, "I find I have to work at that. Once you hear a person's story, it is usually easy to find empathy. But respect can be a harder attitude to generate and maintain." Some noted categories of clients who were difficult for them to respect—for example, cheaters of various kinds, pedophiles, and people whose substance use disorders kept getting the better of them. Given the fact that patients evaluate their therapy by how much they felt genuinely listened to and respected, this work got me thinking about how we conceptualize respect.[30]

I find myself thinking about the idea that respect involves "looking up" at someone. It is not synonymous with admiration, and it is certainly not equivalent to defensive idealization, but it contains the expectation that one can learn from the other, that the other has something of value to teach. It foregoes dominance and embraces an element of submission. It includes a readiness to be surprised, as Donnell Stern,[31] and Theodor Reik before him,[32] have emphasized. It embraces the attitude of humility that has been foregrounded in the writing of almost every great thinker who has tried to define wisdom as opposed to knowledge.

Respect is more about listening than knowing or showing. If any group can bear witness to the beneficent power of being listened to, it is analysts. Perhaps we do so much respectful listening hour after hour that we yearn, when *outside* the office, to have clear opinions and even to pontificate. This may reflect burnout we can all understand, but I think it is a mistake to act uncritically on our own need to dominate discussions with others. Whenever I hear colleagues talk about what we analysts have to *offer* to the larger society, from our unique perspective on human nature, and when we wonder together how to get analytic knowledge out to the wider world, I think we may have it backward. We need to listen more than we need to educate. The only way we will be seen by most of our compatriots as anything but elite liberal scolds is to give them the dignity that comes with our sincere effort to learn how they see the world.

We analysts tend to talk with each other and not with those outside our community. This insularity is not surprising—we have our own peculiar jargon and a specific knowledge base, and when we talk with our colleagues, we do not have to define our terms or defend what we do for a living. But being in an echo chamber is dangerous, and it has already cost us dearly. We need to engage with people and groups that differ significantly from us, assuming that we can learn from the other even if we are in conversation with someone we see as a religious zealot, a bigot, a self-deluded simpleton, or an apologist for terrorism.

Nothing in what I am saying here, by the way, should be understood as discouraging political activity that necessarily finds itself in the paranoid-schizoid position. That is simply the way our system works, and always has: we choose a side, we have our enemies, and we work to get like-minded people in power and frustrate those whose vision differs. But in the professional, private, and public spheres outside electoral politics, we have to do better at respecting even those whose views we abhor. Otherwise, we will languish in our bubble.

Ongoing self-scrutiny and acknowledgment of limitation

It has been critical in the evolution and reputation of psychoanalysis as a discipline, as in the development of any field nourished by the curiosity of the scientist, for us to learn to stress how much we do *not* know. And, as leading analytic voices have been reminding us for a couple of decades, we have come to agree that the *clinical* attitude of "not knowing" is crucial to a sensibility that promotes healing. In an age of treatment by acronym, when governments, corporations, and some professional guilds badger us to treat all human suffering with the latest quick fix that seemed to work in the psych lab or the pharmaceutical trial, we need to talk back to the powerful and insist on honesty about the limitations of what we know. In this context, Neil Altman,[33] Usha Tummala-Narra,[34] Malin Fors[35] and others emphasize that cultural competence is not so much about mastering a subject area as retaining an openness to learning, a willingness to let ourselves be taken over by an intersubjective process that will psychologically enrich both our patients and ourselves.

Many of us in the helping professions came to our vocation at least partly out of curiosity about differences among human beings. Although Fonagy and his colleagues have framed the capacity to mentalize as a developmental attainment that gets organized in early childhood, it is also a lifelong, never-ending process. In fact, one of the pleasures of being a therapist is that one's capacity to imagine minds different from one's own continues to grow and become more nuanced with every professional experience. Supervision and consultation in human relations fields often involves stretching the capacity to mentalize—whether it is to imagine what it would be like to be psychotic, or addicted, or stuck in a post-traumatic loop; or to imagine what it would be like to be an adoptee, or a triplet, or a kid who is bullied, or a Syrian exile, or a rape victim, or an elderly person facing dementia. It never ends. And neither should our efforts to keep taking seriously other perspectives that may seem alien. Or our obligation to be unflinchingly honest about the less palatable aspects of our own psychologies. We need to embrace those realistically and without shame if we are to avoid the attractions of a sense of moral superiority and refrain from projecting our disowned negative self-states on devalued others. If the arc of the universe does bend toward justice, it will only be because enough people in every generation do not take that arc for granted and continue to face painful truths not only about the other but also about the self. In closing, let me recall Freud's profound belief, for which I suggest that there is immense evidence, perhaps especially lately, that civilization is not an automatic or inevitable arrangement for human beings.[36] Civility is fragile. Governments may be more fragile than international corporations. The work never stops.

Notes

1 I am grateful to Malin Fors for conversations that have kept me abreast of current psychological literature relevant to othering. I appreciate also the helpful reflections on this chapter from my political scientist daughter, Susan McWilliams, and my husband, Michael Garrett.
2 C. Wright Mills, *The Power Elite* (Berkeley: University of California Press, 1956).
3 Carey McWilliams, *A Mask for Privilege: Anti-Semitism in America* (Boston: Little, Brown, 1948).
4 Carey McWilliams, *Prejudice: Japanese-Americans, Symbol of Racial Intolerance* (Boston: Little, Brown, 1944).
5 Carey McWilliams, *North from Mexico: The Spanish-Speaking Peoples of the United States* (Philadelphia: Lippincott, 1949).
6 Carey McWilliams, *Factories in the Field: The Story of Migratory Farm Labor in California* (Boston: Little, Brown, 1939).
7 Carey McWilliams, *Brothers Under the Skin: African-Americans and Other Minorities* (Boston: Little, Brown, 1943).
8 Wilson Carey McWilliams, *The Idea of Fraternity in America* (Berkeley, CA: University of California Press, 1973).

9 Sigmund Freud et al. "Totem and Taboo," in *The Standard Edition of the Complete Psychological Works of Sigmund Freud,* vol. 13 (London: Hogarth Press and the Institute of Psycho-Analysis, 1913), 1–161.

10 Daniel J. Gaztambide, "'A Psychotherapy for the People': Freud, Ferenczi, and Psychoanalytic Work with the Underprivileged," *Contemporary Psychoanalysis* 48, no. 2 (2012): 141–165.

11 Sigmund Freud et al. "Lines of Advance in Psychoanalytic Therapy," in *The Standard Edition of the Complete Psychological Works of Sigmund Freud,* vol. 17 (London: Hogarth Press and the Institute of Psycho-Analysis, 1918), 159–168.

12 Alfred M. Freedman, "The Future of Psychoanalysis as a Profession," *Journal of the American Academy of Psychoanalysis* 2, no. 1 (1974): 27–40.

13 Melanie Klein, "Notes on Some Schizoid Mechanisms," *International Journal of Psycho-Analysis* 27 (1946): 99–110.

14 Peter, Fonagy et al., *Affect Regulation, Mentalization, and the Development of the Self* (New York: Other Press, 2002).

15 Henry D. Schlinger, "Theory of Mind: An Overview and Behavioral Perspective," *The Psychological Record* 59, no. 3 (2009): 435–448.

16 Klein, "Notes on Some Schizoid Mechanisms," 99–110.

17 Jessica Benjamin, "Beyond Doer and Done To: An Intersubjective View of Thirdness," *Psychoanalytic Quarterly* 73, no. 1 (2004): 5–46.

18 Thomas H. Ogden, "On the Dialectical Structure of Experience—Some Clinical and Theoretical Implications," *Contemporary Psychoanalysis* 24, no. 1 (1988): 17–45.

19 Jaak Panksepp, "The Long-Term Psychobiological Consequences of Infant Emotions: Prescriptions for the 21st Century," *Neuro-Psychoanalysis* 3, no. 2 (2001): 149–178.

20 Paul K. Piff et al., "Higher Social Class Predicts Increased Unethical Behavior," *PNAS* 109, no. 11, (2012): 4086–4091.

21 Mark Twain, "Concerning the Jews," *Harper's New Monthly Magazine,* Sept. 1899, 527–535.

22 Elyn R. Saks, *The Center Cannot Hold: My Journey Through Madness* (New York: Hyperion, 2008).

23 Jaak Panksepp and Lucy Biven, *The Archeology of Mind: Neuroevolutionary Origins of Human Emotions* (New York: Norton, 2012).

24 Jonathan Shay, *Achilles in Vietnam: Combat Trauma and the Undoing of Character* (New York: Scribner, 1994). Jonathan Shay, "Moral Injury," *Psychoanalytic Psychology* 31, no. 2 (2014): 182–191.

25 Drew Westen, *The Political Brain: The Role of Emotion in Deciding the Fate of the Nation* (New York: Public Affairs, 2007).

26 Jan Anderson et al., "Understanding Suicidal Behaviour in Young People Referred to Specialist CAMHS: A Qualitative Psychoanalytic Clinical Research Project," *Journal of Child Psychotherapy* 38, no. 2 (2012): 130–153.

27 Steven Pinker, *The Better Angels of Our Nature: Why Violence Has Declined* (New York: Viking, 2011).

28 Irwin Hirsch, Coasting in the Countertransference: Conflicts of Self-Interest Between Analyst and Patient (New York: Analytic Press, 2009).

29 Oren Blass, "Respect for the Patient: A Qualitative Study," PhD diss. (Rutgers University, 2006).

30 Mary Leamy, et al., "Conceptual Framework for Personal Recovery in Mental Health: Systematic Review and Narrative Synthesis," British Journal of Psychiatry 199, no. 6 (2001): 445–452.

31 Donnell Stern, "The Social Construction of Therapeutic Action," Psychoanalytic Inquiry 18, no. 2 (1996): 265–293.

32 Theodor Reik, *Listening with the Third Ear. The Inner Experience of a Psychoanalyst* (New York: Farrar, Straus, and Giroux, 1949).

33 Neil Altman, "Black and White Thinking: A Psychoanalyst Reconsiders Race," *Psychoanalytic Dialogues* 10, no. *4* (2000): 589–605.
34 Pratyusha Tummala-Narra, *Psychoanalytic Theory and Cultural Competence in Psychotherapy* (Washington, DC: American Psychological Association, 2016).
35 Malin Fors, *A Grammar of Power in Psychotherapy: Exploring the Dynamics of Privilege* (Washington, DC: American Psychological Association, 2018).
36 Sigmund Freud, et al. "Civilization and its Discontents," in *The Standard Edition of the Complete Psychological Works of Sigmund Freud*, vol. 21 (London: Hogarth Press and the Institute of Psycho-Analysis, 1930), 59–145.

References

Altman, N. (2000). "Black and white thinking: A psychoanalyst reconsiders race. "*Psychoanalytic Dialogues*, 10(4), 589–605.

Anderson, J., Hurst, M., Marques, A., Millar, D., Moya, S., Pover, L., & Stewart, S. (2012). "Understanding suicidal behaviour in young people referred to specialist CAMHS: A qualitative psychoanalytic clinical research project. "*Journal of Child Psychotherapy*, 38(2), 130–153.

Benjamin, J. (2004). "Beyond doer and done to: An intersubjective view of thirdness. "*Psychoanalytic Quarterly*, 73(1), 5–46.

Blass, O. (2006). "Respect for the patient: A qualitative study. " Unpublished doctoral dissertation, Rutgers University.

Danto, E. A. (2005). *Freud's free clinics: Psychoanalysis and social justice, 1918–1938.* New York: Columbia University Press.

Fonagy, P., Gergely, G., Jurist, E. I., & Target, M. (2002). *Affect regulation, mentalization, and the development of the self.* New York: Other Press.

Fors, M. (2018). *A grammar of power in psychotherapy: Exploring the dynamics of privilege.* Washington, DC: American Psychological Association.

Freedman, A. M. (1974). "The future of psychoanalysis as a profession." *Journal of the American Academy of Psychoanalysis*, 2(1), 27–40.

Freud, S. (1913). *Totem and taboo.* Standard Edition, 13. London: Hogarth Press, 1–161.

Freud, S. (1918). *Lines of advance in psychoanalytic therapy.* Standard Edition, 17. London: Hogarth Press, 159–168.

Freud, S. (1930). *Civilization and its discontents.* Standard Edition, 21. London: Hogarth Press, 59–145.

Gaztembide, D. J. (2012). "A psychotherapy for the people: Freud, Ferenczi, and psychoanalytic work with the underprivileged." *Contemporary Psychoanalysis*, 48(2), 141–165.

Hirsch. I. (2009). *Coasting in the countertransference: Conflicts of self-interest between analyst and patient.* New York: Analytic Press.

Klein, M. (1946). "Notes on some schizoid mechanisms." *International Journal of Psycho-Analysis*, 27, 99–110.

Leamy, M., Bird, V., Le Bontillier, C., Williams, J., & Slade, M. (2011). "Conceptual framework for personal recovery in mental health: Systematic review and narrative synthesis." *British Journal of Psychiatry*, 199(6), 445–452. doi:10.1192/bjp.bp.110.083733.

McWilliams, C. (1939). *Factories in the field: The story of migratory farm labor in California.* Boston: Little, Brown.

McWilliams, C. (1944). *Prejudice: Japanese-Americans, symbol of racial intolerance.* Boston: Little, Brown.

McWilliams, C. (1946). *Southern California country: An island on the land.* New York: Duell, Sloane & Pearce.

McWilliams, C. (1948). *A mask for privilege: Anti-Semitism in America.* Boston: Little, Brown.

McWilliams, C. (1949). *North from Mexico: The Spanish-speaking peoples of the United States.* Philadelphia: Lippincott.

McWilliams, C. (1943). *Brothers under the skin: African-Americans and other minorities.* Boston: Little, Brown.

McWilliams, W. C. (1973). *The idea of fraternity in America.* Berkeley, CA: University of California Press.

Mills, C. W. (1956). *The power elite.* New York: Oxford University Press.

Ogden, T. H. (1988). "On the dialectical structure of experience—Some clinical and theoretical implications." *Contemporary Psychoanalysis,* 24, 17–45.

Panksepp, J. (2001). "The long-term psychobiological consequences of infant emotions: Prescriptions for the 21st century." *Neuro-Psychoanalysis,* 3, 149–178.

Panksepp, J. & Biven, L. (2012). *The archeology of mind: Neuroevolutionary origins of human emotions.* New York: Norton.

Piff, P. K., Stancato, D. M., Côté, S., Mendoza-Denton, R., & Keltner, D. (2012). "Higher social class predicts increased unethical behavior." *PNAS,* 109, 4086–4091. doi:10.1073/pnas.111837310.

Pinker, S. (2011). *The better angels of our nature: Why violence has declined.* New York: Viking.

Reik, T. (1949). *Listening with the third ear. The inner experience of a psychoanalyst.* New York: Farrar, Straus.

Saks, E. R. (2008). *The center cannot hold: My journey through madness.* New York: Hyperion Press.

Schlinger, H. D. (2009). "Theory of mind: An overview and behavioral perspective. "*The Psychological Record,* 59, 435–448.

Shay, J. (1994). *Achilles in Vietnam: Combat trauma and the undoing of character.* New York: Scribner.

Shay, J. (2014). "Moral injury." *Psychoanalytic Psychology,* 31(2), 182–191.

Stern, D. B. (1996). "The social construction of therapeutic action." *Psychoanalytic Inquiry,* 18(2), 265–293.

Tummala-Narra, P. (2016). *Psychoanalytic theory and cultural competence in psychotherapy.* Washington, DC: American Psychological Association.

Twain, M. (1899). "Concerning the Jews." *Harper's New Monthly Magazine,* September, 527–535.

Westen, D. (2007). *The political brain: The role of emotion in deciding the fate of the nation.* New York: Public Affairs.

11

AFTER THE WORLD COLLAPSED

Two Culturally Embedded Forms of Service to Others Following Wide-Scale Societal Traumas[1]

Doris Brothers and Koichi Togashi

"If I sleep for an hour, 30 people will die." These dramatic words were uttered by Adolfo Kaminsky to explain why he had stayed awake for two days and nights in order to forge passports for Jews desperate to flee from the Nazis.[2] Even after WWII ended, Kaminsky, who accepted no payment and sought no acclaim, forged passports that saved the lives of thousands of people caught up in a variety of life-or-death struggles.

This chapter represents our attempt to understand what moves survivors of horrific wide-scale societal traumas, like Mr. Kaminsky, to sacrifice their own well-being in their efforts to help others in a wounded society. We are particularly interested in how responses of this kind reflect the culture in which the traumatic experience occurred. Rather than seeing altruistic acts in the aftermath of a devastating societal trauma as a result of what is known as "survivor guilt," we suggest that culturally influenced efforts to memorialize the cataclysm and to repair and sacralize that which was so brutally injured reflects a renunciation of self-centered individuality and an embrace of a profound sense of relational connectedness. Turning to a research study of survivors of the 9/11 terrorist attacks in New York and the survivors of the Great Hanshin-Awaji Earthquake in Japan, we examine the differences and similarities in the responses of members of both groups, and illustrate two culturally embedded forms of service to others following wide-scale societal traumas. We then attempt to understand aspects of the ethical philosophy of Levinas in terms of his devastating experience of the Holocaust as a form of service to others in the West, and the ethical responsibility of selflessness[3] as a form of service to others in the East. We then offer examples from our analytic practices.

Forms of service to others following wide-scale societal traumas

Mr. Kaminsky's actions seem to exemplify what is usually meant by the term "altruism" or "selfless concern for the well-being of others."[4] Controversies about the nature of altruism or selflessness abound in philosophy and psychology. Is it an inborn human characteristic with evolutionary advantage for the survival of the human species? Or is it, as Nietzsche suggests, degrading and demeaning to oneself, a hindrance to self-development and creativity? While Victor Frankl,[5] writing about acts of altruism in the Nazi concentration camps, suggests that finding some measure of meaning through caring for others was necessary for survival, Tvetan Todorov, who has also written about altruism in the camps, argues that the reward for altruism "lies in the act itself; in caring for another, one continues to care for oneself as well."[6] We have wondered if the sort of mutual caring that Todorov alludes to—even when it entails the sacrifice of one's own life—might provide the sublime experience, often called love, that we find only in connection to another when his or her well-being means more to us than our own.

We have all heard stories of people who have sacrificed their own lives to save another's in the immediacy of some imminent mortal threat: soldiers shield comrades against bullets or explosives with their own bodies; firefighters enter blazing buildings to help those trapped inside; passengers jump into the sea to rescue a shipmate who falls overboard. But it is not only when another person's life is at risk that altruistic behavior seems to arise; it is also a common response among those whose homeland has been gravely threatened in some way.[7] This finding aligns with Mark Freeman's contention that it is not only the human Other that draws us out of ourselves, but that we sometimes give priority to non-human Others. For Freeman, "the Other is constituted and defined essentially by its power over me, its capacity to call forth my attention and desire."[8] Art and nature are his examples of nonhuman Others that wield this power. Perhaps we can understand the altruistic responses following some wide-scale societal trauma by viewing the wounded homeland as a nonhuman Other.

Many attempts have been made by such writers as Freeman, Todorov, and Frankl to find universal meanings in the behaviors involved in services to Others, or altruistic behavior. And many psychology researchers have sought to show that it is innate. However, there are new psychological findings that lend weight to the idea that specific relational contexts may powerfully affect the meanings of acts of services to the others, or altruism. For example, in a 2006 study, eighteen-month-old toddlers were found to be willing to give a helping hand to experimenters without being prompted. This expression of service to the Other or altruistic behavior in such young children supported the assumption of an innate disposition for this behavior. But Barragan and Dweck, two graduate students at Stanford, wondered if, by engaging in a few minutes of play with the toddlers, the researchers had primed them toward acts of service to the Other, or altruistic behavior. They conducted a study that compared toddlers who engaged in reciprocal play with the researchers with toddlers who engaged in parallel play with them. Those who engaged in reciprocal play were three times more likely to help the researchers. Carey interpreted the results to mean that this behavior may be governed more by relational contexts than by instincts.[9]

We would go one step further than Carey by suggesting that since our relationships are profoundly affected by the society in which our lives are inextricably embedded, every act of service to others is given meaning by the cultural contexts in which the act arises. A study on wide-scale societal traumas that we have conducted[10] supports the idea that the meanings of any given act and the precise form it takes may be quite different from culture to culture. For the first two phases of our study we conducted in-depth interviews of eight survivors of the 9/11 terrorist attacks on the World Trade Center in New York, and nine survivors of the Great Hanshin-Awaji Earthquake in Japan. We found that, in the aftermath of these events, a great many of those interviewed had responded altruistically. It may well be that volunteering to participate in our study reflected their determination to be of service.

On September 11, 2001, nineteen militants associated with the Islamic extremist group al-Qaeda hijacked four airplanes and carried out suicide attacks against targets in the United States. Two of the planes were flown into the twin towers of the World Trade Center in New York City, a third plane hit the Pentagon just outside Washington, D.C., and the fourth plane crashed in a field in Pennsylvania. Almost 3,000 people were killed during the 9/11 terrorist attacks. The Great Hanshin earthquake occurred on January 17, 1995, in the southern part of Hyogo Prefecture, Japan. It measured 7.3 on the Richter scale of force. By May 19, 2006, 6,434 people lost their lives, three people were missing, and 40,092 people were injured.[11] It is considered Japan's worst earthquake in the 20th century after the Great Kanto earthquake in 1923, and before the Great East Japan Earthquake in 2011.

The fact that the American participants had been subjected to trauma inflicted by humans and the Japanese participants were subjected to trauma caused by a natural disaster undoubtedly played a role in some of the differences we found between the two groups. Nevertheless, the answers given to our research questions by the participants in both groups closely correspond to differences that psychologists, sociologists and anthropologists have found between American and Japanese cultures. For the most part, these differences pertain to the value American people tend to place on individuality and the value that Japanese people tend to place on "collectiveness." The sense of collectiveness among Japanese people is reflected in the Japanese word "*wa*," which according to Sakisaka means: "making oneself pure enough to reflect others' minds."[12] This idea is also expressed in a Japanese word that is associated with Buddhist tradition: "*ichiren-takusho*,"[13] which means having one's share of the shared life space.[14]

This difference seems apparent in answers we received to our study question "In what way do you experience yourself as a survivor?" The Americans all found some way to see themselves as survivors, while almost none of the Japanese did. Many of the Japanese said that they could not call themselves survivors because others had suffered more devastating effects of the earthquake than they had. We imagine that the Americans saw themselves as survivors because they based their answer on their own traumatic experiences without much consideration for the traumas of others, while the Japanese, who experience all human beings and creatures in this world as part of the bigger flow of the cosmos, may have felt compelled to think of their own experiences in terms of the comparative effects of the earthquake on others. However, one American participant who identified as a Buddhist, when asked if he considered himself a survivor, responded: "Aren't we all?" He recalled "the sense of solidarity" that New Yorkers felt in the immediate aftermath of the 9/11 attacks.

Another striking difference between the two groups involves our finding that only one of the Americans spoke of the need to keep the memory of 9/11 alive in the next generation, while all of the Japanese emphasized feeling that it was their duty to tell young people about the earthquake. Here is how one of the Japanese participants, a kindergarten teacher, expressed this need:

> we should tell what happened to the next generation as a lesson. We have a mission. I thought at that time we were allowed to live—not saying we were selected—but we slept together and some of us might have passed away. It was possible…I heard of parents who lost their children who were sleeping by their side in the same bed. So I felt I was allowed to live. It means to me that I have to leave something to the next generation. It is my duty to let the next generation know what happened.

Other Japanese participants indicated that it was not just because they and their family members had survived when so many others were killed that they felt a moral obligation to inform the next generation about the earthquake; it was the acts of giving that were performed by and for others that needed to be remembered. One woman linked her gratitude for the help she received when her house was rendered unlivable by the earthquake to her need to tell the next generation about the earthquake. She explained that she had conveyed her gratitude to her daughters to help them "become people who can understand such a tragic experience." And presumably also to become people who can prioritize others at such times.

Many members of both groups responded to the disasters by devoting themselves to some form of service to survivors. One American newscaster volunteers every year to host a commemorative 9/11 telecast. An American lawyer worked pro bono to secure monetary benefits for those who lost family members in the World Trade Towers. An American mental health practitioner provided her massage-therapy services to survivors without payment. Many of the Japanese participants sheltered and fed other survivors in their own homes. One Japanese restaurant owner re-opened his restaurant in a new location two weeks after the earthquake because he felt that it was his responsibility to keep one of his workers employed. A Japanese priest worked to fight the fires that broke out in the immediate aftermath of the earthquake.

We suspect that in the immediate aftermath of a severe societal trauma occurring anywhere in the world, the sense of collectiveness among the survivors and the need to be of service to others may be especially great. However, the duration of time that such feelings last may depend on the relative strength placed on collectiveness in each culture. Immediately after the 9/11 attacks, American survivors may have felt as intimately connected to members of their wounded society as the Japanese, but because Americans do not share a cultural pride in their collectiveness, they may have felt no need to urge the next generation to remember.

The ethical philosophy of Levinas

The injunction never to forget, indeed, the "moral imperative to remember" is very much associated with the Holocaust. We believe it may be possible to understand Emmanuel Levinas's focus on our infinite responsibility to the Other both in terms of his altruistic response to the devastation wreaked by the Holocaust and as a reflection of the profound influence of his Jewish heritage. As Michael Kigel, the translator of Salomon Malka's biography of Levinas, observes, "Levinas's work is organized around a hidden referent, the Shoah."[15] And after mentioning that Levinas wrote very little about the Nazi horror, Malka notes: "it [the Holocaust] dominated his entire intellectual history and literary career."[16] And although he never wrote about his own experiences at a Nazi work camp, Malka suggests: "The experience of captivity was nevertheless decisive for Levinas, the encounter with the most simple things, the ordeal of loss and of liberty, the sensation of time, deliquescence, misery, absolute passivity, fragility, precariousness—everything that continually tormented his work."[17]

We would suggest that the nonhuman Other that claimed priority for Levinas was neither of his homelands—not Lithuania, the nation of his birth, nor France, the nation where he chose to live after the war; it was the entire world. Among his religious teachers was Rabbi Israel Salanter who added to the Haskalah precept, "Be Jewish at home and human outdoors," with the words: "Be Jewish and human everywhere."[18] Greatly influenced by Franz Rosensweig during his stay in Freiberg, Levinas came to consider the universal and the human, and to see Judaism as a "path to truth." In a discussion with Alain Finkielkraut on the theme of Israel and Jewish ethics that was broadcast on Radio Communautè on September 28th, 1982, Levinas said:

I have always thought of Jewish consciousness as an attentiveness which is kept alert by centuries of inhumanity and pays particular attention to what occasionally is human in man: the feeling that you personally are implicated each time that somewhere—especially when it's somewhere close to you—humanity is guilty.[19]

Levinas seems to suggest that because the Jews have been treated inhumanely for centuries, they are especially conscious of the responsibility each human has for the Other. Perhaps, we could say, that as a Jew who had personally experienced the horror of the Holocaust, his philosophical writings convey the truth of our inescapable relationality.

Like the Japanese, who emphasized the need to keep the memory of their experiences alive in the coming generations, in a text titled "Nameless," Levinas[20] wrote:

We must henceforth, in the inevitable resumption of civilization and assimilation, teach the new generations the strength necessary to be strong in isolation and all that a fragile consciousness is called upon to contain at such times. We must—in reviving the memory of those non-Jews and Jews, who, without even knowing or seeing one another, found a way to behave amid total chaos, as if the world had not fallen apart—remembering the resistance of the Maquis, that is, precisely a resistance having no other source but one's own certainty and inner self; we must, through such memories, open up a new access to the Jewish texts and give new priority to the inner life.[21]

The Maquis mentioned by Levinas were rural guerilla bands of French Resistance fighters during WWII. Operating in the remote regions of Southern France they bravely aided in the escape of many Jews and downed Allied airmen. Here, Levinas is asserting the need to keep the memory alive for coming generations—not merely that the Holocaust had occurred but how some behaved in a collapsing world—that is, altruistically.

Ethical responsibility of selflessness

As our study confirms, many Japanese people say that it is their duty to do something for others—even to their own detriment. It is well known that in Japan there is a strong cultural mandate to educate children to think about others before themselves and to be concerned about how other people feel about them. This type of education has profound cultural meanings that *have become deeply embedded in their ethical values.* As Watsuji [22] and Sagara [23] *argue, this type* of generosity, which is based on the *makoto* form of sincerity, has been considered to be one of the essential virtues of Japanese morality. In business, too, it is considered one of the highest moral values for people to put their customers' (unspoken) needs ahead of their own economic benefit.[24]

We would say that the *makoto* form of moral value is not necessarily the same as altruism among Westerners or even Levinasian ethics, which requires a person to respond to the call of the Other. While Levinasian ethics is inherently different from an egocentric morality, the term, altruism, a priori includes differences between self and other. In this ethic, the person who gives service to the Other recognizes the radical alterity of the Other, which can never be reduced to one-self or any other beings in the world. In contrast, while there are many forms of Japanese ethics, according to the *makoto* form, there is no difference between self and the other, or self and the world; or to put it more strongly, there is no sense of self and the other or self and the world.

According to the *makoto* ethic, when people do something for others while sacrificing their own well-being, they often do so for the "Way of Heaven," which includes themselves, others, and all beings in this world. In this sense, they do not act for others, nor do they sacrifice themselves. But they act by trusting in the will of Heaven, believing that doing so is their role.

Many of the Japanese earthquake survivors we interviewed said, "I felt I was allowed to live." This indicates that they were guided by a metaphysical principle by means of which they see acts of service to others as a moral responsibility in keeping with the Way of Heaven, that is, the moral value of selflessness and otherlessness. According to this moral value, they do not conceptualize them-selves before or after encountering others; they do not recognize the radical alterity of the Other, but see self and the world as inseparable.

A Japanese psychiatrist, Uchinuma, who studied culturally-bound anthro-pophobia, taijin-kyofu—an extreme, pathological form of shyness and timidity—suggests that this syndrome is an expression of a culturally unique interpersonal conflict. For him, the conflict emerges in the extremes of the interpersonal situation, such as "self-centeredness vs. other-centeredness,"[25] "selfishness vs. selflessness,"[26] and "separation vs. merger."[27] A unique contribution of his theory is understanding the treatment process to be one of ethical development in which a feeling of shame is transformed to a feeling of embarrassment, then to a feeling of guilt, and finally to a state beyond right and wrong. On this account, shame and guilt are experientially close and located in one developmental line. He suggests that a therapeutic moment is often built in a non-conflict space between the two extremes of the interpersonal situation; the space in which patients sur-render themselves by releasing a preoccupation with self, other and society.

Nakakuki,[28] in his cross-cultural psychoanalytic study, maintains that maso-chism should not be considered to be psychopathological or a defense. He believes that it has a healthy form and its own developmental line. While his discussion is framed in terms of a classical, one-person perspective—it considers the development of aggression in an intrapsychic mind—his article is innovative because he maintains that self-sacrificing acts by Japanese people should be con-sidered as emerging in a specific cultural and relational context. He stresses that acts of service to others and selflessness among Japanese people are not defenses as argued in Western psychoanalysis, but reflect a healthy need which emerges in human minds for its own sake. Japanese people, according to him, are guided by a moral value to maintain the collective union of the society.

Togashi, in his study of patients who feel "guilty of being" and who believe that they cause trouble to others simply by being in this world, discusses this type of moral value in Japan:

> The ethical dimension in these models is different from that in Western psychoanalytic models in which the moral imperative for patients is understood to be having an integrative self that allows them to take responsibility for deliberation, choice and action.[29] In Japanese models, on the other hand, the moral ideal for patients is considered to be attaining the state of selflessness. It is not until patients relinquish their preoccupation with themselves that they can achieve a state beyond good and bad, or right and wrong. It is no wonder that these treatment models do not include a process for working through transference, for dealing with transference means that patients are expected to focus on themselves and others.[30]

The interview responses of both the American and Japanese participants in our study suggest that, for them, acts of service to others do not necessarily serve as defenses or coping processes for recovering from massive disasters. Rather, reward is experienced in the act itself. We do not wish to generalize our findings to all those who identify themselves as American or Japanese. However, despite the different cultural meanings that their acts of service held for the American and the Japanese participants in our study, we do not believe that their acts served defensive purposes. Rather, we believe that as moral acts that define human beings they were experienced as profoundly rewarding. It is an expression of being human in connection to an Other when that Other's well-being means more than one's own. These are deeply culturally embedded moral acts by human beings.

Clinical vignettes

In order to illustrate two culturally embedded forms of service to others following wide-scale societal traumas, we describe how an American and a Japanese patient responded to wide-scale societal traumas with acts of service to others.

Lena

Lena was born some 45 years ago into a WASP family that could trace its roots back to the Mayflower. Shortly after her mother died when she was nine years old, her father married Alice, a coldly ambitious woman, who seemed to believe that attuned responsiveness to a child's needs for mirroring and idealization amounted to coddling them. She mocked the tears Lena shed over the loss of her beloved mother and viciously demeaned her as "a trust fund baby" because of the small fund that her mother had set up for her.

When her father, an emotionally remote man who had become increasingly alcoholic after his first wife's death, moved the family to Nepal where he had business interests, Lena fell in love with the country and its people. She was delighted by what she called the Nepalese attitude of "radical worthiness" by which she meant that no matter how physically or intellectually challenged a person was, he or she would be included in the community. For the first time, Lena said she felt accepted for simply being who she was and not because "I had earned my keep." She was enthralled with the history of Nepal and often spoke with village elders about their religious rituals and beliefs.

After the family returned to America, Lena, with little help from her family, applied and was accepted into an Ivy League college where she majored in comparative religion. Within a year of graduating, she married a rather self-involved older man who was a well-known academic. Never having developed her own talents or interests, she devoted herself to furthering her husband's career and to raising their two children. By the time Lena entered treatment with me (Doris Brothers) her husband had fallen ill and, since he could no longer work, the burden of supporting the family had fallen on her.

Despite what I imagined to be her longings for nurturance and guidance, Lena maintained a polite, compliant but somewhat guarded relationship with me. Although she joined me in examining the conflict between her need to sustain her ties to her stepmother and father by continuing to endorse their ethos of rugged individualism and her longing to recapture the tender mirroring she had lost when her mother died, our work proceeded very slowly.

A shocking trauma served as a much-needed turning point for us. Lena had traveled to Nepal to visit old friends when the devastating earthquake of April, 2015 struck. Terribly worried about her and unable to reach her by phone or email, I contacted her sister who informed me that despite harrowing experiences, Lena had survived. Our reunion was tearful and openhearted. Severely traumatized by her narrow escape from a collapsed building and her flight through streets filled with injured and dying people, she was overcome with memories of her mother's pain-filled last days. She was also filled with grief over the plight of the Nepalese survivors and the destruction of the country she loved.

Lena, clearly moved by my obvious concern for her and my relief that she had survived, tearfully expressed her gratitude for my efforts to reach her and admitted to feeling surprised that she mattered to me. "I guess I thought I was just someone you had to connect with to do your job," she said. When she expressed doubt that I could understand her urgent need to devote herself to helping those devastated by the Nepalese catastrophe, I decided to tell her about the work I had done with a Red Cross team and at a phone center following the 9/11 attacks—my trauma-generated response to the wounding of my beloved city. As we spoke about her fund-raising efforts on behalf of Nepalese survivors, the distance between us seemed to melt away. At last it seemed that we became able to create a "story of us" that allowed us both a sense of twinship and shared history despite our very different backgrounds.

Lena is now building a career as an oral historian of Nepalese religious figures, a path that will help her memorialize what is unique and central to what she feels is precious in Nepal—it's adherence to radical inclusiveness. For Lena, this means feeling a sense of connection and responsibility to all humans. Lena's commitment to provide an enduring account of the works of those who have shaped Nepal's religious culture reflects her determination to serve her beloved chosen homeland at a time when it is suffering from economic and political upheaval and the lingering effects of a devastating natural disaster. Nepal is the non-human Other she serves with heartfelt devotion.

Aki

Aki is a single, Japanese female in her forties. She was in her mid-twenties when the great Hanshin-Awaji Earthquake struck her region. While all of her family members survived, her divorced father's house was destroyed and the house of her divorced mother and younger brother was burned down. Immediately after the earthquake, she devoted herself to rebuilding her parents' homes; shortly after it, she quit her job and founded an organization to educate the younger generation. Her efforts seem to have been aided by her high intelligence.

Aki came to see me (Koichi Togashi) about fifteen years after the earthquake, complaining about a sense of powerlessness and meaninglessness that emerged after her organization had been taken over by someone else. She held an executive position and had a good reputation in the organization even after she lost the position of president. However, when she found that she could no longer tolerate the change in its basic philosophy of education for the younger generation, she quit.

The history of her career is interesting. Even though Aki graduated from one of the most intellectually rigorous universities in Japan, she had obtained a low-level position in a mediocre company where she worked until the Great Earthquake. Having lacked confidence in her abilities, she felt that her position was appropriate. However, after the quake, she came to feel that her fate and role was to do something for other people. She believed that founding an organization to educate the younger generation would be the best way to meet the "Will of Heaven." She was not religious or spiritual, but she felt strongly that this was what she should do. She did not feel herself to be a person who could support others, but rather it was simply her role in the world after the earthquake.

Aki's mother was judgmental and often belittled her; her father was psychologically and economically weak and indifferent. Aki never felt loved by them. Still, she felt that she had to help them to rebuild their lives. She told me, "I think that

I was lucky in a sense, because the earthquake gave me a chance to see myself as a person who did something for others. I do not like my parents, but I felt confidence in myself after I devoted myself to working for them. Without these experiences, I would not have founded an organization to educate people."

During five years of psychoanalytic psychotherapy on a once-a-week basis, face-to-face, Aki and I tried to find the meaning of her working for the younger generation. We finally understood that she did not feel that she had been given any roles or jobs by the "Willl of Heaven," but she felt that the earthquake had given her a job in the world. She was not depressed because someone took over her organization, but she felt she lost her role in this world. Working through this, Aki finally enrolled in a training program to become a professional supporting disabled people. She emphasized that she just accepted her fate.

We believe that although Lena and Aki both devoted themselves to helping others wounded by wide-scale societal traumas, the meaning of their forms of service reflect very different culturally influenced moral values. For Lena, raising money to aid in the post-earthquake recovery in Nepal reflects the Western value of prioritizing the needs of others who have suffered societal disasters, that is, altruism; Aki's effort to educate people represents her surrender of herself to the Way of Heaven by releasing a preoccupation with herself, other and society

Conclusion: altruism and remembering

In conclusion, we would like to offer some thoughts about the possible culturally specific meanings of longings to memorialize wide-scale traumatic events as well as desires to forget them. An aspect of traditional Japanese morality holds that for some Japanese people, remembering a societal trauma involves reverence for the acts of service to others that were offered in keeping with the "Way of Heaven," that is, the shared moral value of selflessness and otherlessness. For some Americans, on the other hand, remembering their societal traumas is often mixed with pain and guilt. As Roger Frie[31] has pointed out, knowing and not knowing often go hand in hand in the aftermath of societal traumas. By remembering the trauma of 9/11, Americans not only become aware of their shared victimization but also of their shared responsibility for their hurtfulness toward others. Many Americans cannot remember 9/11 without becoming aware that the attackers saw them as evil enough to warrant their destruction and that the retaliatory actions taken by Americans caused death and suffering to countless people. The desire to remember may well conflict with the desire to spare the next generation what may be almost unbearable to remember.

Notes

1 This chapter is supported by The Hirao Memorial Foundation of KONAN GAKUEN for the Humanities and Social Sciences and Grant-in-Aid for Scientific Research(C),

Japan Society for the Promotion of Science, The Ministry of Education, Culture, Sports, Science and Technology, Japan

2 Pamela Druckerman, "If I Sleep for an Hour, 30 People Will Die," *New York Times*, Oct 2, 2016.

3 Koichi Togashi, "Surrender to the Psychoanalytic Zero: The Analyst's Taking Responsibility, Telling, and Being Makoto" (presentation, Taiwan Self Psychology Conference, Taipei, Taiwan, 2017).

4 Concise Oxford Dictionary, 9th ed., s.v. "Altruism."

5 Viktor Frankl, *Man's Search for Meaning* (Boston: Beacon Press, 2006).

6 Tzvetan Todorov, *The Conquest of America: The Question of the Other* (New York: Harper Perennial, 1996), 89.

7 E. Straub and J. Vollhardt, "Altruism Born of Suffering: The Roots of Caring and Helping After Victimization and Other Trauma," *American Journal of Orthopsychiatry* 78, no. 3 (2008). Alexandra Hartman and Benjamin Morse, Wartime Violence, Empathy and Intergroup Altruism: Evidence from the Ivoirian Refugee Crisis in Liberia, May 2015. http://cega.beerkely.edu/assets/miscellaneous_file/119_-_HartmanMorseVio-lenceEmpathy-May_2015-ABCA.pdf. Accessed October 2017.

8 Mark Freeman, The Priority of the Other: Thinking and Living Beyond the Self (New York: Oxford University Press, 2014), 118.

9 Bjorn Carey, "Stanford psychologists show that altruism is not simply innate," *Stanford Report*, December 18, 2014.

10 Koichi Togashi and Doris Brothers, "Trauma Research and Self Psychology: How 9/11 Survivors Integrate the Irrationality of Wide-Scale Trauma" (presentation, 38th Annual International Conference on the Psychology of the Self, Los Angeles, CA, October 17, 2015).

11 The Great Hanshin-Awaji Earthquake Memorial Disaster Reduction and Human Renovation Institution "Disaster Reduction and Human Renovation Institution Pictorial Record 1995.1.17" (May, 2016).

12 Yutaka Sakisaka, *Wa no Kozo* (Tokyo: Hokuju Shuppansha, 1979), 40–41.

13 Koichi Togashi, "Placeness in the Twinship Experience," in *Kohut's Twinship Across Cultures: The Psychology of Being Human*, K. Togashi and A. Kottler (New York: Routledge, 2015), 109.

14 Hazel R. Markus and Shinobu Kitayma, "Culture and the Self: Implications for Cognition, Emotion, and Motivation," *Psychological Review* 98, no. 2 (1991), 228.

15 Salomon Malka, *Emmanuel Levinas: His Life and Legacy* (Pittsburgh: Duquesne University Press, 2006) xi.

16 Ibid, xviii.

17 Ibid, 80.

18 Ibid, 17.

19 Sean Hand, *The Levinas Reader* (Oxford: Blackwell, 1999) 290.

20 Emmanuel Levinas, *Proper Names*, trans. Michael B. Smith (London: Athlone Press, 1996) 121–122.

21 Salomon Malka, *Emmanuel Levinas: His Life and Legacy* (Pittsburgh: Duquesne University Press, 2006) 82.

22 Tetsuro Watsuji, *Nihon Rinri Shisoshi, Vol 2* (Tokyo: Iwanami Shoten, 1952).

23 Toru Sagara, *Seijitsu to Nihonjin* (Tokyo: Perikansha, 1980).

24 Kenji Morita, *Sekimon shingaku to kindai: Shisoshigaku kara no kinsetsu* (Tokyo: Yachiyoshuppan, 2012).

25 Y. Uchinuma, *Taijinkyfu no Ningengaku* (Tokyo: Kyobundo, 1977) 159.

26 Ibid, 84.

27 Ibid, 69.

28 M. Nakakuki, "Normal and Developmental Aspects of Masochism: Transcultural and Clinical Implications," *Psychiatry* 57, no. 3 (1994).

29 William W. Meissner, *The Ethical Dimension of Psychoanalysis: A Dialogue* (Albany New York: State University of New York Press, 2003).
30 Koichi Togashi, "Beyond the Guilt of Being: Surrender to the Psychoanalytic Zero" (presentation, 14th Annual IARPP Conference, Sydney, Australia, 2017).
31 Roger Frie, *Not in My Family: German Memory and Responsibility After the Holocaust* (London: Oxford University Press, 2014).

References

Cheney, David (ed.). *Broad's Critical Essays in Moral Philosophy*. London: Allen & Unwin, 2013.

Carey, Bjorn, "Stanford psychologists show that altruism is not simply innate," *Stanford Report*, Dec 18, 2014.

Druckerman, Pamela, "If I Sleep for an Hour, 30 People Will Die," *New York Times*, Oct 2, 2016.

Frankl, Viktor. *Man's Search for Meaning*. Boston: Beacon Press, 2006 (Originally published 1946).

Freeman, Mark. *The Priority of the Other: Thinking and Living Beyond the Self*. New York: Oxford University Press, 2014.

Frie, Roger. *Not in My Family: German Memory and Responsibility After the Holocaust*. London: Oxford University Press, 2017.

Hand, Sean (ed.). *The Levinas Reader*. Oxford: Blackwell, 1989.

Hartman, Alexandra and Benjamin Morse. "Wartime Violence, Empathy and Intergroup Altruism: Evidence from the Ivoirian Refugee Crisis in Liberia." May2015. http://cega. beerkely.edu/assets/miscellaneous_file/119_-_HartmanMorseViolenceEmpathy-May_2015-ABCA.pdf. Accessed October 2017.

Levinas, Emmanuel. *Proper Names*. Translated by Michael B. Smith. London: Athlone Press, 1996.

Malka, Salomon. *Emmanuel Levinas: His Life and Legacy*. Pittsburgh: Duquesne University Press, 2006.

Markus, Hazel R. and Shinobu Kitayma. "Culture and the Self: Implications for Cognition, Emotion, and Motivation." *Psychological Review* 98, no. 2(1991): 24–253.

Meissner, W. W. *The Ethical Dimension of Psychoanalysis: A Dialogue*. Albany: SUNY Press, 2003.

Morita, Kenji. *Sekimon Shingaku to Kindai: Shisoshigaku Kara no Kinsetsu*. Tokyo: Yachiyoshuppan, 2012.

Nakakuki, M. "Normal and Developmental Aspects of Masochism: Transcultural and Clinical Implications." *Psychiatry* 57, no. 3(1994): 244–257.

Sagara, Toru. *Seijitsu to Nihonjin*. Tokyo: Perikansha, 1980.

Sagara, Toru. *Nihonjin no Kokoro to Deau*. Tokyo: Kadensha, 1998.

Sakisaka, Yutaka. *Wa no Kozo*. Tokyo: Hokuju Shuppansha, 1979.

Straub, E. and J. Vollhardt. "Altruism Born of Suffering: The Roots of Caring and Helping After Victimization and Other Trauma." *American Journal of Orthopsychiatry* 78, no. 3 (2008): 267–280.

Todorov, Tzvetan. *The Conquest of America: The Question of the Other*. New York: Harper Perennial, 1996.

Togashi, Koichi. "Placeness in the Twinship Experience." In *Kohut's Twinship Across Cultures: The Psychology of Being Human*, by K. Togashi and A. Kottler, 107–117. New York: Routledge, 2015.

Togashi, Koichi. "Beyond the Guilt of Being: Surrender to the Psychoanalytic Zero." Paper presented at the 14th Annual IARPP Conference, Sydney, Australia, 2017.

Togashi, Koichi. "Surrender to the Psychoanalytic Zero: The Analyst's Taking Responsibility, Telling, and Being Makoto." Paper presented at the Taiwan Self Psychology Conference, Taipei, Taiwan, 2017.

Togashi, Koichi and Doris Brothers. "Trauma Research and Self Psychology: How 9/11 Survivors Integrate the Irrationality of Wide-Scale Trauma." Paper presented at the 38th Annual International Conference on the Psychology of the Self, Los Angeles, CA, October 17, 2015.

Uchinuma, Y. *Taijinkyfu no Ningengaku*. Tokyo: Kyobundo, 1977.

Watsuji, Tetsuro. *Nihon Rinri Shisoshi,* Vol 2. Tokyo: Iwanami Shoten, 1952.

INDEX